FROM APARTHEID TO DEMOCRACY

RHETORIC AND DEMOCRATIC DELIBERATION
VOLUME 11

EDITED BY CHERYL GLENN AND J. MICHAEL HOGAN
THE PENNSYLVANIA STATE UNIVERSITY

Editorial Board:

Robert Asen (University of Wisconsin–Madison)
Debra Hawhee (The Pennsylvania State University)
Peter Levine (Tufts University)
Steven J. Mailloux (University of California, Irvine)
Krista Ratcliffe (Marquette University)
Karen Tracy (University of Colorado, Boulder)
Kirt Wilson (The Pennsylvania State University)
David Zarefsky (Northwestern University)

Rhetoric and Democratic Deliberation is a series of groundbreaking monographs and edited volumes focusing on the character and quality of public discourse in politics and culture. It is sponsored by the Center for Democratic Deliberation, an interdisciplinary center for research, teaching, and outreach on issues of rhetoric, civic engagement, and public deliberation.

A complete list of books in this series is located at the back of this volume.

FROM APARTHEID TO DEMOCRACY

DELIBERATING TRUTH AND RECONCILIATION
IN SOUTH AFRICA

KATHERINE ELIZABETH MACK

The Pennsylvania State University Press | University Park, Pennsylvania

An earlier version of some material in chapter 2 appeared in "Remembering Winnie: Public Memory and the Truth and Reconciliation Commission of South Africa," in *Global Memoryscapes: Contesting Remembrance in a Transnational Age*, edited by Kendall R. Phillips and G. Mitchell Reyes (Tuscaloosa: University of Alabama Press, 2011).

An earlier version of some material in chapter 3 appeared in "Hearing Women's Silence in Transitional South Africa: Achmat Dangor's *Bitter Fruit*," in *Silence and Listening as Rhetorical Arts*, edited by Cheryl Glenn and Krista Ratcliffe (Carbondale: Southern Illinois University Press, 2011).

The illustrations in chapter 4 appeared in Jillian Edelstein, *Truth and Lies: Stories from the Truth and Reconciliation Commission in South Africa* (London: Granta Books, 2001). Reproduced by permission.

Library of Congress Cataloging-in-Publication Data

Mack, Katherine Elizabeth, 1974– , author.
 From apartheid to democracy : deliberating truth and reconciliation in South Africa / Katherine Elizabeth Mack.
  pages   cm — (Rhetoric and democratic deliberation)
Includes bibliographical references and index.
ISBN 978-0-271-06497-0 (cloth : alk. paper)
ISBN 978-0-271-06498-7 (pbk. : alk. paper)
1. South Africa. Truth and Reconciliation Commission.
2. Rhetoric—South Africa.
3. Deliberative democracy—South Africa.
4. Reconciliation—Social aspects—South Africa.
5. Post-apartheid era—South Africa.
6. Apartheid—South Africa.
I. Title. II. Series: Rhetoric and democratic deliberation.

DT1974.2.M33 2014
305.800968—dc23
2014023266

Copyright © 2014 The Pennsylvania State University
All rights reserved

Printed in the United States of America
Published by The Pennsylvania State University Press,
University Park, PA 16802-1003

The Pennsylvania State University Press is a member of the Association of American University Presses.

It is the policy of The Pennsylvania State University Press to use acid-free paper. Publications on uncoated stock satisfy the minimum requirements of American National Standard for Information Sciences—Permanence of Paper for Printed Library Material, ANSI Z39.48–1992.

In memory of my father,

ALAN G. MACK,

*for inspiring in me a zest for life, and
for supporting my curiosity and wanderlust
no matter where they took me.*

CONTENTS

Preface | *ix*

Acknowledgments | *xiii*

Introduction: The Rhetoricity of Truth Commissions | 1

Chapter 1: Localizing Transitional Justice | 15

Chapter 2: Ambivalent Speech, Resonant Silences | 31

Chapter 3: Contesting Accountability | 60

Chapter 4: Imagining Reconciliation | 97

Conclusion | 125

Notes | *129*

Works Cited | *135*

Index | *143*

PREFACE

> And why does it always have to be people like me who have to sacrifice, why are we always the ones who have to make concessions when something has to be conceded, why always me who has to bite her tongue, why?
>
> —PAULINA IN ARIEL DORFMAN'S *Death and the Maiden*

It might seem odd to begin a book about the South African Truth and Reconciliation Commission (TRC) with a discussion of a play set in "a country that is probably Chile" by a Chilean playwright (ix). Allow me to explain why I do so. *Death and the Maiden*'s clear articulation of the challenges inherent to any truth-seeking process has made references to it almost clichéd in scholarship on transitional justice. In the epigraph above, Paulina asks why she should not take revenge against the man who raped and tortured her. She ventriloquizes the frustration of survivors of human rights violations who reject the "justice" a truth commission offers: justice in the form of a truthful account and acknowledgment of the abuse that victims suffered rather than punishment of those who did or supported that abuse. Ironically, perhaps, Paulina also expresses the resentment of some perpetrators, who claim that they acted in good faith and for a righteous cause and should therefore not be required to disclose the details of their actions before a commission. Suffice it to say, truth commissions never satisfy all parties.

Death and the Maiden is relevant to my project in other ways as well. The Chilean truth commission influenced the form and ideology of the South African commission, a transnational circulation of ideas that I discuss in detail in chapter 1. More importantly, Dorfman's motivations for writing *Death and the Maiden*, and the play's circulation, underscore this project's argument about the tight braid of cultural and political projects. Dorfman hoped that *Death*, like Aristotelian drama, would be "a work of art that might help a collective to purge itself, through pity and terror, in other words to force the spectators to confront those predicaments that, if not brought into the light of day, could lead to their ruin" (74). The "uptake" of *Death and the Maiden* testifies to its rhetorical force (Warner 87). In his foreword to the TRC *Report*, written in part to address the Commission's detractors, Chairperson Desmond Tutu writes, "In Ariel Dorfmann's [sic] play, *Death and the Maiden*, a woman ties up the man who has injured her. She is ready to kill him when he repeats his lie that he did not rape or torture her. It is only when he admits his violations that she lets him go. His admission restores her dignity and her identity. Her experience is confirmed as real and not illusory and her sense of self is affirmed" (1: 7). Here Tutu seeks to persuade critics of the TRC's argument that truth constitutes a satisfying alternative to retributive justice. In so doing, he seriously misinterprets Paulina's response. Roberto's forced confession does not restore her dignity and identity. She appears as angry and vulnerable at the end of the play as she does at the beginning. While she is persuaded to release Roberto unharmed, Paulina's desire for vengeance remains unquenched. In her final lines of the play, she asks, "What do we lose? What do we lose by killing one of them? What do we lose? What do we lose?" (66). For my purposes here, Tutu's misreading of the play matters less than his use of it to legitimate the TRC's approach to victims and perpetrators. His citation exemplifies the interplay of political and cultural processes to which *From Apartheid to Democracy* draws attention.

In the following pages, I demonstrate how rhetoricians can, and why they should, read diverse texts—legal, testimonial, fictional, and visual—as equal participants in political projects. Victims and amnesty applicants, as well as the artists who represent and respond to the TRC in their creative work, share a commitment to its project of imagining a new South Africa. By including these generically varied receptions of the TRC process, *From Apartheid to Democracy* offers what Jeffrey Walker calls a "sophistic history of 'rhetoric' [in that it] includes 'poetry' and 'poetics' as essential, central parts of 'rhetoric's domain" (ix). As Walker demonstrates, epideictic discourse, like the more practical civic oratory traditionally associated with rhetoric, also "calls its audience to acts of judgment and response" (viii).

I characterize TRC participants' and respondents' arguments about the past as public memory. This term foregrounds their (paradoxical) orientation toward the present, communalism, and dynamism. Memories tell as much about the present as about the past, if not more: "[they are] a perpetually actual phenomenon, a bond tying us to the eternal present" (Nora 8).

Memories are born of individual perceptions but also of shared social processes. Uptake of the past, be it contentious or harmonious, unifying or divisive, constitutes those who remember as a contingent public. While communal remembrance is "a crucial aspect of our togetherness" (Phillips 4), it is also always open to "contest, revision, and rejection" (2). The "public" of public memory thus indexes the inherently communal nature as well as the ongoing contestation that characterize remembrance, while "memory" calls attention to the presentist orientation and personal stakes of any engagement with the past.

I conceive of public memory as a process rather than an object. Instead of seeking memories' essential meaning, form, or beginning, I track their uptake and evolution across time and genre. Rhetorical hermeneutics, a form of cultural rhetoric studies "that takes as its topic specific historical acts of interpretation within their cultural contexts," provides one way of doing so (Mailloux 56). Rhetorical hermeneutics examines interpreters' relationship to a text as well as the relationships among interpreters. Indeed, "for rhetorical hermeneutics, these two problems are ultimately inseparable" (50). The metaphor of "conversation" captures the dialogism of public memory (Mailloux, Bruffee). When possible, I comment on the social locations and political orientations of TRC participants and respondents to illuminate the various sources of their arguments.

ACKNOWLEDGMENTS

This book has been a long time in the making. Without Susan Jarratt's mentoring, endless encouragement, and incisive comments, I wouldn't have finished my PhD, let alone become a professor and published this monograph; I owe her my biggest debt of gratitude. With patience, humor, and tact, Steve Mailloux pushed me to be more theoretically sophisticated and precise; he also convinced me that everything is indeed rhetorical. I thank Inderpal Grewal for asking tough questions and building my confidence as a scholar. A special thank you also to Alexandra Sartor, a lively interlocutor, thoughtful reader, conference companion, and, not least, a steadfast friend. Many others at UC Irvine helped along the way, especially Jonathan Alexander, Amitabha Bagchi, Paul Dahlgren, Philomena Essed, David Theo Goldberg, Daniel Gross, Lynda Haas, Laura Knighten, Jane Newman, and Piper Walsh. My writing partners, Matthew Pearson and Alexandra Sartor, consistently provided thoughtful feedback.

For transformative conversations about matters intellectual, professional, and personal, I owe an enormous debt of gratitude to Marjorie Jolles and Shevaun Watson. You two provide different and wonderful models of what it means to be scholars, teachers, and administrators. You are also always one step ahead of me, making my path through academia (and life) that much easier.

Over the years, workshops and panels with John Ackerman, Jim Beitler, Robert Hariman, John Lucaites, Kendall Phillips, Mitchell Reyes, Susan Romano, Patrician Stevens, and Bradford Vivian helped me refine my thinking about the relationship between rhetoric and public memory. An internship with the International Center for Transitional Justice under the direction of Louis Bickford and conversations with Priscilla Hayner gave me a practitioner's perspective on the field of transitional justice and South Africa's TRC's influence on its development. I am grateful to Jillian Edelstein, Carnita Ernest, Cecyl Esau, Terry February, George Hallett, Oupa Makhamelele, and Njabulo Ndebele, who generously allowed me to ask questions about their work and their vision for the new South Africa.

For doling out criticism and encouragement in equal measure, Jeffrey Montez de Oca and Stephany Spaulding, my friends and writing partners at UCCS, deserve special mention. I thank the entire English department, especially Traci Freeman, Ceil Malek, Michelle Neely, Kirsten Ortega, and Ken Pellow, for their support. I also wish to thank Christina Martinez, who has yet to deny a request to purchase materials for UCCS's Kraemer Family Library. A grant from the Committee on Research and Creative Work and the office of LAS Dean Peter Braza provided additional material support.

Anonymous reviewers provided feedback that greatly improved this manuscript. I am grateful for their thoughtful and generous revision suggestions, which I have incorporated to the best of my abilities. I also thank Kendra Boileau and Cheryl Glenn for their support of this project and superb editorial guidance. I extend my gratitude to Laura Reed-Morrisson and to the rest of the staff at Penn State University Press whose work made this book possible.

Relationships outside of the academy sustained me throughout the long gestation of this project. In different ways, Cathy Costello, Marcela Díaz, Andrew Dibben, Henrik Fett, Jack and Cynthia Goldberg, Candace and Ryan Hewitt, Kristy Mack-Fett, Cindy Maguire, Rob McCallum, Bryan McGlynn, Priti Patel, Cancion Soto, John Standish, and Mariann Youmans have kept me afloat. Dominik and Tatiana Fett, you are a constant source of delight. My parents—Karin and Ed Costello, Alan Mack, and Deena Goldstone—nurtured my curiosity and supported my passions from the very beginning. Finally, Minette and Owen Church brought Andrew Agustín into my life: words can't capture my gratitude.

INTRODUCTION:
THE RHETORICITY OF TRUTH COMMISSIONS

In April 1994—after forty-five years of institutionalized white supremacy, which left lasting and deep scars—nearly twenty million South Africans participated in the country's first truly democratic elections. Nelson Mandela, a political prisoner for twenty-seven years, won the elections in a landslide, becoming South Africa's first black president. This dramatic transition to democracy, captured by photographs of snaking lines of voters, guaranteed that South Africa would occupy the world's spotlight. The creation of a new democracy did not in itself erase the history of violence. Through a public and participatory process, the new government created a number of mechanisms for dealing with the past, one of which, the Truth and Reconciliation Commission (TRC), has received the lion's share of attention. South Africa's interim constitution guaranteed some form of "conditional amnesty" for those who had committed human rights abuses in defense of and in opposition to apartheid. It did not, however, specify the nature of the body that would grant those amnesties. The TRC emerged as a "third way" (Boraine, "Truth and Reconciliation"), an alternative to either Nuremberg-style prosecutions or a blanket amnesty. The TRC's architects drew on the insights of international human rights actors as well as South African nationals (Goodman). Though a vexed endeavor in ways that *From Apartheid to Democracy* examines, the TRC nevertheless played a crucial role in South Africa's transition from apartheid.

Truth commissions are an inherently rhetorical and now ubiquitous mechanism for "dealing with the past."[1] They constitute a novel genre of "public persuasion" in that they seek to "advance a cause" or "overcome an impasse" (Zarefsky 30)—typically involving a political transition—by redressing past wrongs through mechanisms such as truth telling, amnesty, and reparations. While they date from the late twentieth and early twenty-first centuries, truth commissions echo the earliest rhetoricians' faith in the ability of speech to create community and dispel violence.

Indeed, they seem motivated by an Isocratean insight: "Since there is innate in us the ability to persuade each other and to reveal to ourselves the things we wish, not only have we put off the life of wild beasts, but we have come together and founded cities; we have established laws and discovered arts, and for nearly all the things we have contrived, *logos* had been our fellow worker" (*Nicocles*, § 6). Truth commissions marshal *logos*, our "fellow worker," to facilitate a political transition in a variety of ways. They might do so by gathering information for concurrent or future prosecutions; by producing an account of past violations in the hopes of "closing the book"; by showcasing, via a commission's historical inquiry and process, the new government's commitment to transparency, human rights, and the "rule of law"; or, in the case of South Africa's Truth and Reconciliation Commission, by promoting a national discourse of reconciliation. While the specific goals and mechanisms of truth commissions vary, all (1) exist only temporarily, (2) investigate a defined time period in the recent past, (3) focus on gross violations of human rights as defined by humanitarian law, (4) place a high value on listening to victims, and, finally, (5) submit a final report that accounts for their activities and findings.

Attempts to address a legacy of human rights violations date back to the Nuremberg and Tokyo trials following the Second World War. The emergent field of transitional justice finds its origins in these postwar experiments in justice. Its practitioners assume that "confronting the past" is a necessary component of a successful transition from authoritarian rule to democracy or from a period of conflict to peace and stability (Bickford, "Transitional Justice" 1045). Because transitional justice "confronts the past" in order to promote justice and to facilitate a transition, its practitioners consider a range of mechanisms in addition to traditional prosecutions. As Bickford notes, these include reparations policies, reconciliation initiatives, institutional reforms, and, of course, truth commissions (1046).

Truth commissions lie at the nexus of debates about how to balance competing demands for truth, justice, and reconciliation. Contingent conditions—a new and fragile government, the threat of a return to violence if prosecutions are an option, and the lack of a strong judicial system—can make retributive justice measures, such as prosecutions, unfeasible. These pragmatic concerns often lead to the decision to hold a truth commission. At a minimum, a truth commission serves to increase public awareness of the abuses committed during the time period covered by its mandate. In some instances, it can illuminate facts about abuses that the former regime kept hidden from the majority of the population. In many cases, however, a truth commission simply acknowledges the truth of abuses that were widely known by the majority of the population but actively denied by the government. Citizens in a repressive environment often fear the consequences of speaking publicly about abuses or are legally prevented from doing so by gag orders. The fear of attracting attention and becoming a victim oneself, and official policies that discourage or ban truth telling, generates what Yael Danieli calls a "conspiracy of silence" (qtd. in Hayner, *Unspeakable* 135). A truth commission breaks the silence. Ideally, it heralds the transition to a new political order by acknowledging the government's responsibility for or complicity in the abuses. The president emeritus of the Open Society Institute, Aryeh Neier, suggests that a truth commission's "acknowledgment implies that the state has admitted its misdeeds and recognized that it was wrong" (34). This official acknowledgment ostensibly enables the new government to gain the trust of citizens who have lost confidence in political institutions and processes. In so doing, the truth commission helps draw a line between the past and the present. For these reasons, some practitioners and human rights activists now consider truth commissions a helpful counterpart to, though not necessarily a substitute for, traditional prosecutions.

Pragmatism alone, though, has not fueled the surge of truth commissions in the last thirty years. In some instances, human rights activists and academics contend, truth commissions might better serve the needs of victims and societies transitioning from a period of violence or mass atrocity, even when prosecutions are possible. As legal scholar Martha Minow observes, "litigation is not an ideal form of social action" ("Hope" 238). Trials can retraumatize victims who must share their experiences in an adversarial context. They tend not to promote truth telling on the part of perpetrators who, out of self-protection, seek to obscure the details of their past. Finally, given their aim of attaining an individual verdict of guilt or innocence, trials do not typically produce a compelling picture of the myriad individuals, practices, and ideologies that created the enabling conditions for and context of abuse. Truth commissions, proponents suggest, instead address victims' desire to tell their stories and generate a historical narrative about the recent past that acknowledges human rights abuses. By creating a safe space wherein victims can testify about their experiences, they meet what Priscilla Hayner describes as a "very basic need by victims to recount their stories of violence and survival" (*Unspeakable* 136). Legal and narrative theorist Teresa Godwin Phelps suggests that the distinctive setting provided by a truth commission can "allow for fuller transformative and constitutive storytelling beyond the scope of any trial" (67). During a trial, perpetrators testify, but they provide only the facts that will serve their case. A truth commission has the power to establish broader parameters for perpetrators' testimony, furthering the potential for the "transformative storytelling" to which Phelps refers. South Africa's TRC distinguished itself from prior truth commissions through its individualized amnesty program, which encouraged perpetrators as well as victims to tell their stories. Following the TRC's example, several subsequent truth commissions have incorporated perpetrators' storytelling into their mandates.

The hybrid form and multiple goals of truth commissions make them prime targets of criticism. Truth commissions generate "genre confusion" precisely because they are "an imperfectly realized hybrid genre, spanning the state inquiry, human rights report, and official history" (Gready 20). According to their critics, truth commissions either do too little, or, more frequently, seek to do too much; that is, they set goals that they either should not or simply cannot realize. On practical grounds, some argue that truth commissions should limit themselves to fact-finding, rather than interpretation or evaluation. Doing so, these critics suggest, would enable a commission to frame its investigations and findings as objectively as possible, thus promoting consensus around its findings regarding human rights violations. José Zalaquett, a human rights activist and commissioner on the Chilean National Commission on Truth and Reconciliation, for example, suggests that truth commissions "should concentrate largely on facts, which may be proved, whereas differences about historical interpretation will always exist" (qtd. in Maier 265). Public intellectual and politician Michael Ignatieff similarly argues that "all that a truth commission can achieve is to reduce the number of lies that can be circulated unchallenged in public discourse," that it "can only winnow out the solid core of facts upon which society's arguments with itself should be conducted" ("Articles" 113). Legal scholar Henry Steiner posits, echoing Ignatieff,

> [p]erhaps truth commissions should have this same attitude, holding to the role of truth-tellers in the flat sense of doing their best to record who did what to whom and when, period. Were they characteristically to engage in social analysis, by identifying structural phenomena underlying violations, and by proposing deep changes in a society's socio-economic organization, they risk being viewed as but another voice in a world of disputed opinions and theories about

justice, development, whatever. Their reports might lose distinctiveness and a sense of objectivity by being absorbed into the broad play of political ideas and historical debate. (16)

Steiner, like Zalaquett and Ignatieff, proposes that truth commissions not engage what rhetoricians recognize as the *stases:* arguments at the level of value, cause and consequence, and procedure and proposal.

On intellectual grounds, some scholars doubt a truth commission's ability to negotiate the competing demands of politics and scholarly inquiry. Charles S. Maier lauds a truth commission's ability to gather the raw material of a dark period of history, but he argues that it is ill equipped to engage in the historian's craft of "moral sifting" (268): "Historians, I believe, will have to use this material, but integrate it into a different framework" (273). Indeed, historians Mahmood Mamdani, Colin Bundy, and Alexander Neville attribute what they characterize as South Africa's truth commission's "compromised historical account" to the compromised nature of the political transition itself. Meanwhile, philosophers tend either to identify the logical fallacies in the ideology of truth commissions, which they attribute to its "public and political purposes" (Holiday 56), or to impose coherence and consistency onto that ideology. For example, Daniel Herwitz attributes a philosophical coherence to the TRC's "epistemic regime" that glosses over its significant and unresolved contradictions (41). Psychologists are dubious about the healing effects of truth commissions. They observe that truth telling in the context of a truth commission might serve some victims' desire to share their stories and the nation's need for a fuller account of the abuses of the past, but does not address the deeper psychological effects of trauma. Whether in praise or blame, these scholars apply academic criteria to the work of truth commissions.

Rhetoricity of Truth Commissions

These varied critiques simultaneously highlight and disavow the inherent and inevitable rhetoricity of truth commissions. Truth commissions are neither the unsullied brainchild of theorists nor the polished machine of technocrats. They are rhetorical experiments, real-world efforts to enact change in the uncertain realm of contingent human affairs via our primary medium of exchange: language. Because truth commissions are mandated to investigate contested narratives, and, in some instances, to promote reconciliation among adversaries, they must negotiate the demands of multiple publics—a rhetorical process that involves fostering complex and ever-changing networks of identification among stakeholders. While a truth commission's mandate sets it in motion, it does not fully control participants' inquiries into the meaning of the past and its bearing on the present and future. No matter a truth commission's ideological imperatives and maxims—"revealing is healing" or "let it out"—individual victims and perpetrators find ways to mold the commission's process to suit *their* needs and to tell the stories *they* feel need to be told. The commission's rhetoric becomes an inventional resource, not a determinant of participants' arguments about the past. Truth commissions also provide a window onto the relationship between language and subject-formation. When participants speak before a truth commission, we witness the dynamic exchange between their pretransitional ways of knowing and being and those made available by the truth commission and the new democracy. The tension between these participants' and the commission's notions of what aspects of the past should be remembered, and how, makes the public hearing a particularly dynamic site for rhetorical analysis.

Acknowledging that truth commissions are live and motivated rhetorical events that occur at a particular moment in time and place, and that they aim to create both a productive "truth" about the past and democratic subjects, reframes practitioners' and academics' critiques. A rhetorician assumes that however narrow a truth commission's mandate, it will inevitably grapple with arguments occurring at different levels of *stasis:* What happened in the years covered by the mandate? What caused those events to take place? What value should be assigned to those events and the actors behind them? And what, if anything, should be done in the present to redress identified wrongs and injustices? From a rhetorical perspective, then, attempts to distinguish "facts" (Ignatieff) and "truth-telling" (Steiner) from "social analysis" are untenable. Truth telling, even in a "flat sense" (Steiner), is inevitably an assertion of value and cause because the statement occurs in language. Consider, for example, the differences between two statements that might plausibly appear in a truth commission's final report: "Activists killed civilians during the armed phase of the anti-apartheid struggle" vs. "Militants murdered civilians during the armed phase of the anti-apartheid struggle."[2] South African poet and journalist Antjie Krog pointed to the inescapable rhetoricity of language and the challenges that rhetoricity poses for a so-called truth commission when the idea of a South African TRC was first proposed. Krog asked,

"Must the commission be called a 'truth commission'? I am not trying to smuggle in confusion here but want to stress the ambiguity of language: it signifies more than a mere dictionary explanation. To examine the question allows one to recognize the complexities of dealing with the world. I feel it would be presumptuous and naïve to set up a commission and claim it could find and tell 'The Truth'" (in Boraine and Levy 116–17). Even when truth commissions limit their intended goals to fact-finding, they place themselves in the realm of analysis and interpretation. The mandate of a truth commission prioritizes the investigation and acknowledgment of certain "truths" over others. These choices reflect its architects' "opinions and theories" about ethical and philosophical issues regarding truth, justice, and "the good." A commission's chosen focus also calls attention to, or diverts attention from, the "structural phenomena underlying violations." By exclusion or inclusion, then, a commission necessarily engages in the "play of political ideas and historical debate" (Steiner). More importantly, the commission sets the stage for the participants in its process to do the same.

The architects of the TRC hoped that its work would be invitational, relational, and quite literally world making. In his introduction to the TRC-founding act, Minister of Justice Dullah Omar described the future commission as facilitating the construction of "the historic bridge of which the Constitution speaks." According to Omar, this metaphorical bridge would help transport South Africans from "the past of a deeply divided society ... towards a future founded on the recognition of human rights, democracy, and peaceful co-existence" (Republic of South Africa). The TRC's highly public process, a feature that distinguished it from prior truth commissions, was to play a crucial role in the construction of this "bridge" (Hayner, "Same Species" 37). As Erik Doxtader explains, "the TRC was envisaged as a public good, a transparent and inclusive body whose work was to be guided by a norm of publicity, an expectation that speech would help open democracy's commons and build collective interest from old divisions" (*With Faith* 257).[3] The Promotion of National Unity and Reconciliation Act charged the TRC not only with the historical task of depicting the "causes, nature, and extent" of the human rights violations that occurred during a particular time period, but also with gathering the "motives and perspectives" of victims and perpetrators through investigations and hearings. This situation of contingent truth seeking calls to mind the Sophistic emphasis on the role of human perception as the primary source of knowledge, on the significance of speaking before others, and, finally, on the necessity of group deliberation (Jarratt xviii). The architects of the Commission hoped that victims' and perpetrators' narratives and their "public acknowledgement" by the Commission would "restore the dignity of victims and afford perpetrators the opportunity to come to terms with their own past" as well as foster an "understanding of our divided pasts" (TRC, *Report* 1:49). Consciously or not, they operated on the rhetorical faith that the language elicited by the TRC would have material effects; it would transform not only the individual participants in the TRC process but also the South African society that bore witness to them. The TRC's attempt to create a public for the new nation—one comprising individual citizens engaged in reasoning about the significance of South Africa's recent past—reveals much about the relationship of language practices and the formation of publics.

From Apartheid to Democracy conceives of the South African TRC as a rhetorical event in three specific senses of the term "rhetorical," none of which precludes the others. First, the TRC was premised on arguments about the *dunamis* (power, potential) of language as described above— rhetoric as constitutive. Second, the Commission's architects, and subsequently the Commission itself, sought to persuade various publics of language's transformative effects so as to stave off calls for other forms of dealing with the past and to facilitate South Africa's (relatively) nonviolent transition—rhetoric as persuasion. Third, and most centrally for this project, the TRC sought to generate "public debate, public participation and criticism" (TRC, *Report* 1: 104)—rhetoric as argument. A rhetorical approach to the TRC yields an intriguing set of questions: How does a truth commission promote identification amid competing truth claims and arguments occurring at different points of *stasis*? In a civic setting that is premised on the sharing of personal stories, what relates and separates the rhetorics of the civic and the personal? How do the dynamics between the participants in a truth commission process, and the constraints produced by their ideological and sociohistorical contexts, construct this novel rhetorical situation? Which of the Commission's arguments did different South African publics seek to contest, and how did these publics voice their counterarguments within the public hearings? Finally, how did this argumentation continue both beyond and outside of the Commission's formal process in genres not typically perceived as rhetorical, such as the novel and the photographic essay?

From Apartheid to Democracy joins a lively scholarly conversation about the TRC. Some studies of the Commission use empirical methods, employing "rigorous and systematic social science methods" (Gibson 3) or "more comprehensive and scientific assessment" (Chapman and Van der Merwe viii), to determine whether the TRC was a success. As their titles imply, *Overcoming Apartheid: Can Truth Reconcile a Divided Nation?* (Gibson) and the edited collection *Truth and Reconciliation in South Africa: Did the TRC Deliver?* (Chapman and Van der Merwe) exemplify this vein of scholarship.[4] These empirical studies do a certain kind of work, but a rhetorical mode of analysis is especially suitable for a rhetorical situation. *From Apartheid to Democracy*'s rhetorical approach answers the question of the TRC's "success" by arguing that the Commission provoked contentious debate and thus contributed to the creation of an agonistic deliberative public sphere. Here I draw both on political theorist Leigh A. Payne's claim that "contentious debate enhances democratic practices by provoking political participation, contestation, and competition" (3) and on rhetorician Patricia Roberts-Miller's positive valuation of agonistic over irenic deliberation. In contrast to irenic deliberation, which strives toward consensus and thus has the tendency to stifle disagreement and critical perspectives, agonistic deliberation "raises interesting questions, brings up injustices, or draws attention to points of view that had been obscured" (Miller 12). In the absence of absolute knowledge of the good, just, or right—that is, in the world of contingent human affairs as opposed to that of certain *a priori* truths—agonistic deliberation creates the optimal conditions in which to think through issues and determine courses of action.[5]

While *From Apartheid to Democracy* argues that agonistic deliberation characterized the TRC process, the Commission itself had both irenic and agonistic aims. The very title of its establishing Act, "Promotion of National Unity and Reconciliation," suggests its irenic impetus (while also betraying its humility about the possibility of achieving that aim through the use of the word "promotion"). At the same time, the Commission encouraged "public participation and scrutiny . . . [to help] the nation to focus on values central to a healthy democracy: transparency, public debate, public participation and criticism" (TRC, *Report* 1: 104). As Claire Moon demonstrates, a tension existed "between the homogenizing *discourse* of national unity and reconciliation, on the one hand, and the pluralizing *process* of the TRC on the other" (8, emphasis in original). While Moon focuses on the Commission's production of that "homogenizing discourse," I show how its public process created openings and opportunities to subvert its irenic aims and deliberate agonistically: participants and respondents challenged the TRC's assumptions, called attention to its omissions and blind spots, and insisted that it recognize perspectives on the past that emphasized difference, especially concerning race. Thus while the TRC might be deemed a failure because empirical surveys demonstrate that South Africans are not fully reconciled, or that they feel that the "truth" of the past still eludes them,[6] it was generative in that its very failure to achieve these idealistic goals provoked valuable contestation in its public hearings and in their literary and photographic receptions long after its official process had concluded.

In its insistence that agonistic contestation characterized the TRC's public hearings and continued in their imaginative reception, *From Apartheid to Democracy* parts company with scholars who argue that the Commission allowed only certain statements while precluding others. For example, philosopher Daniel Herwitz, echoing historians Deborah Posel and Colin Bundy, claims that "the terms of the commission constrained the possibility and appropriateness of victim (and perpetrator) testimony, so that were one unable to abide by them, one would have to bow out of the proceedings altogether" (40). Herwitz suggests that the Commission's "epistemic regime" was so powerful that victims and perpetrators whose perspectives on the past did not align with its reconciliatory agenda would voluntarily exclude themselves from its process (41). Drawing on a rhetorician's sensitivity to the productive and interpretive art of a range of argumentative modes and genres, I show how contestation, though not always explicit or verbal, characterized both the public hearings and the creative work that responded to them. *From Apartheid to Democracy* builds on the work of scholars who show how the TRC's public process enabled participants to influence its direction and outcomes. While Sanders examines how the TRC "altered its course in response to the testimony that it led" (9), and Goodman and Cole analyze the emotional and community-building effects of the Commission's performative dimensions, I focus on the hearings and their imaginative reception as forums of contentious debate that enriched and deepened the truth and reconciliation process that the TRC set in motion. This agonistic contestation did not subvert or thwart the Commission's aim of constructing a bridge toward "a future founded on the recognition of human rights, democracy, and peaceful co-existence," but rather signaled movement in that direction (Republic of South Africa).

In addition to adding this fine-grained rhetorical analysis of the agonistic deliberation that the Commission provoked to interdisciplinary scholarship on the TRC, *From Apartheid to Democracy* contributes to the growing body of rhetorical scholarship on South Africa. Philippe Salazar, Thomas Moriarty, and Erik Doxtader have already made the case that the new South Africa should occupy a central place in the "imagined global geography" (Hesford 788) of twenty-first-century rhetoric and composition studies. While these scholars focus on a range of spheres, political figures, and historical phases of the transition from apartheid to democracy, their interests converge on the ways in which South Africans came to accept the norms of new South Africa, namely, the valuing of deliberation, rather than violence, as a means to resolve conflict. In *An African Athens*, Philippe Salazar calls the post-apartheid South Africa "a signal terrain for rhetoric studies" (ix) and compares it to classical Athens, noting that in each site "the contest of words is a matter of national interest" (xviii–xix). He claims that the rhetorical nature of the transition "imbued [South Africans] with a sense of the inner dignity—the ethos—of deliberation as a human right, or deliberation as the fundamental right that gives shape to other rights" (165) and analyzes the post-apartheid government's attempt to create a rhetorical culture thus distinguished by its valuing of deliberation in "the search for a common denominator" (165). Thomas A. Moriarty's *Finding the Words* similarly calls attention to the creation of a deliberative culture in post-apartheid South Africa, though he focuses more narrowly on the role of South African political leaders in forging it. Moriarty argues that they "moved the country out of the realm of violent conflict and into the realm of rhetorical conflict" (4). He shows how their rhetorical constructions fostered the belief that negotiations and electoral politics are "the method for resolving differences and achieving social and political change in the country" (11). Finally, Erik Doxtader's *With Faith in the Works of Words: The Beginnings of Reconciliation in South Africa, 1985–1995* excavates the roots of this novel rhetorical culture by tracing the history and rhetorical purchase of the term "reconciliation" before the advent of democracy. Doxtader's history explains why, in South Africa, reconciliation is best understood as "a call to speak and the calling of speech . . . a practice of exchanging words in the name of fostering interaction and composing relationships that do not rest on the necessity of violence" (286). Thus defined, the rhetoric of reconciliation creates opportunities for identification and persuasion and also fosters the rhetorical culture that Salazar, Moriarty, and Doxtader describe, rather than marking its achievement.

From Apartheid to Democracy likewise argues that the valuing of rhetorical deliberation in post-apartheid South Africa places it in the center of twenty-first-century rhetorical studies. The task at hand, however, is to examine the contested terms and values that emerged from the new nation's "search for a common denominator" (Salazar 165). Richard Marback's *Managing Vulnerability: South Africa's Struggle for a Democratic Rhetoric*, which I was delighted to read as I was preparing this manuscript for publication, complicates these earlier studies' discussion of the deliberative culture of the new South Africa. Marback rightly observes that democratic participation requires not only a high degree of inclusion but also a "sensitivity to vulnerabilities," so that "democratic citizens come to share the burden and risk of belonging" (10). Marback's investigation of the reciprocal relations of vulnerability and sovereignty complements my analysis of the persistence of dissent in post-apartheid South Africa. *From Apartheid to Democracy* tracks the TRC's elaboration of arguments about truth and reconciliation, and participants' and artists' responses to those arguments, to show how the Commission's irenic impetus toward "national unity and reconciliation" was troubled at various axes of struggle, especially race and gender.

Chapter Overview

Chapter 1 sets the stage for this analysis. In it, I analyze the proceedings of two Justice in Transition conferences to reveal the interplay of national and international arguments about truth telling that led to the particular form and distinctive rhetorics of the South African TRC. While the Commission's focus and goals evolved over the duration of its existence, certain of its key claims, what Paul Gready calls the TRC's "meta-message" (71)—namely, those concerning the healing power of speaking one's truth, the accountability of individual perpetrators, and the desirability of reconciliation—circulated with enough coherence and consistency to provoke the critical receptions that the subsequent chapters examine. *From Apartheid to Democracy* focuses on these highly publicized receptions of the Commission's meta-messages by oft-cited victims and notorious perpetrators—so publicized, in fact, that their TRC hearings generated imaginative responses.

Chapters 2 through 4 exemplify the argument that the TRC's public dimensions—in the dual sense of the hearings being open to the public and of their subsequent uptake and circulation—generated agonistic deliberation that began in the TRC hearings and continued in their imaginative receptions. Each of these chapters focuses on a particular *topos* (place of argument) that the TRC introduced into circulation: accountability, speech and silence, and reconciliation. I understand *topoi* to be "bioregions of discourse" that become recognizable as *topoi* when they function as inventional resources for rhetors (Eberly 6). My analysis travels across time, space, and genre, following various lines of reasoning. I first examine each *topos* as it was established by the TRC. I then note how it sprouted in its travels from the TRC mandate to the commissioners' statements during the public hearings and finally to the *Report*. I examine varied receptions of the Commission's process that stem from these *topoi*, including those of participants in the public hearings and select literary and photographic texts that represent or explicitly reference the TRC process. These receptions contribute to the "cultural conversation" about South Africa's past that the TRC helped to instigate (Mailloux 54). My method is inspired by that of anthropologist Fiona Ross, who "trac[es] the shifts of interpretation, the processes of social reworking, [and] the grounds of acceptance on which narratives come to rest" (102). Unlike Ross, who studied the reception of women's TRC testimonies in their hometowns and the effects of this reception on their everyday lives, I track the evolution of these *topoi* from the public hearings into a range of imaginative texts. These "imaginative combinations" provide insights and make arguments that were difficult to express during the public hearings due to the rhetorical and ideological constraints of the TRC process (Ndebele, "Memory, Metaphor" 21).

Chapter 2, "Ambivalent Speech, Resonant Silences," interrogates the assumptions about speech, dignity, and selfhood that informed the hearings of the TRC's Human Rights Violations Committee, and, more specifically, the special women's hearings that the TRC held to counter the silence of women victims of apartheid-era violence. How did women survivors of sexual violations challenge the TRC's assumptions about their needs and healing process, best exemplified by the TRC's maxim "revealing is healing"? After tracing the ideological origins of the Commission's approach, I examine the experience of one woman deponent, Thandi Shezi, with the TRC. I then follow the arguments around the *topos* of speech and silence into Achmat Dangor's novel, *Bitter Fruit* (2001), which shows how, *contra* the TRC's logic, a woman's decision to maintain a public silence can simultaneously facilitate and reflect her growing independence and sense of agency. This chapter challenges the logic of human rights discourse and the Western rhetorical tradition, both of which equate discourse and the speaking subject with power and presence.

Chapter 3, "Contesting Accountability," examines the conflict between the Commission and anti-apartheid activists' ways of framing the past and determining accountability. I outline the historical and ideological origins of the TRC's unwillingness to address the effects of apartheid's systemic racism and its concomitant focus on the individual perpetrator. I then ask how black perpetrators, in particular, responded to the constraints imposed by the Commission's liberal, and thus race-blind, ideology. To answer this question, I analyze the testimonies of two well-known and controversial figures, former Umkhonto we Sizwe[7] soldier Robert McBride and Winnie Madikizela-Mandela, Nelson Mandela's former wife. I then follow arguments around the *topos* of accountability into Njabulo Ndebele's novel *The Cry of Winnie Mandela* (2003). This chapter demonstrates how and why the TRC's approach conflicted with anti-apartheid activists' understanding of the collective struggle to end apartheid.

Chapter 4, "Imagining Reconciliation," examines TRC participants' visual and verbal arguments around the *topos* of reconciliation as they appear in Jillian Edelstein's photographic essay, *Truth and Lies: Stories from the Truth and Reconciliation Commission in South Africa* (2001). As in the previous chapters, I begin with an analysis of the Commission's complex, and at times contradictory, arguments about reconciliation, focusing particularly on its linking of reconciliation to democratic praxis. I then show how the individuals whose portraits and testimonies appear in Edelstein's *Truth and Lies* complicate the TRC's vision by differently "imagining" both the process of reconciliation and the nature of democratic relations in the new South Africa that the TRC sought to create (Asen 351). Drawing on Robert Asen's understanding of the "collective imaginary" as a source of "topics of discussion" (351), and Barbie Zelizer's argument that images invite speculation by "activat[ing] impulses about how the 'world might be' rather than how 'it is'" (164), I suggest that Edelstein's photographs function rhetorically by inviting speculation about the emergence of democratic norms and the possibilities for coexistence in the new South Africa. *Truth and Lies* thus showcases rhetoric's function as an art of invention "capable of creating new versions of the real and the valuable" (Atwill 206). Finally, the conclusion considers the methodological implications of my study by further elaborating on the importance of reading across genres in politically contentious situations.

I

LOCALIZING TRANSITIONAL JUSTICE

The transnational circulation of people and ideas across cultural and geographic contexts has created new situations in which persuasion can occur. Rhetoric happens when rhetors take up arguments and tropes from this global flow to effect change or achieve identification in a particular location or situation. Rhetorical scholars have urged that attention be paid to rhetoric's now "wider ecology" (Edbauer 9) and to the ways that the "global turn requires a comparative-historical frame and a broader understanding of culture, text, context, and the public sphere than what traditional rhetorical and ethnographic criticism provides" (Hesford 790). Despite these appeals, the field still tends to produce studies of purportedly bounded situations and locales, predominantly in the United States and Europe. For rhetorical scholars to understand late twentieth- and twenty-first-century events, we need to attend to the effects of the convergence of the global and the local that transnationalism makes possible. One way to grasp the rhetorical effects of the transnational "ecology" of rhetoric, particularly in sites beyond the field's traditional areas of focus, is to study truth commissions.

While the form of the truth commission is now global—countries in Africa, Asia, Latin America, and North America have held truth commissions, and currently there are calls for a national truth commission on torture in the United States—that form becomes rhetorically significant when it is used to effect change in a particular place, time, and situation. Analyzing the interplay between the generic form of the truth commission and the specific purposes that are ascribed to it in a given place and time can deepen our understanding of rhetoric in the era of transnationalism. The TRC offers a fruitful site through which to consider the implications of this transnational ecology because it is a site where local, national, and global discourses converged and interacted with the explicit intention of creating South Africa's new democracy. The participants in the TRC process spoke (or remained silent) as individuals with different sociocultural, political, and religious identifications, as South African citizens invested in the future of a particular nation-state, and as cosmopolitans versed in the global discourse of human rights.

This chapter analyzes the genesis of the South African TRC. One of the unique characteristics of the TRC—its acknowledgment of four different kinds of truth—emerged from the transnational exchange of ideas about how best to deal with a violent past. Scholars and practitioners of transitional justice have criticized the TRC's "typology of truths" (Posel 155). I return to the specifics of their criticism later in this chapter. For now I want only to emphasize that the Commission's complex approach to truth emerged not from academe, but from a tense and constraint-laden political context. That it was internally inconsistent and worked at times at cross-purposes is thus not surprising. From a rhetorical perspective, the coherence of the TRC's approach to truth matters less than the lines of reasoning and possibilities of identification and persuasion that it made possible at a particular moment in time. After briefly reviewing the history of the negotiations that led to South Africa's transition from apartheid to democracy, this chapter analyzes the contributions of participants at two Justice in Transition conferences that were held prior to the creation of the TRC in February and July of 1994.[1] It then describes the TRC's distinguishing features and the time line of its process to set the stage for the subsequent chapters' analysis of the agonistic deliberation that the TRC's varied, and at times contradictory, claims about truth and truth's effects inspired during its public hearings and in their imaginative receptions.

Negotiating the Transition from Apartheid to Democracy

That the TRC was a response to the particularities of a negotiated transition, not the realization of an abstract theory of truth and reconciliation, helps explain the complexities and contradictions of its mandate and process. Erik Doxtader's *With Faith in the Works of Words* provides a richly detailed history of the decade-long series of negotiations that lead to the end of apartheid. In the history that follows, I cover some of the same ground, but with a focus on the ways in which the TRC resulted not only from negotiations *within* South Africa but also from the insights gained from other nations' experiments with "dealing with the past" and the influences of global human rights rhetoric. Like Claire Moon, I locate the TRC's "genesis at the intersection between both global and local narratives" (18). While Moon synthesizes the scholarship of transitional justice to support this assertion, I examine actual South Africans' uptake of international arguments about transitional justice through an analysis of the transcriptions of two Justice in Transition conferences. Attending to the specific concerns of these conference participants reveals the particular ways in which global arguments about truth, justice, and reconciliation take root and are transformed in a local context.

The challenge of assigning accountability—or granting amnesty—for abuses committed against and in defense of the system of apartheid vexed the earliest phases of the transition.[2] It is important to note here that South Africa did not undergo a revolution (De Lange 20). By entering into negotiations with the apartheid government, the African National Congress (ANC) acknowledged the legal framework of apartheid despite its political position regarding the system's illegitimacy. Tension arising from this acknowledgment permeated the transitional talks and continued throughout the TRC process (De Lange; Asmal, Asmal, and Roberts). The "talk about talks" that initiated the transition began in 1984, when representatives of the National Party (NP), which had held political power continuously since 1948 and was responsible for instituting apartheid, made contact with the still-imprisoned future president, Nelson Mandela. In February 1990, President F. W. De Klerk, a "reformer," released Mandela, who had spent twenty-seven years in prison as a political prisoner; removed the ban on the ANC as well as other anti-apartheid political parties; and passed the Indemnity Act. The Indemnity Act of 1990 empowered the president to grant indemnity from prosecution if he was "of the opinion that it is necessary for the promotion of peaceful constitutional solutions in South Africa or the unimpeded and efficient administration of justice" (qtd. in Sarkin-Hughes 38). Popular perception was that this first Indemnity Act was targeted primarily at anti-apartheid activists who could not claim immunity (Ntoubandi 156). Negotiations between the NP and the various anti-apartheid parties continued in fits and starts during the two-phased Convention for a Democratic South Africa (CODESA) from December 1991 through May 1992. The Boipatong massacre on 17 June 1992 signaled the nadir of the efforts to negotiate; the Bisho massacre on 7 September of that same year served as an impetus to jump-start them. Later that September, the NP and ANC signed a Record of Understanding that laid the basis for the resumption of negotiations after the breakdown of CODESA. Though the Record of Understanding guaranteed the release of an additional five hundred ANC political prisoners, it did not include an amnesty provision for government forces or for members of the white right, who consequently pressured the government to expand the Indemnity Act of 1990. Their efforts led to the passage of the Further Indemnity Act in October 1992. This act allowed for a panel appointed by the president to grant pardons for past abuses in secret hearings and, not surprisingly, was heavily criticized by international observers (Ntoubandi 157). The National Executive Committee of the ANC rejected the legality of the Further Indemnity Act outright, insisting not only "that the truth must be known, that it must be complete, and that it must be officially proclaimed and publicly exposed," but also that only a democratically elected government should determine the form such truth telling would take (in Boraine, Levy, and Scheffer 139). Later that year, the "sunset clause," brokered by Communist Party leader Joe Slovo, addressed the ANC's criticism of the Further Indemnity Act by determining that amnesty would be granted only in exchange for full disclosure. The sunset clause laid the groundwork for the Multi-Party Negotiating Forum (MPNF), which convened on 1 April 1993 to write the interim constitution and create transitional political structures that would facilitate the first democratic election.

The interim constitution, ratified on 18 November 1993, sidestepped the vexed issue of accountability for past abuses and the uncertain legal status of the prior indemnity acts. While it required that some form of amnesty be granted, it mandated that the parliament, soon to be democratically elected, would work out the thorny details. The "postamble" of the interim constitution reads:

> In order to advance such reconciliation and reconstruction, amnesty shall be granted in respect of acts, omissions and offences associated with political objectives and committed in the course of the conflicts of the past. To this end, Parliament under this Constitution shall adopt a law determining a firm cut-off date, which shall be a date after 8 October 1990 and before 6 December 1993, and providing for the mechanisms, criteria and procedures, including tribunals, if any, through which such amnesty shall be dealt with at any time after the law has been passed.

The postamble requires some form of amnesty and links it to the general goals of reconciliation and reconstruction, but it does not define "political objective," establish a cut-off date, or provide any guidelines about the form that the amnesty-granting mechanism should take. Most importantly for my purposes here, the TRC itself "was *not* mandated or really even imagined within the interim constitution's post-amble," as Doxtader emphatically states (241). Following the democratic elections of 1994, the parliament engaged in a series of heated debates about the form of the mechanism that would grant the mandated amnesty. The newly appointed minister of justice, Dullah Omar, proposed the idea of a truth commission. Despite repeated assurances, members of the NP and the white right feared that the proposed truth commission would function as a witch hunt. They argued further that a commission would threaten the fragile reconciliation and deepen political divisions. In part to underscore that the TRC would not be "an Orwellian parody where the search for truth becomes a bludgeon to beat one party's version of history into the heads of its opponents" (De Klerk qtd. in Boraine and Levy xviii–xix), the proposal was titled the National Unity and Reconciliation Bill. After much debate, in July 1995, President Nelson Mandela signed into law the Promotion of National Unity and Reconciliation Act, which called for the establishment of the TRC.

The Promotion of National Unity and Reconciliation Act tasked the TRC with accomplishing far more than any prior truth commission. In addition to granting amnesty to individual applicants, the Commission was to analyze the "cause, nature and extent" of gross human rights violations that occurred between 1 March 1960 and 10 May 1994, recommend ways to prevent future violations, and restore the human and civil dignity of victims through testimony and recommendations for reparations. According to Alex Boraine, deputy commissioner, the TRC thus proposed "to help create the conditions for a truly new South Africa" ("Truth and Reconciliation" 142). The Commission had a bigger budget, and greater powers of subpoena, search, and seizure, than any truth commission before or since. The TRC also engaged in a "deliberate policy of maximum publicity" (Minow, "Hope" 238). This policy distinguished it from prior truth commissions, the majority of which conducted private investigations and only then produced written reports for public consumption (Hayner, "Same Species" 37). The TRC was intentionally public in multiple senses of the word: official (state-sponsored), transparent in its operations, open to all South Africans who wanted to attend its hearings, and highly publicized. The Commission sought to cultivate citizen participation throughout its process (TRC, *Report* 1: 53 and 104). It held public hearings for victims, amnesty seekers, and various other sectors (e.g., the media, the judiciary, women) that the general public and the press were encouraged to attend. In addition to these face-to-face public interactions, the Commission's proceedings circulated widely in a variety of media: "The hearings were aired live on the radio for several hours each day, and videotape clips were replayed on the evening television news. The *Truth Commission Special Report*, an hour-long Sunday night television show, had the largest audience of all South African news or current affairs shows" (Hayner, *Unspeakable* 226). The TRC functioned as a "technology of citizenship" (Cruikshank 2), educating and regulating citizens in the capacities and consciousness of liberal democratic governance. To wit, the *Report* claims that "public participation and scrutiny [by the media] . . . helped the nation to focus on values central to a healthy democracy: transparency, public debate, public participation and criticism" (1: 104). The public hearings, in particular, taught participants and observers how to participate in civic affairs in a manner befitting the new democracy. Chairperson Desmond Tutu's reminder to participants at one of the public hearings reveals the Commission's pedagogical intent: "People who may be disagreeing, and may be on all sorts of sides, but one of the things about a new dispensation on all of our democratic and constitutional rights is, is that we have, all of us, points of view which have to be respected" ("Human Rights Hearing"). Finally, the TRC's positing of reconciliation as a goal and as an outcome of its truth seeking also distinguished it from most prior truth commissions (Hayner, "Same Species" 39).[3]

The Commission convened in December 1995 and concluded in 2003 with the publication of the last two volumes of the seven-volume *Truth and Reconciliation Commission of South Africa Report*.[4] Seventeen commissioners, selected so as to represent a range of professions and political parties, headed the TRC's three primary committees—the Human Rights Violations Committee (HRVC), the Amnesty Committee (AC), and the Reparations and Rehabilitation Committee (RRC). The TRC's rhetorics shifted over the course of these eight years in response to the participation of different agents, internal and external to the Commission, as well as to the differing goals and priorities of these three committees. During the first stage of the Commission's development, as the Promotion of National Unity and Reconciliation Act was drafted and the Commission was established, a "political sense of reconciliation" dominated, with nation building as its end (A. Du Toit, "Moral Foundations" 130). According to Andre Du Toit, a professor of political science at the University of Cape Town, the work of the HRVC prevailed during the second stage and a "religious and therapeutic sense of reconciliation" through truth telling took precedence (131). The HRVC offered victims of gross human rights violations the opportunity to relate their accounts of these violations. Of the 22,000 victims who gave statements, roughly 2,000 gave their testimony in the committee's public hearings (Chapman and Van der Merwe 10). As the HRVC hearings concluded, the AC's concerns became central, with a corresponding shift away from storytelling to fact-finding and legal concerns with due process (Gready 56; Simpson 237–38). During this stage, "quasi-judicial and adversarial procedures" dominated (A. Du Toit, "Moral Foundations" 131). The AC required that individual perpetrators—not bodies, parties, or organizations—submit an application for each gross human rights violation for which they sought amnesty. Applicants had to demonstrate that their violations were politically motivated and that they had fully disclosed their nature and extent. The AC received roughly 7,000 applications, of which 1,793 were heard in its public hearings (Chapman and Van der Merwe 11). The RRC was responsible for making recommendations for reparations for victims. The state ultimately paid only a third of what it recommended—R30,000 (about $450) per victim—and it disregarded the RRC's other recommendations (Chapman and Van der Merwe 12). The writing of the *Report* governed the final stage of the Commission's progress. During this stage, the goal of making "victim and perpetrator findings" took precedence (A. Du Toit, "Moral Foundations" 130–31). In chapters 2, 3, and 4, I explore the distinctive ways in which the HRVC and AC, whose processes were more public than that of the RRC, were to serve the Commission's goals of truth and reconciliation.

Global Influences on South Africa's TRC

In form and process, the Commission reflected the priorities and insights of the transnational human rights movement, specifically the global push for truth telling and justice efforts that occurred with increasing frequency in the latter half of the twentieth century. In his foreword to the Commission's final *Report*, written at the conclusion of the TRC process, Chairperson Desmond Tutu invoked remembrance of the Holocaust to justify the Commission's insistence on opening the "wounds" of the past under apartheid: "The past refuses to lie down quietly. It has an uncanny habit of returning to haunt one. 'Those who forget the past are doomed to repeat it' are the words emblazoned at the entrance to the museum in the former concentration camp of Dachau" (1: 7). Remembrance, Tutu suggests, provides the only way to realize the rallying call of the human rights movement: "Never again!" Indeed, several years before the creation of the TRC, Kader Asmal, in his inaugural lecture as professor of human rights at the University of the Western Cape in May 1992, argued forcefully that a human rights culture would not entrench itself in the newly democratic South Africa without some sort of serious reckoning with apartheid. To support his "ten reasons why the book [on the past] must remain open now and for some time after a settlement has been reached" ("Victims" 494), Asmal referenced the efforts of "other places" (499)—Argentina, Chile, the Soviet Union, Czechoslovakia, Germany, and "even the United States" (502)—to confront their pasts. Richard Goldstone, now a judge on South Africa's Constitutional Court, similarly pointed to the instrumental role of the international human rights movement in the struggle to end apartheid to explain his endorsement of the TRC's creation. He claimed, "South Africa is unique in that it is the only country to achieve change as the result of an international human rights endeavor—and we owe a moral duty to pay our dues [sic]" (in Boraine and Levy 122). Goldstone suggests here that South Africa pay its debt to the international human rights community by adhering to one of its central tenets: the need to document, acknowledge, and publicize human rights abuses. Minister of Justice Dullah Omar argued that truth telling served the government's broader goal of creating a "human rights culture" in the new South Africa by "entrenching international norms [of documenting human rights abuses] within the framework of South Africa's domestic jurisdiction" (in Boraine and Levy 2–3). Proponents of the TRC sought to leverage the example set by other countries as well as the dictates of international law to compel South Africa to engage in truth-telling efforts.

Other nations' experiences with "dealing with the past" in the context of a political transition directly influenced the formation of the TRC. The Justice in Transition institute, founded by Alex Boraine in 1994 in response to the controversy surrounding Dullah Omar's proposal for a truth commission, played a pivotal role in bringing these international insights to South Africa. The institute hosted a two-stage conference to explore the different ways in which South Africa could confront its history of human rights violations. The first conference, Justice in Transition, took place in February 1994, when, as Richard Goldstone put it, "the idea of a Truth and Reconciliation Commission seemed like a pipe dream," one that only Alex Boraine had "the faith and confidence to carry through" (in Boraine and Levy 127). This conference "focus[ed] on the experiences of Eastern Europe and Latin America, to give [South Africans] a better appreciation of the complexity and extent of the problem and sharpen our options" (Boraine, Levy, and Scheffer xv). The Institute for Democracy in South Africa website noted that international delegates "from places as varied as Poland, Israel, and El Salvador . . . brought stories and perspective rarely heard in South African discourse." As José Zalaquett observed in his opening remarks, "a pool of world experiences is contributing to an understanding of the lessons to be learned about justice in the process of transition" (in Boraine, Levy, and Scheffer 8).

The majority of the international delegates stressed that the complexities of political transitions preclude strict adherence to absolute principles; compromises, more than ideological purity, characterize political transitions. Zalaquett advised politicians to remember that "they are dealing with an exercise in maximization, not simple righteousness" (in Boraine, Levy, and Scheffer 9). So while Juan Mendez, an Argentine human rights lawyer, advocated the principle of the "duty to prosecute" (90), other international delegates offered advice about how South Africans could make the constitutionally mandated amnesty more palatable to victims. They especially stressed the need to link amnesty to truth telling, so that amnesty would not descend into amnesia. Adam Michnik, a philosopher and theorist of Poland's Solidarity movement, lauded a mutual amnesty's ability to "open up the road to peace," but he hastened to add that "amnesty is not equivalent to amnesia and thus the past must be carefully written up and remembered" (18). Roberto Canas, a member of the negotiating team that ended the civil war in El Salvador, likewise stressed the importance of truth telling: "For a peace settlement to be solid and durable, it must be based on truth" (54). Here we see the origins of the argument that South Africa's mandated amnesty, when linked to truth telling through the requirement of full disclosure, could strengthen the new democracy. Indeed, Albie Sachs, a legal academic who served on the national executive of the ANC, reminded the international delegates, "The amnesty is balanced out with the concept of reconciliation and reconstruction. It is not a reconciliation to bury and forget the past . . . it is to assume responsibility for the past and correct the imbalances and injustices" (128). The TRC commissioners would later elaborate on Sachs's argument, presenting amnesty not as a compromise to be accepted with gritted teeth, but as the grist of reconciliation.

Localizing Global Rhetorics of Truth and Reconciliation

The South African attendees expressed gratitude to the international delegates for sharing their experiences and insights, but they also insisted on the complexity of the South African context. Mary Burton, president of the anti-apartheid organization Black Sash (1986–90) and future TRC commissioner, said, "I have wanted to call out during the conference: 'Yes, but you don't quite know what it's like for us. You don't understand the complexity of the things in which we are involved'" (in Boraine, Levy, and Scheffer 121). Burton went on to describe the Afrikaner concentration camps of the Second Anglo-Boer War (1899–1902) and the psychic effects of that experience on later generations of Afrikaners. Wilmot James, executive director of the Institute for Democracy in South Africa, urged attention to the effects of three hundred years of colonialism on social inequalities (134). Others pointed to more recent historical events and factors that would, or should, distinguish South Africa's efforts to "deal with its past." Andre Du Toit noted that state violence under apartheid took a different form than it did under South American dictatorships (130–33), while Albie Sachs, in reference to the entirety of the apartheid system, insisted that "anything that caused severe pain on the basis of racial domination must be part of the mandate [of the proposed TRC]" (146). All expressed their newfound appreciation for the "magnitude of the task ahead" (120), describing the conference as a "rich but also confusing, even contradictory, experience. There has been an overload of relevance" (130–31).

After the democratic elections in April 1994, the newly elected parliament began to debate the terms and implications of the postamble, specifically Minister of Justice Dullah Omar's proposal for a TRC. In July, the Justice in Transition institute held a second conference, the South African Conference on Truth and Reconciliation, "to encourage discussion and debate so that misgivings and misconceptions can be fully dealt with and so that maximum consensus can be reached concerning this extremely important and sensitive proposal" (Boraine, Introduction xxi). Participants at this conference began the process of localizing the insights offered by the international delegates at the first conference by considering their *kairos* (timeliness) and *to prepon* (fit) for South Africa. As Kader Asmal stated, "We will be guided, to a greater or lesser extent, by experiences elsewhere. . . . But at the end of the day, what is most important is the nature of our particular political settlement and how best we can consolidate the transition in South Africa" (in Boraine and Levy 27). While the guiding assumptions and final form of the TRC did incorporate the lessons gained from Latin American and Eastern European transitional experiences, they also reflected the unique historical and sociocultural context of South Africa.

Building on the concerns expressed at the first Justice in Transition conference, South Africans at the second conference again questioned whether and how the proposed truth commission could address the particularities of the South African context. The anti-apartheid activist Mamphela Ramphele, now vice chancellor of the University of Cape Town, asked whether the language of human rights, such as "crimes against humanity" and "human rights violations," would adequately encompass the destruction wrought by apartheid or too narrowly define the scope of responsibility for that destruction (in Boraine and Levy 32–36). Ramphele wondered whether it would create a narrow "truth," one that would exclude many victims from its purview and exculpate those "silent voters who did not stand up and say 'no!' loudly enough" (36). While endorsing the proposed truth commission, Willie Esterhuyse, a professor of philosophy, voiced the concerns of many in the white Afrikaner community about South Africa's adoption of a mechanism that was developed to address the legacy of Latin American dictatorships. Esterhuyse pointed to the factors that, in the eyes of white Afrikaners, distinguished apartheid from those dictatorships—namely, that apartheid took place under a limited democracy and that both the government and "anti-apartheid" activists committed atrocities (31). Esterhuyse further noted that the Roman Catholic influence in Latin America made "confessions and repentance semi-public affairs," whereas in South Africa the guiding principle is "confess your sins privately and live accordingly" (31). Finally, he suggested that the "ugly face of truth" might threaten the fragile reconciliatory process already under way (32). Esterhuyse concluded his remarks by again endorsing the proposal for a TRC while cautioning that its architects should include "a cross-section of interest groups" (32).

Other South African participants sought to localize the human rights rhetoric, particularly the imperative to document and acknowledge past wrongs. They drew connections between the absence of truth telling about events in South Africa's past and social relations in the present. Antjie Krog followed Mary Burton in referencing the abuses suffered by Afrikaners in the concentration camps, but she did so to endorse Omar's proposal for a truth commission. Presenting a counter-factual, she suggested that the lack of recognition of the Afrikaners' "intrinsic humanity" and "equality," evidenced first by their imprisonment in concentration camps and then again by the absence of truth telling about their suffering, contributed to the inhumane mindset of apartheid: "Wasn't the mere fact that the abuses of the [Anglo-Boer] war were never exposed perhaps not a key factor in the character that formulated apartheid's laws? . . . Perhaps if compensation had been experienced not only in material terms but also through the recognition of the intrinsic humanity and equality of all inhabitants then South Africa's history would have looked different (in Boraine and Levy 112–13). Had the English acknowledged the extent of their wrongdoing, Krog suggests, perhaps the Afrikaners would have been less likely to imagine and enforce the dehumanizing system of apartheid. Febe Potgeiter, deputy secretary-general of the African National Congress Youth League, considered the implications of Krog's argument for South Africa's future by linking analysis of the abuses of the more recent apartheid past to the creation of a different culture for the "new" South Africa. He observed, "In the process of identifying where boundaries have been over-stepped, we will be redefining our common understanding of a human rights culture" (23). In his response to the South African attendees, Dullah Omar echoed Krog's and Potgeiter's understanding, asserting that "the proposed commission should be seen as part of the attempt to build a new society" (130). Despite some misgivings, then, the South African conferees generally agreed that the proposed truth commission's critical and moral inquiries into the past would serve the goals of the new South Africa.

Prior truth commissions, along the lines advocated by Ignatieff and Steiner, had sought the most basic form of truth: a "record of who did what to whom and when" (Steiner 16). The TRC, in contrast, acknowledged truth's inherent rhetoricity by acknowledging and theorizing four kinds of truth: forensic, social, narrative, and healing. With the exception of forensic truth, the Commission's four-pronged typology recognized the role of human perception and language in the production and effects of truth claims. Participants at the South African Conference on Truth and Reconciliation first introduced the notion of multiple truths. Albie Sachs distinguished "microscopic" truth ("factual, verifiable and can be documented and proved") from "dialogic" truth ("the truth of experience that is established through interaction, discussion, and debate"), and he argued that the latter should be the TRC's "primary concern" (in Boraine and Levy 103). Sachs's "microscopic" truth became, in the language of the TRC, "forensic or factual truth," which encompassed "the familiar legal or scientific notion of bringing to light factual, corroborated evidence, of obtaining accurate information through reliable (impartial, objective) procedures" (TRC, *Report* 1: 111). The Amnesty Committee's quasi-juridical function made it rely most heavily on this form of truth. The TRC's notion of "social or dialogic" truth echoed Sachs's language almost exactly. The final *Report* defines it as "the truth experience that is established through interaction, discussion, and debate" (1: 113–14). The TRC's public process facilitated the making of "social truth."

At the same conference, Antjie Krog presaged the TRC's notion of "narrative" truth. She pleaded for the proposed truth commission to allow for the "uninterrupted telling of experiences as perceived by the victims" (in Boraine and Levy 116). The TRC heard Krog's plea. "Narrative truth" informed the "victim-centered approach" of the HRVC, wherein deponents had the "right to tell their stories of suffering and struggle" (TRC, *Report* 1: 53). According to the *Report*, "narrative truth" coincided with the "value [that] continues to be attached to oral tradition" in South Africa (1: 112–13). Through the extensive use of simultaneous interpretation, the TRC also heeded Krog's proposal that it record these stories "with respect to the individual's language, vocabulary, accent and rhythm" (in Boraine and Levy 116).

The fourth truth, "healing and restorative truth," furthered the Commission's goal of reconciliation as well as its attempt to foster a culture of human rights. The *Report* explains that "[healing truth] places facts and what they mean within the context of human relationships—both amongst citizens and between the state and its citizens—[and] contributes to the reparation of the damage inflicted in the past and to the prevention of the recurrence of serious abuses in the future" (1: 114). Healing truth worked in tandem with the Commission's embrace of *ubuntu*, a Nguni term typically translated as "humanness."[5] In the section entitled "*Ubuntu*: Promoting Restorative Justice," the TRC *Report* defines *ubuntu* as a "traditional African value" that "expresses itself metaphorically in *umuntu ngumuntu ngabantu*—'people are people through other people'" (1: 127). Nosisi Mpolweni of the Xhosa department of the University of the Western Cape describes the social relationships that lie at the heart of *ubuntu*: "The African kind of interconnectedness . . . opens up all the time, it broadens. First we take care of the person next to us, then it opens up to the family, you share, then it grows to the community. Whatever we do, we don't do it alone" (Krog, Mpolweni, and Ratele 202). In her explanation of the term, Pumla Gobodo-Madikizela, former TRC commissioner and now a professor of psychology at the University of Cape Town, similarly emphasizes the roots of *ubuntu* in African culture and its role in repairing and sustaining relationships. She states, "The emphasis of *ubuntu* is on social relationships that are based on cooperation for the good of the community. *Ubuntu* is part of the deep cultural heritage of African people" (Gobodo-Madikizela 163).

There are ongoing debates about whether *ubuntu* is, in fact, part of Africans' "deep cultural heritage." In his memoir *No Future Without Forgiveness*, TRC Chairperson Desmond Tutu claims that it is consistent with the "African *Weltanschauung*" in which "harmony, friendliness, community are great goods. Social harmony for us [Africans] is the *summum bonum*— the greatest good" (31). Like Tutu, South African theologian Reverend Wesley Mabuza, director of the Institute for Contextual Theology, states that there is "a strong link between their religious understanding of reconciliation and their African cultural roots" (qtd. in Van der Merwe 2). Mabuza asserts that *ubuntu* stems from the "African mind": "I need to say that this idea that there is secular on one side and religious on the other is a western approach. For us it is an *ubuntu* situation. Whether you are religious or not, what is the human thing to do in this situation? From the African mind I would have problems with this demarcation" (qtd. in Van der Merwe 2). Mark Sanders argues that *ubuntu*, defined as "an African ethos of reciprocity," guided the HRVC hearings by positioning the Commission as a sympathetic substitute for those perpetrators who would not claim responsibility for the human rights violations about which victims testified (9). In so doing, he argues, the TRC "generalized perpetratorship and reparative agency" (9). Other scholars, however, tend to view claims about *ubuntu*'s indigeneity and pervasiveness among African peoples with a great deal of skepticism. Yianna Liatsos suggests that *ubuntu* was promoted and cultivated by the TRC commissioners to "affirm an organic affinity between 'African ways' and the Christian message of forgiveness and redemption that Tutu and the Act advocated for post-apartheid South Africa" ("Keeping Faith"). Drawing on his research in urban black South African communities that maintain strongly retributive and violent justice practices, Richard Wilson claims that "[*ubuntu*] became the Africanist wrapping used to sell a reconciliatory version of human rights talk to black South Africans" (13).

Whatever its origins, appeals to *ubuntu* did appear in the earliest phases of South Africa's transition from apartheid and continued to appear well after the conclusion of the TRC process. The 1993 Interim Constitution and the preamble of the National Unity and Reconciliation Act both contain the following oft-cited statement about what the new South Africa would require: "There is a need for understanding but not for vengeance, a need for reparation but not for retaliation, a need for ubuntu but not for victimization." *Ubuntu* was a key feature of Chairperson Tutu's rhetoric during the TRC public hearings, and, as mentioned previously, "*Ubuntu*: Promoting Restorative Justice" is the title of a section of the final *Report*. The *Report* goes so far as to suggest that "a spontaneous call has arisen among sections of the population for a return to *ubuntu*" (1: 127), a claim it supports by quoting the testimony of Susan van der Merwe, whose husband allegedly died at the hands of Umkhonto we Sizwe, the armed wing of the ANC. In her testimony excerpted in the *Report*, Van der Merwe references *ubuntu* as the source of her belief that "every person's life is too precious" (1: 128). The *Report*'s strategic excerpt supports the TRC's claim about both the ubiquity and indigeneity of *ubuntu* in South Africa. It also underscores its nonracialism—Van der Merwe's whiteness does not prevent her from affirming this "African" concept. The final *Report* also cites the statement of Cynthia Ngewu, whose son was among the "Gugulethu Seven" killed by the police in 1986: "We do not want to return the evil that perpetrators committed to the nation. We want to demonstrate humaneness towards them, so that they in turn may restore their own humanity" (5: 367). These presumably unsolicited statements of *ubuntu* provide support for the *Report*'s assertion that South Africans concurred with its understanding that there was a "need for *ubuntu* but not for victimization" (Republic of South Africa). The commissioners undoubtedly used *ubuntu* as a rhetorical resource to explain and justify "healing" truth and its relationship to the goal of reconciliation. But once the term *ubuntu* circulated, participants and critics of the TRC defined it in their own ways. For my purposes here, the authenticity or origins of *ubuntu* matter less than its function as a *topos*, or place of argument, for participants in and respondents to the TRC process.

The TRC's truth typology produced a tangled knot more than a seamless weave. Criticism of what historian Deborah Posel calls the Commission's "wobbly, poorly constructed conceptual grid" of truths abounds (155). Some argue that the TRC's major dilemmas resulted from the fact that "the two processes—quasi-judicial fact-finding versus victim-centered storytelling—were fundamentally irreconcilable, and for a simple reason: different kinds of truth were at stake" (Simpson 238). Anthony Holiday argues similarly: "The former set of [forensic] facts served the interests of the TRC's truth-gathering task, while the latter [psychological] set, once bared in public, would be grist to the mill of national reconciliation" (54). Still others argue that the TRC never intended for the truths to cohere.

To wit, Daniel Herwitz proposes that the Commission's typology was instrumental, "operat[ing] as a homily throughout the proceedings" so as to facilitate the movement from truth to reconciliation (16). More recently, Paul Gready, while generally laudatory of the TRC framework (56), has cautioned against the embrace of a "banal post-modern" conception of truth that does not "confront and refute" obviously untrue narratives and perspectives (73). Gready notes that "simply mapping contradictory truths potentially enriches difference," and he chastises "writers and critics" who, consciously or not, provide "ammunition" for such an approach (71, 73). Gready writes primarily for scholars and practitioners of transitional justice and human rights. He seeks to draw general insights from the South African experience about the usefulness of truth commissions as a transitional justice mechanism.

My aim in the following chapters is not to judge the consistency or coherence of the TRC's truth typology—the job of the philosopher or historian. Nor is it to evaluate the typology's usefulness as a tool of reconciliation—the job of a scholar or practitioner of transitional justice. My interest instead lies in the ways in which the Commission's engagement with different kinds of truth, as well as its claims about truth's varied effects, generated contestation in the public hearings and spawned a range of imaginative receptions of the TRC process. A cultural rhetoric approach that reads across genres is able to capture this ecology of truth claims, as it occurs at the interstices of, and traverses, institutional, political, and cultural realms. The imaginative texts that I examine do not offer ambiguous postmodern conceptions of truth but rather make pointed arguments about the limitations, strengths, and unanticipated effects of the Commission's process and arguments. Because the HRVC and AC emphasized different kinds of truth and made different arguments about the effects of those truths on TRC participants and South African society at large, I address their work in different chapters. The HRVC, whose work dominated the first year and a half of the TRC process, prioritized narrative truth and suggested that it would culminate in a healing truth for individuals and those who bore witness to their stories. To this claim, captured in the slogan "speaking is healing," I now turn.

2

AMBIVALENT SPEECH, RESONANT SILENCES

Memories, like stories, can never be free.

—SARAH NUTTALL

I am not going back there. Pray to God that I am not asked to appear before the TRC again. Yes, going to the TRC was a victory. It was a victory in that I found the courage to confront my rape. It gave me a platform to share my grief. It made me talk. Hopefully, I will heal in time.

—THANDI SHEZI

The Commission's work relied on giving words to experience. Yet, women's "silence" can be recognised as meaningful. To do so requires carefully probing the cadences of silence, the gaps between fragile words, in order to hear what it is that women say.

—FIONA ROSS

Scholars and human rights activists agree that telling one's story does not necessarily promote long-term psychic recovery or healing (Hamber). However, they have found that doing so fulfills a basic human desire to "break the silence." As Priscilla Hayner explains, "truth commissions seem to satisfy—or at least *begin* to satisfy—a clear need of some victims to tell their stories and be listened to" (*Unspeakable* 135). Those commissions that hold hearings aim to create the conditions for "free speech" by providing victims with the opportunity to share their stories before a sympathetic audience. The validation that results from speaking (and from being heard) ostensibly contributes to the restoration of victims' dignity and also promotes their inclusion in the national community from which they had been excluded, thus contributing to a truth commission's nation-building project. These scenes of "free speech" intrigue rhetoricians, who share with truth commissions a faith in the transformative and dignifying power of speech. Speaking freely about the past, though, proved to be more difficult than the TRC had anticipated for both the perpetrators and victims of apartheid violence. In this chapter, I take up the *topos* of speech and silence in relation to women survivors of apartheid violence. Women survivors worked within and against the Commission's assumptions about the significance of the violations they suffered, about the spaces wherein they would want to speak their memories, and about the meanings of their silences. Some did so within the space of the Commission's Women's Hearings, while others did so by refusing to speak—by remaining silent. Their participation in the TRC process traversed the spectrum of speech and silence, revealing the rhetorical resonance of each.

Reading across time, context, and genre, beginning with the texts generated by the TRC and then considering various nonfiction and imaginative receptions of its process, creates a nuanced portrait of the rhetorical situation generated by the Human Rights Violations Committee (HRVC) and women's responses to it. In this chapter, I first provide the theoretical foundation of the TRC's belief in the causal relationships among voice, dignity, and citizenship. I then demonstrate how these beliefs shaped its engagement with women participants who tended to speak about the violations suffered by the men in their lives, rather than their own direct experiences. Women's silences about their direct experiences of human rights violations threatened to obstruct the TRC's truth-gathering and nation-building project. Commissioner Mapule Ramashala observed, "If women do not talk then the story we produce will not be complete" (qtd. in Ross 22). The Commission thus made special efforts to get women to speak through the creation of Women's Hearings. Thandi Shezi, a woman survivor, testified at these hearings in 1997. While Shezi was not a public figure prior to her appearance before the TRC, since testifying she has figured in scholarly articles, a documentary, and a play about women's experiences in detention and the psychic effects of testimony.[1] She thus became a public figure in the sense that her story has circulated widely and been appropriated to support a variety of arguments about the effects of public truth telling and the TRC process. Shezi engaged in a series of conversations with journalist Pamela Sethunya Dube in 2001 in which she reflected both on her experiences in detention and on her experience testifying before the TRC. These conversations took textual form in Dube's "The Story of Thandi Shezi." Despite the lapse in time and the intimate, unofficial nature of these conversations, I show how the TRC's arguments about voice, agency, and identity influence both Dube's framing of "Story" and Shezi's contributions to it. My analysis demonstrates the persistence and continuing power of the TRC's claims about voice and silence to shape practices of remembrance. At the same time, I demonstrate how in the Women's Hearings and the conversation with Dube, Shezi complicates those claims by asserting her identity as a survivor, not a silenced or voiceless victim, and by challenging the Commission's interpretation of the effects of her speech and of the meaning of her silences. While the Commission contoured what participants said within and beyond the hearings, it did not fully control their speech.

The remainder of this chapter offers insights into why some women would choose not to participate in the TRC process—that is, why they would choose to maintain silence. I argue that these women's silences do not necessarily or always signify voicelessness or a lack of power. Silence poses a methodological challenge; by its very nature, it eludes analysis. One way to gauge the rhetorical power of silence is by attending to its effects—both institutional, as in the TRC's Women's Hearings, and literary, as in Achmat Dangor's *Bitter Fruit*, a novel that explores the complicated origins, evolution, and effects of the silences that the TRC sought to break. Lydia, the main female character in *Bitter Fruit*, refuses the TRC's invitation to speak about her apartheid-era rape, and, in so doing, challenges its assumptions about the relationship between speech and selfhood while simultaneously resisting inscription into its nation-building project. This chapter on the *topos* of speech and silence aims to complicate both the TRC's idealized notions of "free speech," as well as its critics' claims of total foreclosure, in addition to demonstrating the resonance of silence as a "specific rhetorical art" (Glenn 2).

I Speak, Therefore I Am: The TRC's Theoretical Assumptions About Voice and Agency

The TRC's heady rhetoric about the transformative potential of victims' stories weaves together diverse discourses that nevertheless all hinge on the assumed relationship between speech and selfhood. From ancient times to the present, Western political theorists have linked speech to action and civilization. The rhetorical philosopher Isocrates (ca. fourth century B.C.E.) boldly asserted, "Of all human capabilities [speech] is responsible for the greatest goods. . . . If one must summarize the power of discourse, we will discover that nothing done prudently occurs without speech (*logos*), that speech is the leader of all thoughts and actions, and that the most intelligent people use it most of all" (*Antidosis,* §§ 251–57). Roughly two thousand years later, philosopher Hannah Arendt echoed Isocrates with her claim that speech enables human existence: "With word and deed we insert ourselves into the human world" (156–57). In the Western tradition, speaking confirms one's humanity, intelligence, and agency. Civilization itself, it would seem, requires humans who speak.

Psychoanalytic discourses similarly link memory, voice, and narration to one's psychic well-being. By the late nineteenth century, what anthropologist Rosalind Shaw describes as "a dominant memory discourse of therapy and remembering" had emerged (7). This discourse builds on claims about the pernicious effects of repressed memories; the difficulty of articulating traumatic experiences; and the benefits afforded to victims of trauma who successfully narrate their experiences of abuse. According to this theory, the creation of narrative order transforms what was once formless, unspeakable, and unmanageable into a coherent story. The process of creating and then narrating this story to oneself and to others ostensibly restores the agency that the trauma threatened or destroyed. The work of psychiatrist Judith Hermann and legal theorist Teresa Godwin Phelps conveys this chain of assumptions: that personal and political trauma affects victims in similar ways—by inhibiting their ability to speak—and that psychological recovery entails the recovery of speech. They logically posit "coming to speech" as an essential component in the reconstruction of traumatized persons and societies.

The assumed relations between speech and subjectivity coalesce in much of the literature on rape and its aftermath. Feminist philosopher Louise Du Toit asserts that "the loss of self and world is thus in both rape and torture accompanied by a loss of voice, by a loss of agency and self-extension which is carried or embodied by the ability to speak" (267). Here Du Toit collapses the distinction between voice, agency, and self-extension; the loss of one necessarily entails the loss of the others. Though she writes about the rape epidemic in South Africa, her assertion could appear in feminist literature about rape victims anywhere in the world. In her opening statement at the Women's Hearings in Johannesburg, Thenjiwe Mtintso, a commander in Umkhonto we Sizwe and herself a survivor of detention and interrogation, expresses this same *doxa* of feminist scholarship and conveys its centrality to the work of the TRC: "[This hearing] is the beginning of giving the voiceless a chance to speak, giving the excluded a chance to be centred and giving the powerless an opportunity to empower themselves" (TRC, *Report* 1: 110). For Mtintso, as for Du Toit, speech, selfhood, and empowerment are inextricably linked.

The right to speak one's own story in one's own "voice" has become a priority in legal and political arenas as well, notably in human rights activism and one of its primary genres, the testimonial. Indeed, the thirty clauses of the International Declaration of Human Rights can be interpreted collectively as an effort to protect the individual's ability to narrate her story (Slaughter 413–14). Human rights activists encourage "promotions of human welfare that tend both to encourage and to foster the human voice speaking itself" (415–16). While the right to produce one's own life narrative constitutes an end goal of human rights activism, life narratives also function as tools of advocacy to promote and defend other kinds of human rights claims (Schaffer and Smith 1). Much of the scholarship on life narratives as tools of human rights advocacy focuses on their production, reception, and circulation (5). Paul Gready examines the problematic effects of an "increasingly globalised public sphere" on the "politics and ethics" of self-narration (76). Yazir Henry, a participant in the hearings of the HRVC, provides a deeply personal account of the (mis)appropriation and circulation of his TRC testimony by the South African journalist and poet Antjie Krog as well as by other media. He writes, "The lack of sensitivity with which my story was treated once it left the confines of that space and became part of the public domain was immediately apparent. . . . It was out of my control and done without my permission" (169). Experiences like Henry's illustrate the complications that can arise when one speaks one's story, even in the ostensibly safe space of a truth commission hearing. This chapter takes up the problematics of testimony at an earlier stage—not once the life narrative is appropriated by others and circulates, but rather at the moment the testimony is elicited, and the request fulfilled ambivalently, or when the request to testify is outright refused. Before turning to these two possible responses to the call to speech, I analyze how these various discourses about the value of speech and the concomitant problem of silence converged in the work of the TRC.

According to the TRC, silencing and voicelessness were the result of the objectification that victims suffered. Victims were first and foremost the *objects* of perpetrators' violations, not the *subjects* of survival of these violations.[2] The Commission sought to validate and acknowledge "the individual subjective experiences of people who had previously been silenced or voiceless" (TRC, *Report* 1: 112). Per the Promotion of National Unity and

Reconciliation Act, it did so "by granting them the opportunity to relate their own accounts of violations of which they are the victim." Victims' "own accounts" consisted not only "of [their] individual subjective experiences," but also of the form in which those accounts were relayed; they were to contribute "their own stories in their own languages" to what the Commission called "the South African story" (1: 112). Recounting their experiences of abuse before a public audience ostensibly "restor[ed] the human and civil dignity of such victims" (Republic of South Africa). At the same time, their stories contributed to the TRC's goal of truth recovery. Indeed, the Commission subsequently claimed the interrelatedness of these processes in its final *Report*: "Establishing the truth [of South Africa's violent past] could not be divorced from the affirmation of the dignity of human beings" (1: 114). Thus the TRC linked the truth-telling and restoration-of-dignity components of its mandate. For victims' dignity to be restored, according to the logic of the TRC, they not only had to speak about their violations—to move from silence to speech—but had to do so in the public realm of the hearings of the HRVC. The *Report* asserts that the *"public unburdening of [victims'] grief"* and subsequent *"public recognition"* (1: 128, my emphasis) enacted the transformation of knowledge into acknowledgment, a process that it explains as follows: "Acknowledgment refers to placing information that is (or becomes) known on public, national record.... Acknowledgment is an affirmation that a person's pain is real and worthy of attention. It is thus central to the restoration of the dignity of victims" (1: 114). This notion of "truth as acknowledgment" lay at the heart of the HRVC's engagement with victims (A. Du Toit, "Moral Foundations" 132–34).

Authorizing those who were ostensibly invisible and voiceless under apartheid to speak in the official realm of the hearings also cultivated victims' identity as citizens. The *Report* claims that public truth telling "help[ed] citizens to become more visible and more valuable citizens through the public recognition and official acknowledgement of their experiences" (1: 110). Through the public hearings, the Commission sought to instill in victims a newfound trust of the state and the inclination to participate in civic affairs. Victims learned how to perform in their capacity as fully enfranchised citizens in South Africa's new democracy. At the same time, their participation in this state-sponsored exercise helped legitimize the new government. Elizabeth Povinelli's insight that liberal forms of recognition, such as that offered by the TRC, are conditional—"as long as real economic resources are not at stake"—and thus "cunning" here proves apt

(17). The TRC offered victims who testified neither revolution nor a radical redistribution of resources, but rather sympathetic recognition and (limited) monetary compensation.

In addition to promoting victims' healing, the restoration of their dignity, and their ability to perform as citizens, public storytelling also served the Commission's nation-building goals. Phelps explains how such public storytelling fosters what she describes as "wider healing": "If the stories are told publicly, they have the potential to construct meaning for individuals and also for nations" (60). The presence of victims' narratives in the broader "story" of South Africa made that story more meaningful and emotionally resonant, especially to those who might otherwise deny the abuses of the apartheid era. The *Report* recalls their didactic and emotional effect: "[Victims' stories] provided unique insights into the pain of South Africa's past, often touching the hearts of all that heard them" (1: 113–14). The broader historical narrative subsumed individuals' stories, making them the "pain of South Africa's past," a shared legacy of the entire nation. Like the public speech that forms the "common world" in Hannah Arendt's metaphor of "the table," victims' stories formed a historical narrative that the Commission hoped would gather South Africans of all backgrounds around the "table" of the new nation (48). The Commission's transitional logic thus required speaking subjects whose voices would speak the new nation into being.

Breaking Women's Silence: The TRC Women's Hearings

From January 1996, the TRC's official starting date, through December 1997, when the work of the HRVC concluded, the Commission gathered and processed about 21,000 victims' statements.[3] Not all of those who provided statements and desired to speak at the public hearings had the opportunity to do so. The Commission selected those deponents who were representative of the demographic of the population of the region where the hearing was taking place and whose stories represented varied perspectives on the violence and the types of human rights violations that had occurred there (TRC, *Report* 1: 146). Lars Buur, an anthropologist and member of the regional Investigation Unit of the TRC based in Johannesburg, describes the TRC's information management system as a "bureaucratic machinery of truth production," with its attendant categories, codes for violations, controlling vocabularies, and demand for "in mandate" statements (67).

Statement takers' questions shaped victims' narratives even before they were recorded on the Commission's official protocol, which itself, due to time constraints, became shorter and more formulaic over the course of the Commission's process. Commissioners' questions during the hearings themselves also constrained participants' narratives. Victims were asked to provide basic biographical information and were then invited to discuss the circumstances and context of the violation. The Hearings concluded with the commissioners' asking victims what they wanted from the Commission (Krog, Mpolweni, and Ratele 85). The various stages of the Commission's work transformed victims' narratives into *"signs* of gross human rights violations under apartheid, inscribed in statement protocols, the database, investigative reports, the Commission's archives, the final report, and, ultimately, the national archives" (Buur 80). Participants in the Commission's process had to negotiate between the stories they wanted to share and the primarily forensic report the Commission could hear, quantify, and incorporate into its final *Report*. Deponents contended with these constraints by offering layered testimonies that conformed to, but also exceeded, the narrow boundaries established by the Commission's mandate and process (Fullard; Ross; Krog, Mpolweni, and Ratele).

Several months into the HRVC hearings, a gendered pattern of testimony became apparent. While more women were testifying than men, they were doing so as so-called secondary witnesses, speaking as relatives and/or dependents of victims rather than speaking of "their experience as direct victims" (TRC, *Report* 4: 283–84). While the *Report* explains that "over the life of the Commission, commissioners distinguished less and less between what were originally perceived as 'primary' and 'secondary' victims" (4: 283), there was no shift in the Commission's definition of gross human rights violations. For example, in the Commission's modified approach, the widow of a man who was murdered would be considered a "primary" victim of a gross human rights violation because of the killing's financial impact on her. In another example, the *Report* refers to a woman who was threatened by the police at whose hands her sister had died days earlier. It observes that this woman was initially a "secondary" victim, but could easily have become a direct target of a gross human rights violation, and, thus, a "primary" victim (4: 284). In both examples, the Commission focuses on violations of bodily integrity and their (potential) effects. It does not focus on non-physical violations, nor does it focus on the apartheid system that led to violations of bodily integrity, provided the rationale for doing them, and protected those who committed them.

The Commission misconstrued women's testimony about others as constituting silence about the abuses they suffered themselves. Anthropologist Fiona Ross shows how "secondary" witnesses embedded personal narratives about a variety of violations and modes of resistance into their testimony about family members. In other words, she shows how women were, in fact, *speaking* their stories, and that the Commission simply proved unable to *hear* them (Ross 28). As the suffering heads of fractured families, and often the primary breadwinners, women were not only the direct victims of the violation of bodily integrity that befell the loved one on whose behalf they spoke, but also the direct victims of the system that enabled that violation to happen and whose daily violations they suffered. Many of them might argue that injury to a son or daughter is felt as much, or perhaps even more, than an injury to oneself. The Commission's use of the adjective "direct" to classify experiences of gross human rights violations assumed individuated subjectivities that did not accord with the self-understanding and self-presentation of many deponents, especially women. The TRC's interventions instead created the "woman" victim as a particular kind of harmed subject—one who experienced sexual violations. As Ross explains, "sexual violence was represented in the hearings and in public discourse as a defining feature of women's experiences of gross violations of human rights" (24). Furthermore, the Commission assumed that sexual violations were something "about which women *could* and *should* testify, and about which they *would* testify under certain conditions" (24).

Women's silence about their so-called direct experiences of abuse hindered the Commission's construction of a unifying historical narrative and threatened the national community the Commission hoped that narrative would cultivate. The Commission thus set about creating propitious conditions for women's testimony about the sexual violence they had experienced. "Gender and the Truth and Reconciliation Commission," a paper that Beth Goldblatt and Sheila Meintjes delivered at a workshop on the TRC and gender that was held in anticipation of the public hearings phase of the Commission's process, offered the Commission specific recommendations about how to do so. Goldblatt and Meintjes urged the Commission to reconsider the questionnaires used by statement takers so as to elicit more details about women's experiences; not to probe too deeply for graphic details, and yet not to avoid "embarrassing" or "private" subjects like sexual abuse; and to offer closed hearings, staffed only by female commissioners, so as to make it easier for women to speak of experiences not commonly discussed around men. They also called for special hearings in which women and/or community leaders could give testimony on behalf of women who were not comfortable speaking before the Commission. In response to Goldblatt and Meintjes's recommendations, the Commission amended the form used to record statements; held special workshops in which participants explored ways to bring more women into the process; and conducted Women's Hearings in Cape Town, Durban, and Johannesburg (TRC, *Report* 4: 283). Despite the TRC's stated aim of creating a space wherein these women could share their "individual subjective experiences" (1: 112), the commissioners in the Women's Hearings sought to shape the focus and content of women's testimony so as to serve the TRC's broader aim of constructing a serviceable truth for the new South Africa. In the following section, I show how one woman, Thandi Shezi, negotiated the TRC's assumptions about what and where she should remember and challenged its interpretation of the meaning and effects of her speech and silence.

Thandi Shezi: An Ambivalent Speaker at the Women's Hearings

Thandi Shezi became involved in the struggle to end apartheid while still in high school. She describes her activism as a "family thing," as both her sister and brother were already in exile when she "became active in the ANC" (qtd. in Dube 125). In 1982, she joined the ANC underground. In that capacity, she provided assistance to people who were being evicted and also participated in the ANC's campaign of "soft targets" by doing reconnaissance work and transporting weapons (Shezi). At the time of her arrest, Shezi was secretary-general of the Soweto Youth Congress (SOYCO) and had completed military training in Botswana. In her interview with Dube, she claims proudly, "Up until the day of my arrest in September 1988, I was ready to fight to the end" (qtd. in Dube 125). In mid-September 1988, however, the police descended on Shezi's family home and interrupted that "fight." The officers beat Shezi and her cousin in front of her mother and children before taking her to John Vorster Square, a prison outside of Johannesburg. During her interrogation, Shezi was beaten again, tortured, and gang-raped. Shezi was then imprisoned for four months until she managed to send a message to her family about her whereabouts through a fellow prisoner. Her family contacted a lawyer, who secured her release.

In 1997, Shezi was invited to speak about her experience at the TRC's Women's Hearings in Johannesburg. During the hearing, the commissioners' questions construct her as a "naturally gendered *victim* of violence" (Ross 25, my emphasis), not as a lifelong anti-apartheid activist and survivor. In her opening remarks, Commissioner Joyce Seroke reminds Shezi that she has been chosen to speak because she was a victim of "violations of bodily integrity" and must speak only "in brief" about her activist history: "Thandi, you are coming to relate to us about September 1988. Just in brief, if you can tell us, what happened up until when you were detained and you ended up in jail" (Shezi). For the TRC, Shezi's history of political activism serves only as a prelude to her detention and torture. In addition to framing her as a victim, the commissioners emphasize the rape over all the other violations that Shezi experienced. After listening to Shezi's testimony, Commissioner Mkhize states, "Thandi, it does seem that in all the painful experiences you went through, it seems the rape experience was the most painful one, that you cannot be able to go through [sic]." Shezi might well agree that the rape constituted the worst of the violations she experienced while in detention. My intention here is not to challenge that interpretation, but rather to demonstrate how the commissioners' questions shaped Shezi's recollection and the meaning she ascribed to it, as when Commissioner Seroke asks Shezi a leading question about the effect of the rape on her gender identity: "How did you feel about your womanhood when you were violated in this way by the police?" The question assumes that Shezi's womanhood existed in a particular form prior to the violation, and further, that the rape inevitably altered that prior form.

Shezi resists this winnowing of attention to the day of the rape and the concomitant deflection from the other aspects of her experience and identity. Later in her testimony, she attempts to convey the important role she played in the underground struggle. In response to Commissioner Mkhize's question about why she was "trusted in that male dominated area," Shezi describes herself as a comrade about whom others did not need to worry: "Maybe they saw bravery in me. I used to be able to withstand difficulty . . . they knew I was a strong person, I could withstand difficulties" (Shezi). In repeating that she was able to "withstand difficulty," Shezi calls attention to her ability to survive and persist as well as to the significance of her role in the anti-apartheid struggle. Toward the end of her testimony, as part of her appeal to the government to create women's centers, Shezi takes the opportunity to mark women's general contribution to the demise of apartheid: "It would seem in most cases our Government looks after male needs and I think we played a very important role in the struggle and the history." Without directly contesting the Commission's labels and framework, she presents herself and other women as influential actors in South Africa's historical narrative, not only (or primarily) as silenced victims of apartheid.

Shezi furthermore suggests that the silences that the TRC interpreted as voicelessness were in some instances chosen and empowering. She acknowledges that she maintained silence in the first years after her release from prison in part because she felt responsible for the rape's occurrence, an internalization of the "blame the victim" mentality. However, Shezi also shows that "holding it in" was her chosen coping strategy. Glossing Veena Das, Fiona Ross describes this as a "[construction] of agency that does not lie in linguistic competency but in the refusal to allow it; in the ability to *do* something with the experience, namely to hold it inside, silent" (49). Though Shezi recalls that she felt intensely angry, implying that this strategy was not entirely successful, she notes that she was actively "trying to grapple with this painful experience. . . . All along I had thought I could keep this inside myself and just retain it up until I die" (Shezi). At the same time, she explains how her silence stemmed from her concern that her admission would change others' perceptions of her. After speaking for the first time about the rape at the TRC hearing, Shezi states emphatically, "I do want people to empathise with me and share the pain with me." She hastens to explain, however, that she does not want to be seen as merely a victim of rape: "But I do not want them to reduce me to an object and see me as just nothing." Her testimony suggests that, after the rape, she wielded silence strategically to avoid being seen only as a victim of rape and torture. Finally, Shezi explained that her silence while in detention reflected an understanding of and respect for women activists' code of conduct. She recalls, "They used to talk about assault, that they'd been electrocuted and being [sic] insulted also, but they didn't go any beyond that. We didn't discuss about other things." Not talking about the rape confirmed Shezi's belonging in the community of women political activists and reinforced her status as a political actor and survivor.

Shezi found ways to justify both her prior silence as well as her decision to speak, finally, in a context of her choosing. During Shezi's hearing, the chairperson asked her a leading question about the psychological effects of the TRC Women's Hearings: "Do you feel that openness in fact begins to heal? And how do you feel about other women sharing their experiences in this way?" Shezi chose not to answer the question directly. She instead situates the chairperson's decontextualized question by noting the significance of the context in which such disclosure takes place. In her response, she attributes her decision to speak about the rape at the Women's Hearings to her work with Kulumane, a support group for survivors of apartheid-era violence that was formed in 1995 to educate and advocate on behalf of victims.[4] Shezi explains, "What has really helped me is Kulumane Support Group, because I saw other people relating their own experiences in Kulumane; talk about their painful experiences. I then also decided that maybe that's about time I related my experience." Shezi suggests here that speaking *in the presence of fellow survivors* promoted her healing, not the mere act of speaking, especially not to official commissioners who, while sympathetic, represent the state and are mandated to treat her as a victim. Despite Shezi's efforts to mark the effects of the context of her speech on her sense of self and dignity, the chairperson concludes her hearing with a general affirmation of speech: "I think you are an example to other women, of how talking can in fact help to heal so that one can create a sense of self-worth about oneself" (Shezi). Say it and it shall be so.

Reflections on Speech and Identity Outside of the TRC:
"The Story of Thandi Shezi"

"The Story of Thandi Shezi" emerged from conversations that took place between Pamela Dube and Shezi in January and February 2001. In her introduction, Dube contrasts this series of private conversations to Shezi's other experiences of talking about her time in detention, including her testimony at the Women's Hearings. She presents "Story" as an insider's perspective, telling readers that she "spent weeks with Thandi, trying to understand her pain and how she had survived all these years" (117). Dube does not provide details about the context or mode of these conversations. The absence of these details contributes to the informal and intimate tone. Dube implies that, with her, Shezi could indeed speak freely.

However, the text that Dube intersperses throughout "Story," italicized so as to distinguish it from Shezi's words, frames and thus interprets Shezi's remembrances for the reader. Many of these insertions voice critiques of the TRC. In one, Dube claims that "[Shezi] feels betrayed by the TRC" because it did not force Andries van Heerden to acknowledge that he had raped as well as beaten her and other women (127). In another, Dube observes that "for Thandi and many others, [the TRC] did not necessarily hold out the prospect of healing" (128). Other of Dube's insertions, however, draw on and repeat the assumptions of the TRC about Shezi's victimhood and the meaning of her speech and silence. Dube repeats, verbatim, Commissioner Seroke's insinuation that the rape deprived Shezi of her "womanhood": "This is [Shezi's] story. It starts on the day her womanhood was taken from her and her soul and her body ripped apart" (117). This introduction positions Shezi as an objectified and gendered victim. While a differently constrained rhetorical scene than that of the Women's Hearings, this "Story," like all stories, is still shaped and mediated.

As she did in the Women's Hearings, Shezi works within and against those assumptions to forge her identity as a survivor. She remembers herself as powerfully and vocally resistant during the rape and resourceful and clever during her time in detention. In her TRC testimony, Shezi claimed that it was physically impossible for her to speak during the rape: "I had already been injured and the tongue had been torn after the electric shock. So I was in no position to speak at that stage. . . . I was helpless" (Shezi). Here Shezi presents herself as literally voiceless and thus disempowered—the quintessential woman victim from whom the Commission expects to hear. In her interview with Dube, however, Shezi recalls the rape quite differently, going so far as to comment on her discovery of her voice and quoting her verbal resistance to her rapists: "I found my voice and asked them, 'If you hate black people so much, why are you enjoying the body of a black woman?'" (qtd. in Dube 120). In this revised remembrance, Shezi is strong and fearless. Indeed, at the very moment that she claimed literal speechlessness in her remembrance before the TRC, Shezi claims that she "found [her] voice," a voice with which she wryly observed the hypocrisy of the police. With Dube, Shezi also recalls her survival tactics as the rape was taking place: "It was then that I decided: I am not going to give in. I had to fight. Physically, I knew it was impossible. A small voice inside said to me: to survive, you have to remove your soul from your body" (qtd. in Dube 121). My intention here is not to ascertain which of Shezi's remembrances is more truthful or accurate. Rather, I want to call attention to how Shezi takes the opportunity to remember herself either as she actually was or as she would like to have been. Remembrance here becomes a mode of identity-construction in which Shezi highlights her voice and agency. In her revised remembrance with Dube, she spoke, decided, persevered, and, ultimately, survived.

A similarly confident and empowered tone characterizes Shezi's remembrances of her time in detention. She calls herself "an 'expert'" in survival tactics in jail and refers to her various strategies as an "art" (qtd. in Dube 123). Shezi explains to Dube how she coped with an abusive warden by beating her up and making the injuries appear to be the result of the warden's accidental fall on the wet floor of Shezi's cell (122). She also describes the intricate system involving "swinging bags" that she and other women political prisoners devised to get reading materials from the common inmates on the floor below who were allowed newspapers, books, and radios (123). Finally, she explains how she "managed to befriend a prison guard" so that she could have contact with other political prisoners (123). One of these contacts resulted in Shezi's communication with her family about her location and her eventual release from prison. These details of Shezi's resistance and empowerment characterize her as a speaking survivor, not the passive, silenced, and objectified victim imagined by the TRC.

With Dube, Shezi also expresses ambivalence about the TRC process itself. She explains that speaking before the Commission was at once traumatizing and affirming. Shezi states that "[the TRC] made me talk," and she prays that she will not be "asked to appear before the TRC again" (qtd. in Dube 128). Shezi's phrasing hints at the sense of obligation and compulsion experienced by women who wanted to support the TRC process but were reluctant to accept its framing of their past experiences and identities. And yet, despite her marked ambivalence, Shezi says twice that appearing before the TRC was a "victory" (qtd. in Dube 128). Consistent with her remaking of her remembrances of the rape and detention, we witness Shezi's claiming and renaming of her experience before the TRC in ways that serve her present-day needs. She serves as a powerful example of a rhetor who achieves some degree of agency in the face of constraints and controlling assumptions about her selfhood and modes of coping via speech and silence. Shezi's vexed relationship to the TRC helps explain why some women would choose not to participate in its process at all—that is, why they would opt to remain silent.

Resonant Silences in Achmat Dangor's *Bitter Fruit*

By its very nature, silence eludes textual analysis, but it is not without effects. In tracing the fluid relationship between imposed and chosen silences as well as the spectrum of women survivors' engagement with the TRC, I turn now to the novel *Bitter Fruit*. I argue that its representation of the characters Lydia, a willfully silent victim of an apartheid-era rape, and Michael, the "bitter fruit" that results from that rape, challenges the TRC's negotiation of South Africa's relationship to its past, particularly its emphasis on public verbal truth telling as a mode of personal healing and as a mechanism of national reconciliation. *Bitter Fruit* posits silence, writing, and action as alternative responses to abuses that occurred during apartheid, and it suggests that the path leading to the new South Africa will be more circuitous than that envisioned by the Commission.

As a public intellectual, political figure, and established writer, Achmat Dangor is uniquely positioned to offer a novelistic response to the Commission's efforts to break women's silences. Dangor grew up in what he describes as a "staunch, if not dogmatically 'fundamental' Muslim environment" (*Bold Type* interview) in one of the "coloured" townships of Johannesburg. There he witnessed firsthand the forced removals of different "population groups" in response to apartheid government dictates. Dangor claims to have always felt compelled to address the injustices wrought by apartheid, though not necessarily to become an active participant in a postapartheid government: "Politically, I have always been moved by the need to help bring about change, not necessarily to become a functional part of that changed society" (*Bold Type* interview). Despite his stated desire, Dangor has been as politically active during the transition from apartheid as he was during the struggle. He has consistently maintained one foot in South African politics and the other in the realm of letters. In 1981, at the height of mass mobilization and popular participation in the struggle, he founded a black-led development agency, the Kagiso Trust. He was the executive director from the agency's founding until 1991. After the transition, Dangor served variously as the chief executive of the Nelson Mandela Children's Fund and the Mandela Rhodes Foundation; interim director of the World AIDS Campaign; and director of advocacy, communications, and leadership at UNAIDS. He currently serves as the CEO of the Nelson Mandela Foundation, which "contributes to the making of a just society by promoting the vision, values and work of its Founder and convening dialogue around critical social issues."[5] In a *Bold Type* interview about "why he writes," Dangor explained, "From the day I was born until literally 46 years later, I lived in a country that desperately needed change, and desperately resisted change." Most of Dangor's writings are set in South Africa and address the twentieth- and twenty-first-century South African political experience. He has developed a global literary reputation. *Bitter Fruit* was on the 2004 shortlist for the Man Booker prize.

Dangor recalls three specific "flashes of insight" that drove him to remember in the form of the novel *Bitter Fruit* (*Ledge* interview). These "insights" convey his conscious and what he deemed necessary decision to participate in the "cultural conversation" about South Africa's past that the TRC instigated (Mailloux 54). The first "insight" resulted from his frustration with the TRC. He felt that none of the participants in the TRC hearings "grasp[ed] what they're doing. They're taking all of South Africa's history and putting it in the public domain. . . . It was really something that I felt needed to be done from a re-imagined point of view" (*Ledge* interview). Here Dangor insists that the TRC process has only begun the necessary excavation of South Africa's violent past. He suggests that the intensity of the Commission's hearings, and the enormity of its historical endeavor, exceeded the cognitive and affective capacities of those involved. He implies that the TRC's insertion of this history into the public domain might have a similarly numbing effect, providing the public with a litany of stories, one more horrific than the next, but without contextualizing those abuses or inquiring into their reverberations across time and space. Without critiquing the Commission per se, Dangor identifies the need for an imaginative treatment of the "human drama" that its hearings generated (*Ledge* interview), one that will move readers beyond the facts of abuse toward an understanding of those abuses' personal and political consequences. He insists that the arts can contribute to that process by exposing South Africans' "sometimes deliberately contradictory viewpoints" of their past (*Bold Type* interview). Unlike the TRC, which was driven by its *telos* to create an "inclusive remembrance" that would facilitate "the creation of national unity and transcending [sic] the divisions of the past" (TRC, *Report* 1: 116), these imaginative treatments are not obliged to represent, reconcile, or transcend the differences in South Africans' perspectives on the past.

Dangor's "second insight" compelled him to address the "taboo barrier" that prevented South Africans from hearing women's stories of rape and other sexual violations (*Ledge* interview). He refers to this "taboo barrier" as "the soft flesh of South Africa, the parts that we don't want to talk about or feel, the wounds and the bruises" (*Ledge* interview). Here Dangor seems to conceive of South Africa's past as embodied experience, remembered as much in the body as in words. Dangor claims that he had this inspirational "insight" upon concluding that the Commission held *closed* hearings not only because "many of the victims requested it, [but also because] South Africa wasn't yet ready to talk about the dark side of war" (*Ledge* interview). He attributes that reluctance to South Africa's colonial legacy of "the worst kind of Victorian prudery" (*Ledge* interview). Dangor implies that the Commission held the Women's Hearings not only out of respect for women who did not want to speak their stories publicly, but also because it feared challenging the taboo around sexual violations. *Bitter Fruit*, then, constitutes his effort to challenge the prudery that erects those "taboo barriers." The quotation from André Gide that opens part 1 of the novel makes Dangor's intentions explicit: "I will teach you that there is nothing that is not divinely natural.... I will speak to you of everything" (2). *Bitter Fruit* reeks of "mortal belching" (8), "pungent farts" (8), "decaying metabolism" (4), and "overripe figs" (38). It further challenges South African readers' "Victorian prudery" with detailed descriptions of sexual encounters, both gay and straight, often abusive or nonconsensual, and always overlain with issues of power and race.

Dangor's third "flash of insight" concerned his desire to give voice to the stories of women who chose not to participate in the TRC's Women's Hearings, "[women who are] personified—represented—by the character of Lydia" (*Ledge* interview).[6] His representation of Lydia clearly struck a chord with readers. The novel *Bitter Fruit* emerged from the critical responses that Dangor received to a short story that eventually became the first chapter of the novel. The short story ends with Lydia dancing barefoot over shards of glass in response to her husband Silas's announcement that he has seen Du Boise, the policeman who raped her with impunity during the apartheid era. According to Dangor, readers of the short story exclaimed, "What are you going to do now?" and "This is exploitation!" (*Ledge* interview). These readers wanted something other than a representation of a gross human rights violation that irrevocably destroyed the victim, turning her pain into a spectacle that serves only the voyeurism or intensifies the hopelessness of readers. Dangor responded to these vehemently negative responses by writing the novel *Bitter Fruit,* in which Lydia does cope with her trauma, but not by speaking at the TRC's Women's Hearings or by being, in his words, "a Superwoman that overcomes all her traumas by simply ignoring them" (*Ledge* interview). Through its depiction of Lydia's evolution, the novel critiques the TRC's mode and valuation of public remembrance and its concomitant attempts to break women's silence.

Summary of *Bitter Fruit*

Bitter Fruit traces the dissolution of a family literally born of, and ultimately undone by, the violence of apartheid. The action of the novel takes place in 1998, the year after the Commission concluded the hearings of the HRVC and during which it released the first five volumes of its final *Report*.[7] The event that sets the novel in motion and motivates the characters' actions occurred many years earlier, in December 1978, when Silas and Lydia Ali—who are "coloured," according to apartheid-era racial designations—were recent newlyweds, and the apartheid police detained them. Unbeknownst to Lydia at that time, Silas was a member of the African National Congress. During the roundup, Du Boise, one of the policemen, rapes Lydia in a police van while Silas beats helplessly on its sides. In her diary, Lydia recalls the silence that ensued immediately after the rape:

> Silas and I walked down the quiet, peaceful street, both of us silent. He had stopped moaning, but did not know how to reach out and touch me. . . . Perhaps his touch would have drawn me closer to him and to his struggle. . . . But his fear, that icy, unspoken revulsion, hung in the air like a mist. It would enable me to give life to Mikey, my son [the "bitter fruit" of the rape]. At that moment, in Smith Street, Noordgesig, I crossed over into a zone of silence. (129)

While Silas's "fear, that icy, unspoken revulsion" does initially silence Lydia, she is not voiceless. In her diary, she goes on to describe precisely the experience that the Commission will urge her to share at the Women's Hearings. Her diary entries begin on the day after the rape—a gross human rights violation, according to the TRC's interpretation of its mandate—and they end on May 16, the day that "they completed the TRC White Paper, ready to go to the parliament" (134). The entries thus parallel exactly the Commission's mandate and time line.[8] Unlike the voiceless victims of the Commission's rhetoric, Lydia's diary portrays a victim who seeks to verbalize her experience, but who finds herself stymied—trapped in a "zone of silence"—by the discomfort of those who are closest to her (129). Eighteen years later, Silas interrupts that "zone of silence" when he tells Lydia about his chance encounter with Du Boise in a supermarket (129), setting the action of the novel in motion and instigating an argument about the TRC's appeal for public remembrances of violations like the one Lydia experienced. This argument results in yet another series of silences, first imposed but then chosen.

Initially, Lydia is the silenced victim that the TRC envisions. She wants to speak about her experience and is frustrated and disappointed by Silas's and her parents' resistance to doing so. Silas offers several reasons for his refusal to speak about the rape, effectively silencing Lydia. All of his disparate arguments subordinate Lydia's needs and desires to his own or to "the struggle."[9] At first he insists that there "was no need to [talk about the rape]" (13), a claim he quickly modifies by insisting that the initial silence was called for by the political exigencies of that time: "It was a time when, well, we had to learn to put up with those things" (13). Silas does not elaborate on this point, leaving the reader to infer that the anti-apartheid struggle required sacrifice from everyone and that complaints of any variety were not countenanced. His comment hearkens back to an earlier episode in their marriage in which he similarly justified an extramarital affair that he had with "a comrade in the 'movement'" (12). Lydia recalls Silas's self-defense: "People in the underground were in constant danger . . . and this created a sense of intimacy, it was difficult to avoid such things" (13). Silas explained that Lydia "had to be told [this] so that she would understand the 'context,' so that her rage would not be 'misdirected'" (12–13). In other words, he suggested that the psychological demands placed on active agents in "the movement" eclipsed Lydia's personal needs and expectation of fidelity in their marriage. As feminist critics have demonstrated, so-called women's issues—from a politically motivated rape to the interpersonal dynamics of a marriage—are frequently relegated to the sidelines during liberation struggles.[10] Though Silas subsequently acknowledges that he did not have the right to determine whether there was a "need" to discuss the rape, and he never suggests that the rape was an acceptable casualty of the struggle against apartheid, he does maintain the notion that Lydia's personal experience was rightly subordinated at that time to the ostensibly distinct, and more important, movement to end apartheid.

Lydia's sense of being sidelined and disregarded during the anti-apartheid struggle contributes to her decision to maintain silence about the rape even when Silas and the TRC urge her to speak. During the argument that follows Silas's announcement about Du Boise's amnesty application, he tells Lydia, "We have to deal with this" (15). What Silas really means here is that she, Lydia, should speak at the Women's Hearings and thereby deal with her anger and pain. Lydia resents the tardiness of Silas's concern and his reliance on the Commission to facilitate their overdue engagement with its repercussions. She also resents his attempts to make "her pain his tragedy" (127). She reflects bitterly that he only crashed the "zone of silence" into which they had both settled "because of his ego, his concern with *his* suffering" (129, 122). Silas himself acknowledges his tendency to claim Lydia's suffering as his own. When he suppresses an urge to panic at the sight of Lydia's bleeding feet, he tells himself, "He could not—once more—scream and weep louder than her, just as he had done nearly twenty years ago [when she was being raped]" (19).

Lydia also resists having her voice and experience become professional stepping-stones for Silas, who is the liaison between the TRC and the Department of Justice. She recognizes that he is disappointed when she refuses the Commission's offer, as "her appearance would have given him the opportunity to play the brave, stoical husband. He would have been able to demonstrate his objectivity, remaining calm and dignified, in spite of being so close to the victim" (156). She refuses to enable this gendered performance in which her suffering and vulnerability would highlight his strength and reserve. In light of Silas's insistence that she participate in the Commission's process (and the distinct roles that they each would inevitably play in so doing), and given their contentious history concerning the hierarchy of personal and political needs, Lydia's decision to maintain public silence about the rape—not to cope with her anger as Silas demands (and desires)—constitutes a subtle form of rebellion against being told what, why, how much, and when to feel and speak. As Helene Strauss observes in her analysis of Lydia's rejection of Silas's and the TRC's urging that she speak at the Women's Hearings, "Lydia's refusal to let [them] determine the moment of release serves as an attempt at reclaiming female agency amidst the overdetermining constraints of patriarchal benevolence" (para. 4). So often "women's issues" are taken up in the service of a broader agenda in which they have been deemed topical or convenient, not because there has been a foundational shift in priorities and thinking about gender.

Silas becomes the prism through which Lydia evaluates and critiques the TRC. She claims that he is motivated by his fear of chaos, the unpredictable, and the unforeseen. Her skepticism about Silas's way of managing his anxiety shapes her perception of the Commission's work. Lying awake in their bedroom, gazing at its contents, she reflects on what she calls Silas's "rule of law": "This was her husband's world, filled with recorded knowledge, a desperate orderliness of catalogued books and research papers. A history of the world, a *containment* of history, of civilizations won and lost through the rule of law. This was his true north, the rule of law" (155). According to Lydia, Silas relies on history and the "rule of law" to tame those forces that threaten his "desperate orderliness," as if recording and documenting knowledge and events would make them less susceptible to the vagaries of time and human nature.[11] She conflates Silas's "rule of law" with that of the Commission, observing how poorly this approach serves the victims of apartheid: "How little his rule . . . had helped all those 'victims' who had told their stories before the Commission. The brave victims and the wise Commissioners, the virtue of both defined as if by divine decree" (156). Lydia derides the Commission's efforts to contain and control South Africa's legacy of violence and those whose lives that violence shaped and created.

For Lydia, the rape remains an open and present wound. Remembrance is a luxury, one available only to those for whom the wound has sufficiently healed or for whom it was not particularly severe in the first place. In her argument with Silas, she counters his claim that his suffering was equivalent to hers, characterizing his experience as "a memory to you, a wound to your ego, a theory" (14). Lydia points to the permanence and immutability of the rape to challenge the TRC's promise of closure as the result of public testimony. She recalls with more than a hint of sarcasm the words of "the young lawyer from the TRC" in whose eyes she detected "an evangelist's fervour": "This is an opportunity to bring the issue out into the open, to lance the last festering wound, to say something profoundly personal" (156). She confronts the Commission's hyperbolic goals and its rhetoric of transformation with her own assertion that testifying will change "nothing": "It would not have helped her to appear before the Commission, even at a closed hearing. . . . Nothing in her life would have changed, nothing in any of their lives would change because of a public confession of pain suffered. Because nothing could be undone" (156).[12] That Lydia refers to the experience as "a public confession" suggests that she perceives the Women's Hearings more as a trial or church confessional, in which she is the perpetrator/sinner, than as a space of healing in which she is the victim/survivor. She rejects the allegedly therapeutic and ontological effects of public speech that motivate the Commission's effort, countering its rhetoric of transformation with an equally forceful argument about the permanence and immutability of the effects of rape.

Like Thandi Shezi, Lydia hoped to share her experience with interlocutors of her choosing. She did not seek the opportunity to speak before an audience of strangers who represented the state and needed her story to construct a "complete" history for the new nation (TRC, *Report* 1: 112). Having acquiesced to the silence that Silas's initial response to the rape created, she now seeks to maintain it and thus avoid waking her demons. But Lydia's is not an empty or inactive state of silence. With silence, she actively blocks out others and creates an internal world that allows her to move beyond the rape. She reflects on her decision to retreat into silence: "For her to come to terms with what had happened, she would have to seek some inner serenity, lock all her disturbing recollections into that secret crypt in her memory . . . [the CD player that Silas gave her] had become her source of silence, a filter through which she could screen the world" (Dangor, *Bitter Fruit* 122). Within her now consciously chosen silence, shielded from the pressures of Silas and the TRC, Lydia engages in alternative strategies to cope with the rape and its aftermath, ones that do not merely occur outside the official domain of the state, i.e., the TRC's hearings, but rather actively distance her from her family and South Africa's nation-building efforts.

Bitter Fruit offers several variations on the idea of silence as a necessary and sometimes productive "filter" in personal and political life (122), rather than as a condition that signifies absence, voicelessness, and inaction. The novel's silences have diverse effects; they are protective and generative, yet also damaging and stifling. Kate, Silas's friend and colleague, offers one such nuanced perspective on the effects of silence when she contemplates the possibility of Silas's discovery that she and Mikey (Silas's son) are having an affair. Without disregarding the omissions and distortions that silence requires, Kate finds solace in the notion of protective "spheres of silence." She tells herself, "We'll learn, all of us, to live in our spheres of silence, not saying the unsayable, denying everyone the pleasure of seeing us suffer the divine virtue of the brave new country: truth. We have to learn to become ordinary, learn how to lie to ourselves, and to others, if it means keeping the peace, avoiding discord and strife, like ordinary people everywhere in the world" (138). Though "the truth" to which Kate refers is the affair that she is having with Mikey, she alludes to the TRC's aims of public truth telling through her sarcastic references to "the divine virtue of the brave new country: the truth" (138). Her reflections suggest the limitations of the Commission's maxim of "speaking is healing" not only to intimate affairs such as her own, but also to some of the matters that fall directly under its domain. She contemplates the possibility of "*not* saying the unsayable" (138, my emphasis). In her assessment, the new South Africa will have come of age when it can cope with "spheres of silence" (138), perhaps even with lies, on the understanding that while they dissemble and separate, they also help maintain the peace.

Bitter Fruit also provides a platform for Silas's musings on the importance of muffled truths, if not outright silence, at least in political affairs. Taken to an extreme, his approach becomes nothing more than dodging and hedging. For example, Silas advises "his" minister to deflect criticism of the truth and reconciliation process by "spin[ning] even more elaborate webs, words and meanings that turned in on themselves, full of 'nuance and context'" (109). While acknowledging the possibility of abusive evasions such as these, the narrative offers an alternative framework for understanding his approach toward "truth." When Silas refers to his role as a liaison between the Department of Justice and the TRC to explain his reluctance to discuss the rape with Lydia, he indexes the tension between the kind of bold public speech that the TRC elicits, which is comparable to the "naked" exchange that Lydia seeks to have with him, and the muted language, outright silences, or selective amnesia that are required by other aspects of (or parties to) the political transition: "He was trained to find consensus, even if it meant not acknowledging the 'truth' in all its unflattering nakedness" (63). As the "fixer," Silas has to negotiate between the TRC's quest for harsh "truths" and the compromises required by still-powerful parties to the transition. He implies that the aversion to candid talk that culminated in the absolute silence between him and Lydia, and consequently drove a wedge between them, might at the same time have helped safeguard the fragile political transition. In short, particular situations require degrees of silence that entail sacrifices, yet at the same time yield certain benefits. Silas vacillates over the course of the novel, at one moment endorsing silence and evasion, at another encouraging Lydia to speak at the TRC's hearings. His waffling suggests only that, in a time of transition, the calculus of the benefits and pitfalls of frank exchange and silence changes constantly.

The negotiated evasions and forms of silence in the life of the Ali family mirror those that protect the fragile political truce. For example, rather than directly addressing a borderline incestuous episode between Lydia and Mikey, the Alis instead "established a code of silence, a set of mutual understandings . . . whatever happened on *that day* would not be spoken about or even hinted at" (151).[13] According to the "speaking is healing" logic that motivates the Commission's work, their decision not to address this disturbing incident verbally jeopardizes their ability to recover from whatever damage it may have caused to their individual psyches and to their relationships with one another. While *Bitter Fruit* does not celebrate the Ali family's "code of silence" as inherently positive or healing, it offers a nuanced analysis of what transpires within it. The narrator explains how the episode and the ensuing silence transformed the family dynamics: "They would think of it as *that day* in their minds, independently acknowledging that their relationships with each other had started their real transformation when they sat trapped in their separate spaces" (151). The "code of silence" traps and isolates Silas, Lydia, and Mikey from one another and precludes communications that might enable them to reestablish their damaged relationships. In it, they are "unable to reach out to each other, unable to express outrage or assert innocence" (151). At the same time, the "code of silence" prevents potentially destructive exchanges that might place further stress on their already frayed relationships, for they are also "unable to accuse, justify or recriminate" (151). What the hiatus on speech does *not* do, however, is provoke or signal inaction: Silas, Lydia, and Mikey's simultaneous inability to turn *to* or turn *on* one another causes each to turn inward, resulting in the transformation of their understanding of themselves, of their interpersonal relationships, and, for Michael, of his relationship to the TRC and the new South African state.

The Ali family's "code of silence" creates space for Mikey's transformation. The narrator observes the changes that occur within the first month of the silence in the Ali household:

> Michael has a feverish energy that seems to consume his youthfulness. He is taller and leaner, he acquires a dark-clothed attractiveness....
>
> All this in one month. How rapidly the quicklime sets on pauperized emotions! (169)

As with the novel's other treatments of silence, ambiguity marks this description of its effects on Mikey. On the one hand, the "code of silence" instigates his maturation; within it, perhaps as a result of its impoverishment of his emotions, Mikey can become Michael. On the other hand, there are the costs of the silence: the deadening of Mikey's emotions and the severing of his ties to Lydia and Silas. Mikey's foundation, however, consists primarily of "pauperized emotions" buried under "quicklime," leaving the reader to wonder whether his triumph over youthfulness is pyrrhic.

Mikey's transformation begins with his determination to learn more about his family's personal history and its imbrication in the history of

South Africa, topics that heretofore held little interest to him. With obvious discomfort, he observes the parallels between his thinking and that of the TRC: "He can no longer think of the future without confronting his past. Christ, he thinks, I am beginning to sound like Archbishop Tutu" (131). He further disavows the messy and intimate nature of his amateur exploration. The narrator explains, "Michael hates dwelling on the past, looking back is such a fruitless exercise . . . it is one thing to study history, quite another to go and search for 'meaning' in the petty annals of dusty streets. Yet he feels it is something he must do" (181). The personal significance of Michael's endeavor simultaneously drives and repels him. Initially, he attributes his newfound interest in his family history to a desire to disprove Lydia's assertion that he is the product of the rape. However, he quickly discards that explanation, asking himself, "Is it not enough to want to discover your roots simply for the sake of it?" (186). To Silas's relatives, Michael simply says, "I want to find out more about my beginnings" (187). He finally accepts that his quest is driven entirely by his need to know a history that intimately concerns him.

Though Michael struggles to accept his desire to know his personal history, both he and Lydia attribute the Commission's inability to empathize fully to its lack of an intimate connection to the events under its purview. The Commission's limitations are made incarnate in the person of Archbishop Tutu, who, Michael observes, can sympathize but not empathize: "What does *he* know? He has never been raped, nor is he a child of rape" (131). Lydia makes a similar point as she justifies her refusal to speak at the Women's Hearings. She asks Silas, "You think Archbishop Tutu has ever been fucked up his arse against his will? . . . He'll never understand what it's like to be raped, to be mocked while he's being raped, to feel inside him the hot knife—that piece of useless flesh you call a cock—turning into a torture instrument" (16). With Lydia's disavowal of Tutu's attempt to empathize, Dangor might also be calling readers' attention to his novel's inherent limitations as an empathetic witness to the women whose experiences it seeks to represent.

What *Bitter Fruit* does do, however, is give life to aspects of apartheid and its legacy that the Commission's mandate excludes and the silences that those exclusions unintentionally create. Michael's investigation of his family history, for example, takes him on a historical path forged by the forced relocations, a form of human rights violation that fell outside the Commission's mandate. Michael reflects, "Yes, he can write his history and the history of a whole country, simply by tracing his family's nomadic movements from one ruined neighborhood to the next" (186). What most distinguishes Michael's and the TRC's engagement with South Africa's violent past is his response to the historical details that he unearths. For him, learning the truth about his mother's rape is not compensation enough. He decides to kill Du Boise before the Commission responds to his application for amnesty. When he pulls the trigger on Du Boise, he whispers, "My heritage . . . unwanted, imposed, my history, my beginnings" (276). Having dealt with his personal history as he sees fit, Michael completes the transformation that began in the Ali family's "code of silence": "He, too, is going to a death of sorts. Michael is to die; Noor will be incarnated in his place" (277). Rather than accepting truth as a form of restorative justice, as the TRC encourages victims to do, Michael enacts his own brute form of retributive justice, an action that takes him outside the limits of national and family order. After killing Du Boise, he plans an extended exile in India.

Like Michael, Lydia experiences transformation within various silences: one, the "zone of silence" that was initially imposed on her but then maintained by choice, and the other, the mutually agreed-upon Ali family's "code of silence." The layered silences that she experiences facilitate her movement away from South Africa's weighty history and its nation-building effort. For Lydia, they create a safe space, first described in the narrative as a "filter" and later as a "cocoon": "[Lydia] is also rapidly being transformed, terms and thought processes that astonish everyone . . . all look at her as if she is a strange insect emerging from a cocoon . . . wondrous, fearful of her own new wings, Lydia is hesitant at first, speaks as if seeking approval and permission" (170). This figurative language posits silence as a protective barrier that shields its delicate contents from damaging external forces. In a transitional process that mirrors that of the new South Africa, but that occurs on parallel rather than convergent tracks, Lydia emerges from her "cocoon" as an independent woman, increasingly less encumbered by her obligations and commitments as a wife and mother. The narrator observes, "This new and hardened Lydia, acquiring a glib new language. She had her own car now, was free to do things independently . . . she no longer needed him [Silas]" (255). Lydia thus establishes a life that is increasingly separate from that of her family's, using the car to work longer hours in a hospital far from where they live.

In defiance of the Commission's imperative that South Africans verbally confront their recent past and participate in the construction of a more inclusive historical narrative, Lydia, like Michael, instead seeks to distance herself from that past, using silence to do so. Her silence does not signal a negation of the influence of that history or the rape, but rather her decision to establish a different relationship to it. When Silas implores her to talk in a desperate move to save their marriage, she uses silence to deflect his words: "No, no, she is not going to listen to his sordid confessions . . . she remains quiet, hopes that her silence will signal her determination to end their relationship, this marriage that has become a farce" (279). In this instance, the withholding of language communicates more clearly than any words Lydia's resolve to terminate the bonds of family. To underscore her decision, Lydia also decides to unburden herself, literally, of one textual historical record. On the occasion of Silas's fiftieth birthday, she decides to give him the diary that his mother had entrusted to her "for safekeeping" in the early days of their marriage. The narrator relates her thoughts as she considers giving him the diary: "Only women, wombed beings, can carry the dumb tragedy of history around with them. History is a donkey's arse. . . . Hand Silas his heritage, say something short but profound, kiss him on the cheek, then walk away, free of him and his burdensome past" (251). In her reflection, the diary is the repository of a complicated legacy that she no longer feels compelled to address or confront. Her decision to relinquish the diary, and the national history of apartheid South Africa that it contains, mirrors her rejection of the Commission's appeal to collaborate in its creation of an official collective memory for the new South Africa.

Rather than defining Lydia's agency as a "coming to speech," the concluding lines of *Bitter Fruit* suggest that her freedom lies in her newfound ability to disentangle herself from the burdens placed on her by familial relationships and the nation, as represented in part by the TRC's efforts to elicit her story and her participation in the political life of post-apartheid South Africa. Lydia's desired trajectory is the inverse of the Commission's verbal encounter with complicated personal, social, and political histories. She seeks to free herself from public and private "commitments to a past not of [her] choosing" (Vivian 57). The final image of the novel is of Lydia heading toward an unknown future, one bound to neither her biological nor her national family. Nor is it arrived at through speech. Alone in her new car, she drives out of Johannesburg into the veldt: "Time and distance, even this paltry distance, will help to free her. Burden of the mother. Mother, wife, lover, lover-mother, lover-wife, unloved mother" (Dangor, *Bitter Fruit* 281). Quoting a Leonard Cohen song, Lydia hums, "Carry your own burdens, / Mister my friends" (281). While the TRC concerns itself with the accumulation of stories and the construction of an inclusive national narrative, Michael and Lydia each seek to leave that history behind. They do not seek voices with which to articulate the past, nor do they want an official audience to listen to their stories. To be clear, neither disavows its influence; instead, both reject the assumption that the Commission's orchestrated encounter with the past is the only or best way of determining its influence on the present.

Lydia's departure and Michael's self-imposed exile suggest that the transition from apartheid will require a more radical departure from the past than the linguistic rebirth enacted through the public hearings of the TRC. In keeping with *Bitter Fruit*'s metaphor of the national family, this narrative trajectory suggests that the transition will transpire through a variety of communicative acts, including silence, and will entail the dissolution of apartheid-era family structures. Perhaps it is this utter dissolution that Dangor characterizes as "the inevitable heart of decay that seems to be part of the birthing process of all magnificent democracies" (*Bold Type* interview). Dangor's reflection offers a more hopeful perspective than that seemingly offered by the dark conclusion of *Bitter Fruit*. It suggests that the world represented in the novel represents only one phase of a process that might result in the construction of a truly new, but as of yet unrealized, South Africa.

Conclusion

Critic Sarah Nuttall suggests that in telling stories of the past, rememberers are "working out what constitutes a collective, resistance, freedom, place, and survival in the present" (76). The material in this chapter suggests that this "working out" happens as much in silence as it does in speech. Truth commissions, like much rhetorical and feminist scholarship until recently, mistakenly assume that speech necessarily or always dignifies. As the actual survivor, Thandi Shezi, and the imagined survivor, Lydia from *Bitter Fruit*, demonstrate, the relationship between the two is far from simple. What can and should be translated into words depends on the context, the nature of the audience, and one's own integration and understanding of the experience being remembered. Decoupling speech from selfhood enables us to hear both speech and silence differently, with greater sensitivity to what they contain, what motivates them, and what they aim to do.

3
CONTESTING ACCOUNTABILITY

The past is a foreign country: they do things differently there.
—L. P. HARTLEY

The problem was one, at that time, everyone can do anything to anyone because of the situation. That is why we are saying now, we cannot believe it, but we believe it. Because there were many people, even myself, I can do that thing at that time.
—SIZWE MAKANA FROM *Long Night's Journey into Day*

In *Long Night's Journey into Day*, a documentary about the TRC directed by Frances Reid and Deborah Hoffmann, Sizwe Makana seeks to explain why four black youths killed Amy Biehl, a white American Fulbright scholar. Biehl was pulled from her car as she drove through an anti-apartheid rally in which participants shouted anti-white slogans. Makana is incredulous— "we cannot believe it, but we believe it"—and flummoxed: How can she explain and justify her past mind-set and actions in a wholly different present? Like Winnie Madikizela-Mandela, whose testimony this chapter examines in detail, Makana resorts to the phrase "at that time," as if to suggest that her interlocutors could only understand what happened— more precisely, how it could have happened—if they had been there *then*. Makana's inability to explain herself and these events speaks to a central challenge facing the participants in truth commissions: the need to frame and account for one's past actions with terms and from the vantage of the present.

Revolutionary times present particular challenges to individuals' sense of right and wrong, clarifying intentions at one moment while obscuring them the next. In the 1980s and early '90s, during the most violent phase of the anti-apartheid movement, Madikizela-Mandela explains that "the heat was very hot" ("Human"). With this brief description, she seeks to capture a time in which the apartheid government sought to weaken the opposition by using brutally violent measures on the streets and in prisons and by generating paranoia in the anti-apartheid community. Passions and suspicions ran high. At that time, apartheid's defenders and opponents alike were often "caught up in structural processes that both motivate[d] and constrain[ed] their actions, in ways that may not [have been] intelligible to the actors themselves" (Posel and Simpson, "Power" 10). If unintelligible to the perpetrators *then*, these motivations are that much more difficult to articulate and explain *now*, for transitional moments complicate the task of accounting for oneself. Individuals must reflect on their past identifications and justifications in a context of instability, both political and moral. That instability—the absence of stable and clearly articulated norms—serves to highlight the creative work of identity and social construction.

Both the challenges and opportunities of accounting for oneself became readily apparent in the TRC's public hearings for perpetrators. The hearings were structured by what I call the TRC's "rhetoric of accountability," which had diverse, and at times conflicting, ideological origins, including human rights discourse and restorative justice, a quasi-judicial framework that emphasizes perpetrators' acknowledgment of individual responsibility and seeks to promote their reintegration into society. The ANC's liberalism and nonracialism—its bulwark against the collective mentality and racism of apartheid—also had a strong influence on the Commission. The TRC was committed to promoting a new South Africa "founded on the recognition of human rights, democracy and peaceful co-existence . . . irrespective of colour, race, class, belief or sex" (Republic of South Africa). The TRC's norms and values, however, were deeply incongruent with those that structured life under apartheid. Apartheid was a system organized hierarchically by race and predicated on group membership. "At that time," the boundaries separating the private individual from the collective and public self were porous at best. As Sarah Nuttall observes, "the intricate crossing of the individual and social has been subject, in South Africa, to particular pressures and distortions" (76). This "intricate crossing" made it especially difficult for subjects to inhabit simultaneously the individual and nonracial subject position required by the TRC and account for the collective and racialized "I" of the past. The disjuncture between the material realities and ideological frameworks of apartheid and those of postapartheid South Africa vexed the rhetorical scene of the TRC's hearings.

This chapter first provides a brief history of apartheid's racism and racialism. It then explains how the TRC's rhetoric of accountability sought to counter that historical legacy and shape perpetrators' remembrances of the past. It goes on to analyze how two infamous perpetrators of gross human rights violations—Robert McBride and Winnie Madikizela-Mandela—challenged the Commission's rhetoric of accountability in their public hearings. According to apartheid categories, McBride was coloured and Madikizela-Mandela was black. Both experienced the racism and racialism of apartheid and devoted their lives to its downfall. Neither McBride, who had been granted indemnity through earlier negotiations between the ANC and the apartheid government, nor Madikizela-Mandela, who stood little chance of being charged in the civil courts due to her (putative) victims' lack of evidence and money, had to apply for amnesty. Nevertheless, both participated in the TRC process and used the forum provided by its public hearings to call attention to the challenge of accounting for actions committed during apartheid in the social norms and vocabulary of the new South Africa.

While consummate rhetors, McBride and Madikizela-Mandela still contended with the constraints of the TRC's rhetoric of accountability. The final section of this chapter turns to a freer rhetorical scene, one imagined by Njabulo Ndebele in *The Cry of Winnie Mandela*, a novel so closely based on real-world events that Ndebele includes a "Note to the Reader" stating that it is indeed a "work of fiction" (x). *Cry* features an *ibandla* (gathering) of black women who speak of their own struggle during the long years of apartheid and pose questions of Winnie that were left unanswered during her TRC hearing. By enabling the fictionalized Winnie to speak freely about her past, and also explaining why she can do so before the *ibandla* but not before the TRC, *Cry* contributes to the Commission's goal of deepening historical understanding, and, at the same time, suggests how its rhetoric of accountability created constraints that prevented it from fully achieving this goal itself.

Apartheid: Racist and Racialist

Given that the TRC mandate addressed a time period structured explicitly by racialist and racist thinking, one of the most puzzling aspects of its process was its reluctance to use race as an analytic. In the following section, I provide a brief genealogy of South African racial formations and state policy to explain why the ANC adopted a strategy of nonracialism to oppose apartheid and how that ANC strategy eventually led to the TRC's strange silence around race.

As the South African attendees at the Justice in Transition conferences observed, white supremacy in various guises shaped policy in South Africa long before the National Party (NP), which campaigned on the platform of apartheid, won the national elections in 1948. The national scope of apartheid's social engineering project brought tighter enforcement and greater coherence to these earlier segregationist policies, which had differed across regions and municipalities. Apartheid ideology also changed some of the underlying assumptions of these segregationist policies. Before the NP victory in 1948, "cultures were more closely associated with ethno-culture than they were with races" (Macdonald 12). In other words, shared culture, more than skin color, established group membership. This cultural understanding of race shaped pre-apartheid policies toward native Africans in some regions of South Africa, such as the Cape. According to the logic of shared culture, by adopting European cultural practices and values, native Africans could become "less African" and thereby access certain rights, such as the franchise, freedom of movement, and land ownership.

Apartheid sought to replace cultural constructions of race with biological ones. In its ideology, "races were deemed integral categories and were declared to impress distinctive essences on their bearers" (Macdonald 92). The state legally recognized four main "racial" groups: African, Coloured (mixed race), Asian (primarily South Africans of Indian descent), and White. The apartheid state maintained that whites should control the South Africa government due to their inherent superiority, and that their interests should take precedence over those of other racial groups (Thompson 190). In a 1964 speech, Hendrik Verwoerd, prime minister of South Africa from 1958 to 1966 and the primary theorist and architect of apartheid, famously asked, "Is not our role to stand for the one thing which means our own salvation here but with which it will also be possible to save the world, and with which Europe will be able to save itself, namely the preservation of the white man and his state?" (qtd. in Andrews 860). When the Nationalists won the elections in 1948, however, no common white identity existed. Moreover, the bitter memories of the Anglo-Boer wars (1898–1902) were still fresh. British South Africans and Afrikaners had different traditions, languages, and histories in the region. Apartheid policies sought to foster a common white racial identity that would supersede these cultural divisions and thus reinforce white supremacy. At the same time, and counterproductively in some instances to the goal of a common white identity, apartheid policies favored Afrikaners who had long felt discriminated against by British South Africans, and the state actively promoted Afrikaner culture and language (Thompson 188).

The apartheid state argued that different racial groups not only occupied different rungs on the ladder of superiority but also constituted separate nations. This idea was expressed in Verwoerd's policy of "separate development," which held "that races are akin to nations, [and] that they engender primary solidarities, organize society, and establish allegiances" (Macdonald 11). According to the ideology of separate development, native Africans thus did not belong in the (white) Republic of South Africa, but rather in their own homelands, called Bantustans (11). In a twist that benefited the white Republic of South Africa, however, the logic of "race as nation" was not applied equally. Rather than having their own racial nation, black Africans were divided by tribe. Each of the nine tribes occupied its own Bantustan. This division of black Africans served the political interests of the apartheid state by reinforcing putative cultural differences, thereby minimizing the possibility that black Africans would unite around their common experience of white supremacy (13).

Apartheid eventually became a "monstrously labyrinthine system [that] dominated every facet of life" (Posel 1). The following sampling of legislation demonstrates the breadth and depth of apartheid's reach. The Population Registration Act of 1950 was the system's linchpin; it required that South Africans be classified and then register as members of one of the four main racial groups. The Prohibition of Mixed Marriages Act of 1949 and the Immorality Act of 1950 reached into the bedroom, governing personal and sexual relations between the races. Other legislation, such as the Group Areas Act of 1950, dictated where each racial group was allowed to live; this act provided the legislative backdrop to the "forced removal" of black South Africans from desired, often urban, areas to townships outside the city centers or to their newly designated "homelands." The Pass Laws Act of 1952 controlled the movement of black South Africans living outside of the homelands by requiring all those older than 16 to carry a "pass book" that indicated where, when, and for how long they could be in a given area. The Bantu Authorities Act of 1951, as well as the Bantu Education and the Reservation of Separate Amenities Acts of 1953, enforced "separate and unequal" provisions in the realms of education, municipal services, and governance. By 1936, long before the institution of apartheid in 1948, black Africans had lost the franchise in all regions of South Africa. A series of apartheid-era parliamentary acts, beginning with the Separate Representation of Voters Act of 1951, began the process of disenfranchising coloureds and Indians as well. The Suppression of Communism Act of 1951 curtailed political dissent by empowering the government to ban political activity by individuals and groups it deemed Communist, a catchall category that included anti-apartheid activists and actions. This list of apartheid legislation is not exhaustive. It covers only the first few years of the apartheid state. Nevertheless, it demonstrates the extent of the racial and racist thinking underlying the system.

Nonracialism in Post-apartheid South Africa

During the apartheid era, "racism was institutionalized, legalized, and internalized" (Harris et al. 2). As one major way to oppose apartheid, the ANC and other anti-apartheid organizations adopted the ideology of nonracialism. As Kader Asmal claimed memorably in his 1992 inaugural lecture as a professor of human rights law at the University of the Western Cape, "Throughout the history of the resistance movement, the emphasis has been on the golden thread of non-racialism, which has been the foundation of the struggle of the victims and the oppressed" ("Victims" 491). What nonracialism entailed for each organization, and the policies it inspired, changed over the latter half of the twentieth century. Of significance here is the nonracialism that guided the ANC in the 1990s, as it was this version that the TRC mandate reflected and that its process promoted. The ANC leadership envisioned a liberal democratic South Africa. In its inclusive nation-state, "all citizens would have the same political rights; race would not be recognized by the state; universal guarantees for all citizens would render specific protections for minorities unnecessary; and non-racialism would prevail, mostly because race would cease to matter formally" (Macdonald 112). The ANC's nonracial vision thereby countered apartheid's racialism—claims of inherent racial difference—and its racism—state-sanctioned oppression or inequality on the basis of (perceived) racial difference. Political equality and democratic governance, rather than ethnic culture or race, would define post-apartheid South Africa's "universal nation" (108). South Africa's nonracialism coincided nicely with a growing global consensus about the value of human rights. As Richard Wilson explains, "[both] converge on the view that nations must not be constituted on the basis of race, ethnicity, language or religion, but should be founded instead on a 'community of equal, rights-bearing citizens, united in patriotic attachment to a shared set of political practices and values'" (Ignatieff qtd. in Wilson 1). The patriotism trumpeted by the ANC blended its nonracialism with the universal discourse of human rights.

The elections of 1994 seemed to herald the realization of the ANC's nonracial and participatory vision for the new South Africa. South Africans of every hue queued at voting booths to participate in the historic event. President-elect Nelson Mandela, who enjoyed a landslide victory, promoted a new national culture, one reflective of the ANC's liberal, democratic, and nonracial values.[1] Researchers at the Center for the Study of Violence and Reconciliation describe the Mandela government's introduction of a rhetoric that was consistent with the ANC's values: "During the Mandela era (1994–1999), a new vocabulary emerged to describe the social order. The vocabulary spoke of nationhood, unity, racial harmony and reconciliation. South Africa was described as a 'rainbow nation'" (Harris et al. 1). This rhetoric placed constraints on public discourse about South Africa's racialist and racist past by "render[ing] the real, often violent, consequences of race invisible. In the Mandela era, there was little national debate on how race had influenced past human rights violations. There was also little recognition that race continues to shape identity and interactions—violent or not—within the present" (2). The ANC's efforts to excise racialist and racist thinking from the culture and conscience of the new South Africa were based on hopes and desires more than reality. Michael Macdonald points to the circularity of the ANC's reasoning: "Non-racial institutions would dispel racism by ignoring race officially and ignoring race officially would prove that racism had been dispelled. The catch is that the ANC could not and can not prevent South Africans from harboring racial affinities" (112). Race, whether officially recognized or not, continued to figure centrally in South Africans' perceptions of themselves and of one another as well as in public discourse. The government's elision of race from public discourse had particular consequences for the TRC's approach to perpetrators of gross human rights violations.

Nonracialism and the TRC's Amnesty Provision

Despite the centrality of racism and racialism to the ideology and policies of apartheid, neither figured centrally in the TRC's engagement with the past. The TRC instead relied on the complementary discourses of human rights and nonracialism. This framing made it difficult for participants in the TRC hearings to call attention to the systemic racism and racialism of apartheid. Historian Madeline Fullard identifies multiple sources of this displacement of race. She demonstrates how the TRC mandate "decenter[ed] race through the use of descriptors that render[ed] the conflicts of the past unspecific and all-encompassing" (32). The limited time line of the TRC mandate, which did not encompass the entire apartheid era, also narrowed the scope of the inquiry. It tasked the commission with generating "as complete a picture as possible of the nature, causes and extent of gross violations of human rights committed during the period from 1 March 1960 to the cut-off date contemplated in the Constitution [ultimately, April 1994]" (Republic of South Africa). The date of 1 March 1960 refers to the Sharpeville Massacre, in which police shot and killed sixty-nine protesters in a demonstration against the "pass laws." The TRC *Report* justifies the time line by explaining that Sharpeville initiated what were "possibly the worst and certainly, in regard to the wider region, the bloodiest [thirty-four years] in the long and violent history of human rights abuses in this subcontinent" (1: 24–25). As Fullard suggests, the TRC's time line thus "propose[d] a certain circumscription of focus to physical violence" rather than to the diverse violations of the system of apartheid (10). This narrow focus, coupled with the vague language and limited time line of the TRC's mandate, constrained its inquiry into the past.

The TRC also opted for a circumscribed interpretation of "gross violations," one that emphasized acts of physical violence. The Promotion of National Unity and Reconciliation Act defined "gross violations" as "the violation of human rights through the killing, abduction, torture or severe ill-treatment of any person." The TRC could have interpreted the Act's reference to "ill-treatment" expansively, to include a broader range of apartheid abuses, as was advocated by various organizations representing the victims of abuses such as forced removals and Bantu education (TRC, *Report* 1: 64). Indeed, the *Report* itself acknowledges that "conceptually, the policy of apartheid was itself a human rights violation" (1: 29) and that "a deep awareness of this systemic discrimination and dehumanization made it very difficult for the Commission to concentrate only on those whose rights had been violated through acts of killing, torture, abduction, and severe ill-treatment" (1: 63). Notwithstanding these reservations, the TRC ultimately determined that the mandate excluded from explicit consideration the social, legal, psychological, and economic abuses of apartheid. The *Report* concludes that "the Commission resolved that its mandate was to give attention to human rights violations committed as specific acts ... as such, the focus of its work was not on the effects of laws passed by the apartheid government" (1: 63–64). Researchers from the Centre for the Study of Violence and Reconciliation note that these interpretations meant that "the TRC did not engage directly with the institutionalised, structured ways in which racist policies affected and victimized people on a daily basis" (Harris et al. 5). Other scholars have similarly called attention to the ways in which the TRC's interpretation excluded from its purview the daily abuses of apartheid and thus its many victims.[2] In the remainder of this chapter, I argue that the Commission's interpretation also diverted attention from the effects of apartheid on the perpetrators' worldview and actions.

The TRC's Rhetoric of Accountability

Initially, the architects of the TRC linked the constitutional requirement to grant amnesty to the TRC's quest to create "as complete a picture as possible" of South Africa's apartheid past (Republic of South Africa). They hoped that extending amnesty would encourage perpetrators to disclose the full extent of their human rights abuses. This aim was consistent with the human rights movement's imperative to document, acknowledge, and publicize human rights abuses. Applicants were required to "fully disclose" and provide a "political motivation" for the violations for which they sought amnesty (TRC, *Report* 1: 55). To further the aim of full disclosure, only *individuals*—not bodies, parties, or organizations—could apply, and a separate application had to be submitted for each violation for which the applicant sought amnesty.[3] The Commission's emphasis on the perpetrator as an individual agent reflected its reliance on the "liberal, individualist, and legalistic assumptions" of what has come to be known as the "dominant human rights framework" (Nesiah and Keenan 262). Liberal moral individualism remains at the core of the Universal Declaration of Human Rights and the transnational movement that it has inspired. As Michael Ignatieff explains, "rights language cannot be parsed or translated in a nonindividualistic, communitarian framework. It presumes moral individuals and is nonsensical outside that assumption" ("Human" 67). In keeping with this liberal democratic framework, the TRC asked *who*, as opposed to *what*, was responsible for the human rights violations that occurred during the time period covered by its mandate (Fullard 27). In other words, it located power and agency in the individual *qua* individual, rather than in the collective or political system within which she operated under apartheid. It thereby held that individual amnesty applicants could and should be held accountable for their actions.

While the new South Africa might celebrate citizens' individuality, the system of apartheid insisted on collective racial identifications and refused outright to recognize the individual subjectivity of nonwhite South Africans. The disjuncture between the Commission's liberal assumptions and the sociopolitical and ideological history of twentieth-century South Africa is particularly acute. Erik Doxtader observes, "In light of South Africa's complex political history, it is not clear how claims about the capacities and inalienable rights of the self-certain individual fit with the varieties of communalism that have long informed Afrikaner nationalism, ANC ideology, and versions of African humanism that uphold the idea of *ubuntu*" ("Easy" 137). Yet, despite this disjuncture, liberal individualism converged nicely with the nonracialism of the new South Africa. Richard Wilson demonstrates the neat convergence of the individual subject imagined in human rights discourse and the ANC's nonracialism: "Both political philosophies assume South Africa to be a society of individual citizens, not a society of racial communities with group representation and minority rights" (3).

In addition to submitting individual applications, amnesty applicants had to demonstrate that their violations were politically motivated, a determination that the Amnesty Committee (AC) found difficult to make. Martin Coetzee, executive secretary of the AC, explains that the AC recognized as "politically motivated" only those actions taken on behalf of anti-apartheid parties or under the auspices of the national security forces in defense of apartheid. This narrow definition of "political" excluded many actions. Apartheid legislation, such as the Suppression of Communism Act, prevented many organizations from identifying as "political" for fear of repression by the apartheid state. For this reason, resistance often occurred under the banner of informal political parties or nonpolitical organizations, such as labor groups and youth clubs (Fullard 20). While the AC considered criteria such as the perpetrator's motive, the context wherein the act took place, and the proportionality of the act to the objective pursued, it disqualified actions that it determined to be motivated by "personal gain" or committed "out of malice, ill-will, or spite" (Coetzee 185). Most surprisingly, the AC did not consider racism to be a legitimate "political" motivation. The *Report* acknowledges that "the enforcement of apartheid legislation affected every sphere of society," and thus "the political nature of specific acts was hard to define" (1: 82). Yet the Commission "largely excluded racism as a motive for committing gross human rights violations" (Fullard 20). This exclusion was consistent with the TRC's adherence to and promotion of the ideology of nonracialism. It conflicted, however, with the reality of life under apartheid.

Applicants pursuing amnesty for gross violations of human rights were required to make their "public and full" disclosure in public hearings (TRC, *Report* 1: 53). This requirement was not a part of the original amnesty provision agreed upon by representatives of the ANC and the NP. In the initial version of the amnesty provision, all applications were to be presented in closed hearings (1: 53). The objections of human rights groups and other nongovernmental organizations to the idea of closed hearings compelled the architects of the TRC to revise the requirement. The final version of the TRC's establishing act mandated that amnesty hearings concerning applications for gross human rights violations be open to the public (1: 53, 119).

The *Report* subsequently justified the requirement for public hearings by linking it to the notion of restorative justice. According to the *Report*'s definition, restorative justice is a process that "aims at the healing and the restoration of all concerned—of victims in the first place, but also of offenders, their families, and the larger community" (1: 126). A perpetrator's acknowledgment of wrongdoing, or "offender accountability" (1: 126), constitutes one of the process's key components. To reassure angry victims that amnesty was not synonymous with immunity, the *Report* repeatedly points to this component of restorative justice, explaining that "the amnesty provisions in the Act required applicants to declare the nature of their offences—effectively acknowledging their culpability" (1: 119). The TRC hoped that the applicant's public acknowledgment—and the resulting humiliation—would soften the bitter pill of amnesty. In his attempt to refute the claim that the Commission traded truth and reconciliation for justice, Chairperson Desmond Tutu unabashedly calls attention to the role of shame in the TRC's approach to perpetrators. He points to the fact that applicants had to make this admission "in the full glare of television lights," which turned it into "a penalty of . . . public humiliation and exposure," as he writes in his memoir (51). The *Report* makes a similar point, though in gentler terms: "By bringing the darker side of the past to the fore, those responsible for violations of human rights could also be held accountable for their actions" (1: 110). As Yianna Liatsos observes, "the public degradation of perpetrators was in fact rationalized as a means of balancing the otherwise badly unbalanced historical scales" ("Truth" 119).

In short, the Commission hoped that the requirement for "public and full disclosure" would address victims' allegations that the amnesty provision inadequately responded to their demands for justice.

According to the logic of restorative justice, the "public and full disclosure" requirement also served perpetrators and the new nation. It allowed amnesty applicants to bring "the darker side of the past to the fore" and thus "to contribute to the creation of the new South Africa" (TRC, *Report* 1: 110). Their public expression of these dark memories would serve as a form of expiation that would gain them entry as private, moral citizens into the new democratic national body. By accepting their "moral responsibility," perpetrators would simultaneously renounce their past and commit themselves to the values of the new nation (1: 130). This mish-mash contradictory logic, equal parts shame and restoration, revolved around the very same action: the amnesty applicant's public admission of individual responsibility.

The emphasis on individual responsibility in both human rights discourse and restorative justice dovetailed nicely with another of the Commission's ideological sources: the collective wisdom generated after the Holocaust about the causes of systemic human rights abuses. Legal scholar Martha Minow identifies the core assumption of this collective wisdom as "the recognition of individual duties to international norms that transcend national obligations" (*Between* 40). That is, the individual is morally obliged to uphold the norms of human rights when they conflict with the demands of the nation or any other collective to which (s)he might belong. The *Report* indexes the influence of the Holocaust on this line of thought: "The abdication of responsibility . . . [and] moral indifference . . . are all essential parts of the many-layered spiral of responsibility which makes large-scale systematic human rights violations possible in modern states" (1: 131). Here the *Report* implicitly compares Nazi Germany to apartheid South Africa. Both are "modern states" and in each, the *Report* suggests, individuals' outright "abdication of responsibility" or mere "moral indifference" allowed "large-scale systematic human rights violations" to occur. The individuals in this comparison are clearly apathetic Germans and white South Africans or active proponents of Nazism and apartheid, not Jews and other targets of the third Reich or nonwhite South Africans. Nevertheless, the TRC applied the insight about individual moral responsibility to all perpetrators in what came to be described as its "even-handed" approach.[4]

Jus Ad Bellum and Jus In Bello

The Commission took pains to demonstrate that its "even-handed" approach with perpetrators was not indiscriminate—that it did, in fact, make "moral judgments" (TRC, *Report* 1: 65). The *Report* explains that it did so by relying on the distinction between *jus ad bellum* (justice of war) and *jus in bello* (justice in war) (1: 65). *Jus ad bellum* refers to cause—"the justifiability of the decision to go to war" (1: 66). Defenders of apartheid argued that their "just cause" was the fear that Communists would take over South Africa under the guise of the anti-apartheid movement. Anti-apartheid activists argued that apartheid had been found to be a crime against humanity by the General Assembly of the United Nations, clearly giving them "just cause" to fight against it. The Commission ultimately determined that "various parties to the conflicts of the past" did indeed have "just cause," but that they had not all engaged in *jus in bello* (just means)—"how much force may be used in a particular context and ... who or what may be targeted" (1: 67). This distinction enabled the Commission to observe that apartheid had indeed been declared a "crime against humanity," and to describe apartheid as "immoral, illegal, oppressive, and inhuman" (1: 67), while concluding that "not all acts in war could be regarded as morally or legally legitimate, even where the cause was just" (1: 69). Put simply, anti-apartheid activists' cause was just, but not all their actions in the service of that cause were moral or legitimate.

Anti-apartheid activists contested the Commission's assessment, arguing that they had "just cause" and had also engaged in "just means." They noted that their decision to resort to violent means was adopted only after they had exhausted peaceful means of resistance. In 1964, Nelson Mandela, from the dock of his defense case in the Rivonia Trial, presented a sustained explanation of the ANC's decision to turn to violence in the struggle to end apartheid:

> The hard facts were that 50 years of non-violence had brought the African people nothing but more and more repressive legislation, and fewer and fewer rights. . . .
> It was only when all else had failed, when all channels of peaceful protest had been barred to us, that the decision was made to embark on violent forms of political struggle, and to form Umkhonto we Sizwe. (32–33)

In his call for a general amnesty for all "freedom fighters," Letlapa Mphahlele, former director of operations of the Azanian People's Liberation Army, again reminded the Commission of the ANC's reasoning: "Peaceful means were tried as a way of overcoming that system for many years and they failed. In this sense, we were driven to resort to arms. As such, the amnesty sought by the freedom fighters is not a favour. It is a fundamental right" (11). The Commission acknowledged as much (TRC, *Report* 1: 68). Indeed, the *Report* embeds its acknowledgment that the antiapartheid movement exhausted nonviolent "means" before turning to a limited strategy of violence within a section that also states repeatedly that apartheid was "illegal, oppressive, and inhuman" (1: 68). Nevertheless, the *Report* returns to its claim that not "all acts carried out in order to destroy apartheid were necessarily legal, moral, and acceptable" (1: 69).

The TRC's moral and legal reasoning around this particular issue never satisfied those who otherwise endorsed its efforts. Out of frustration with the Commission's approach, ANC legal advisor Matthews Phosa formally announced that the ANC would submit only a party amnesty application to the TRC. In response to this declaration, Archbishop Desmond Tutu threatened to resign as chairperson of the Commission on 31 October 1996. The ANC determined that political exigencies outweighed the cause of justice; after much deliberation, it eventually agreed to withdraw its party application and encourage individual members to apply for amnesty. Writing at the conclusion of the TRC process, Kader Asmal, Louise Asmal, and Ronald Suresh Roberts praise the TRC for "complet[ing] an enormous task with great humanity and strength," but ultimately determine that "[it] failed in its moral judgments of the issues pertaining to the Just War doctrine" (97).[5] The Commission's "failure" in this regard, however, proved generative, as it provoked TRC participants Robert McBride and Winnie Madikizela-Mandela, as well as the novelist Njabulo Ndebele, to expose the shortcomings of the Commission's approach.

Omissions in the TRC's Rhetoric of Accountability

Though the AC sought to avoid the adversarial relations characteristic of a traditional criminal trial, participants and observers claim that the mood of many of the public hearings was in fact antagonistic. Applicants did not try to prove their innocence. However, they did attempt to persuade the commissioners that they had acted on "political" convictions and under the auspices of a body the Commission would recognize as "political." In their attempts to make the applicant ineligible for amnesty, the lawyers opposing the application offered alternative versions of the applicant's motivation or the details of the violation. Moreover, as in a criminal trial, something significant was at stake in the amnesty hearings. Most obviously, amnesty constituted a guarantee that applicants would never have to face legal charges. In this sense, a successful application served a protective function and contributed to applicants' peace of mind. For some perpetrators, a successful amnesty application held symbolic import as well. Though it did not convey individual victims' forgiveness, it represented an official pardon on the part of the new government. Receiving amnesty thus gave perpetrators who were remorseful a symbolic fresh start in the new South Africa. Finally, amnesty decisions constituted a form of judgment, if unofficial, about the legitimacy and morality of past actions.

The problem was that the Commission's rhetoric of accountability left an elephant in the hearing halls: race. The liberal individualism that underlay the TRC's rhetoric of accountability failed to account for apartheid's enforcement of collective racial identities and its regulation of public and private relationships. The freedom to be and to act as an individual agent was precisely what apartheid denied to all South Africans, though most severely to nonwhites. The *Report* acknowledges this, describing apartheid as "systemic and all-pervading" (1: 62). Apartheid's racism and racialism undeniably affected South Africans' motivation to enact political change as well as the "means" that they could take to do so. Nonwhite South Africans bore the material and psychological burdens of apartheid more than whites, and, consequently, felt particularly motivated to bring about its downfall. And, yet, given their political and economic disenfranchisement, they had a limited range of resistance options. White South Africans, in contrast, had the political, economic, and social power to contest or defend apartheid either actively, through political means, or passively, by leaving the country. It is therefore (perhaps) reasonable to compare their blindness and/or apathy toward the abuses of the apartheid system to that of some Germans toward the abuses of the Nazis. But consider the justice of asking members of the Jewish resistance living in the ghettos to face the same charges of human rights violations as Nazi soldiers did. Seen from this perspective, the Commission's "even-handed" approach and focus on individual perpetrators indeed "flattened distinction and context" (Fullard 36).

I turn now to the overt and covert ways in which Robert McBride and Winnie Madikizela-Mandela resisted the TRC's rhetoric of accountability in their public hearings.

The Case of Robert McBride

The arc of Robert McBride's political consciousness and activism, from nonviolent resistance to armed struggle, mirrors that of the ANC. McBride first experienced apartheid while still in the womb. The Group Areas Act of 1950, which established where different races could live, determined that nonwhites could no longer live in the city center or nearby suburbs of Durban. McBride's parents, Doris and Derrick, were forced to move to Wentworth, formerly a Second World War military transit camp, and, at the time of the McBrides' move, an economically depressed, semi-industrialized area on the outskirts of the city (Rostron 26). Wentworth was an area for the coloured population, a racial designation that was often defined negatively. As Marike de Klerk stated, "You know, the Coloureds are a negative group. The definition of a Coloured in the population register is someone that is not black, and is not white and not an Indian. In other words, a nonperson. They are the leftovers" (qtd. in Rostron 31).

As an adult, McBride attributed his first step toward political radicalization to his experience playing for the Northlands, a rugby club that reserved a few spots for nonwhite players. After suffering a racist insult from an opponent and overhearing derisive comments from his own teammates, McBride gave up trying to win whites' approval and acceptance: "'I became,' he says, 'more African than the Africans—a radical black'" (qtd. in Rostron 71).[6] The first elections of the tricameral parliament in 1984, in which coloureds, but not black Africans, had their own House of Representatives, further incensed McBride and other anti-apartheid activists. As McBride's lawyer explained to one of the sisters of the victims of the bombing for which McBride was applying for amnesty, the message of the tricameral parliament was clear to black South Africans: "You're not citizens of this country, you'll never have a right in this country, go to hell" (McBride). In 1985, McBride co-led a boycott of classes, and later a petition effort, to attain better premises at Bechet College, where he was studying to become a teacher. The swift and heavy-handed response, including the banning of the student organization, further pushed McBride toward militancy: "There is just no hope for a so-called Coloured person to really progress independent of the constraints of the authorities. It's designed this way to keep a person just at a certain level where they want you. Well, since we were suspended and banned after dealing with the issue at Bechet in a peaceful, legal manner, I decided that it can't work. You can't progress within the system" (qtd. in Rostron 91). Roughly sixteen months later, Gordon Webster, McBride's friend from Bechet, recruited him into the Special Operations Division of Umkhonto we Sizwe.

As an undercover operative, McBride was primarily responsible for weakening the South African economic infrastructure through targeted bombings. After a string of successful sabotage attacks around Durban, McBride, Greta Apelgren, and Matthew Lecordier decided to bomb the Why Not Bar, a popular bar for off-duty security personnel. They did so, as McBride explained at his amnesty hearing, in response to a decision taken by the armed wing of the ANC "to take the struggle out of the black ghettos and into the white areas" (McBride). The Why Not Bar was next to the Magoo Bar on the Marine Parade, "the heart of the country's leisured sanctuary... [that] in many ways epitomized the middle-class white South African dream: a gregarious trilogy of fun, sun and sport" (Rostron 219). The 14 June 1986 bombing took the lives of three women and injured sixty-nine others (214). McBride was found guilty and given a death sentence, but he was released from death row in 1992 during negotiations between the liberation movement and the apartheid government.

Because of these negotiations, McBride did not have to apply for amnesty. He did so only to show his commitment to the truth and reconciliation process. As a legislator in the national parliament, McBride voted for the Promotion of National Unity and Reconciliation Act. In an interview, he noted that "with all its faults, the Truth Commission is really the only institutional vehicle that addresses the issue of reconciliation" (Reid and Hoffmann). To participate with the TRC was to endorse the new South Africa's government, led by the ANC. McBride's status as a hero of the struggle lent particular symbolic weight to his participation. Commissioner Mary Burton recalls commenting to a member of the South African cabinet, "I just hope that Robert McBride applies for amnesty.... I felt that it would give a wonderful symbol to the commission and that it would encourage others to do so" (Reid and Hoffmann). The "others" to whom Burton refers likewise engaged in violent rebellion against the apartheid government. It was hoped that McBride's attitude toward his past—his willingness to accept the TRC's condemnation of the violence committed by all parties under apartheid—would guide these "others."

Though McBride voluntarily participated in the amnesty process, he insisted on doing so on his own terms. In interviews and, to some extent, during his testimony before the Commission, he articulately and forcefully critiqued the TRC's "even-handed" approach to the violence committed by apartheid's defenders and liberation forces. McBride considered his violent actions justifiable, given that they were directed against an unjust system, and he resented having to apologize for them in the same manner as those who committed violent acts to defend apartheid. Referring to the nearly universal consensus about the righteousness of the Allies' cause during the Second World War, McBride notes pointedly, "There's no person or soldier from the Second World War . . . of the allies, who would like to be associated [with] or even compared to Nazis" (Reid and Hoffmann). He offers a qualified apology to the victims of the Why Not Bar bombing during his amnesty hearing, one that places the loss of individual lives within the context of the broader struggle against apartheid: "It was in a quest for my own freedom, and in a quest to unshackle myself from the Apartheid system, that I brought about the death of your loved ones. For this I am sorry" (McBride). McBride embeds the deaths of these individuals within a noble struggle for freedom and justice, and, through his indirect locution—"brought about" rather than "killed"—he complicates the Commission's simplistic "victim-perpetrator" dyad that decontextualizes and depoliticizes individuals and their actions (Wilson 59). McBride implies that moral reasoning guided his actions during the struggle to end apartheid. As a moral person already, he resents the Commission's efforts to instill in him a new morality.

At the public hearing in which McBride and the other perpetrators of the Why Not Bar/Magoo Bar bombing presented their amnesty application, McBride launches his broader critique of the TRC's rhetoric of accountability. The hearing lasted eight days and garnered a great deal of publicity. Prior to the hearing, McBride met with the families of some of the victims, who agreed not to oppose his application for amnesty. However, the families of several other victims remained steadfast in their opposition. Richard and Prior, the attorneys of these victims and/or their families, sought to prove that McBride's application did not meet the amnesty program's requirement of "political motivation."[7] They had two tacks, or strategies: first, to demonstrate that McBride did not sufficiently research the target site to ensure that it was a legitimate political target and should thus be held responsible for the unintended civilian casualties that resulted; and, second, irreconcilable to the first, to demonstrate that McBride was in fact aware of the civilian presence in the bar (or could or should have been), and that, despite this knowledge, he carried on with the attack. In the first, McBride's ineptness condemns him; in the second, his callousness. While the success of the first argument would compel the AC to deny McBride amnesty, the second offers a different reward. It implies that regardless of the political nature of the violation, McBride's act was immoral. This moral condemnation alone would not constitute grounds to dismiss McBride's amnesty application, but it would serve a secondary function: Richard's clients could at least be satisfied that McBride was toppled from his "hero of the struggle" throne.[8] In calling into question McBride's morality, Richard indirectly attacks its ideological source: the ANC's decision to engage in armed struggle after the apartheid government officially banned the party in 1960. In his response, McBride outlines the assumptions of proponents of the "just war" thesis: that apartheid was unjust; that peaceful resistance was futile; that the avenues of legal recourse were closed; that any actions taken to end it were thus righteous; and, consequently, that those individuals who carried out said righteous actions cannot fairly be held in moral contempt for them. McBride adopts the *ethos* of a soldier who consciously takes the risk of killing himself or others in the service of a greater cause. He states, "I was acting in a military situation. I'm not suggesting either way that I was forced or undue pressure was put on me, I'm saying that I did all of those discussions about killing with myself before I entered Special Ops" (McBride). By defining the struggle against apartheid as a "military situation," he justifies the extreme measures that he took and calls attention to the depth of his moral reasoning.

To underscore the point that he made decisions as a soldier during wartime, rather than contemplating them on a hill as a moral philosopher might, McBride, here the consummate rhetor, concretizes Richard's hypothetical questions. He reminds Richard that the struggle was real, not a hypothetical moral quandary conducted in anticipation of the Commission's requirement that violent actions be proportional to the injustices against which they were directed. McBride explains, "I can't work on hypothesis, I worked from the opposite direction, not from the one you are doing . . . proportionality was never ever part of my discussions with any of the Commanders on the number of policemen or Security personnel to civilians. That was never ever discussed. Because we didn't prepare instructions and operations in anticipation of a Truth Commission" (McBride). McBride's sarcasm suggests the lunacy of implying that soldiers involved in a war, and a "just war" to boot, would have engaged in these kinds of calculations. He states unapologetically in a statement that he read at the conclusion of his hearing, "I fought against a subjugation with utmost dedication and for this I am proud. . . . [Nothing] will make me change my belief that it was correct to fight against a crime against humanity" (McBride). By identifying apartheid as "subjugation" and "a crime against humanity," maintained through violence and repression, he rejects the suggestion that it constituted a political system that one could, or indeed should, have opposed through traditional political channels or with a peacetime morality. Wars require the possibility of human sacrifice in service of a (putatively) greater cause. McBride forces his listeners to apply this principle—killing during wartime is morally justifiable (and at times unavoidable)—to the specific and real situation of apartheid.

McBride further addresses Richard's insinuation of immorality by offering a pragmatic, and yet ultimately moral, defense of his violent actions. He claims that his "immediate reaction [to the casualties caused by the Magoo Bar bombing] was to be obsessed with doing sabotage operations so that I could get rid of apartheid as quickly as possible, because the way I saw it, apartheid was responsible for the tragedy" (qtd. in Edelstein, *Truth and Lies* 133). He takes as a given that apartheid was the source of the violence, and that its rapid destruction, even at the cost of some loss of life, would actually reduce the total number of civilian casualties. According to this perspective, addressing the source of the tragedies—the system of apartheid—was the most expedient way to reduce the loss of life. McBride makes a similarly pragmatic argument when he elaborates on his comment that the ANC was "over-concerned" about the potential for civilian casualties: "Well I think in our endeavour to always maintain moral high ground and to be always correct and 100% pure, we sometimes neglected to effect the struggle in a more realistic way" (McBride). Here he pits idealism against pragmatism and implies that the costs of the former might outweigh those of the latter, i.e., strategic acts of violence would have more quickly brought about the end of apartheid, thereby reducing the *total* amount of human suffering (with the difference being that the suffering caused by the anti-apartheid struggle would be shared more equally between blacks and whites than that inflicted by the apartheid system, which fell disproportionately on nonwhite South Africans).

McBride seeks to demonstrate that his pragmatism about civilian casualties is not irreconcilable with a sincere feeling of sadness about the individual loss of life in the Magoo Bar bombing, nor is it indicative of his immorality. Prior, one of the victims' lawyers, attempts to prove otherwise by showing that McBride's despair at the loss of life in fact caused him to reconsider his stance concerning civilian casualties. As evidence, Prior reads a reflection that McBride putatively provided in an interview with Bryan Rostron, the author of a biography of McBride, *Till Babylon Falls*. In the statement, which appears as a direct quotation, McBride expresses remorse for the death of civilians during the Magoo Bar bombing:

> I was in a state of shock. Before I was just carrying out an operation. . . . I felt terrible, I felt disgusted with myself and ashamed. I felt I would never be forgiven. Before I was doing it for the army, for the freedom of the people. . . . At the time it was quite practical, something to carry out. Afterwards I realised the enormity of the whole thing. The humanness of the suffering came to me. If they had been soldiers, it would have been a legitimate target. Civilians were not a legitimate target. Because they were women, I felt it all the more. I felt I was stooping to the same level as the enemy. I was worried all the time. I was irritable and upset. (Rostron 225)

During the hearing, Prior seems to think that if he can get McBride to verify that he made this statement, he will then have proven that McBride himself admitted that his actions fell outside of the guidelines established by the "political motivation" requirement.

McBride's response, however, thwarts his plan. After questioning the origin and status of the statement as a direct quotation—"I don't recall giving the author such a quotation"—McBride addresses Prior's allegation. He explains that the statement generally summarizes his feelings at the time—"That would sum up the feelings I felt after realising the enormity of what happened"—but then goes on to say that "there are subtle differences and nuances in the semantics there, which are different to what I am saying now" (McBride). Unfortunately, McBride does not elaborate, leaving the listener to determine what those "subtle differences and nuances" are. McBride might be implying that Rostron's transcription of his statement is inaccurate: that is, that he might have said something like this, but not exactly. Or he might be saying that the statement is correct as it stands, but that he has in fact changed his thinking and is attempting to say something different now in his amnesty hearing: that is, that the tragic outcome of the bombing and his immediate emotional response no longer compel him to regret his involvement.

The remainder of McBride's testimony supports this latter interpretation. He asserts that, before the event, his commitment to the struggle propelled him to act as he did. Afterward, in the face of the human cost, he questioned his logic and actions. Now, however, with the benefit of time and distance, he sits comfortably with his initial motivations. McBride takes up Prior's hypothetical scenario concerning the number of policemen in the Magoo Bar to convey the complexity of his moral reasoning: "I just want to extend it [Prior's hypothesis] a little bit. If [there were] a hundred people in the bar, and I had firm knowledge [they] were all policemen, were all generals and I hit the bar and they all died as enemy personnel, I would still not be happy about it because those would have been fellow South Africans I'd been injuring or killing" (McBride). While remaining resolute about his decision in this hypothetical situation, McBride does reiterate his discomfort about the loss of life, even of those he considers "enemy personnel." He "would not be happy about it," but he does not say he would do otherwise. However, he does clarify that he would not knowingly have sacrificed civilian lives. Had he known that the bar was filled primarily with civilians, he would have called off the operation. In other words, his decision to bomb the Magoo Bar was not casual or indiscriminate. McBride states, "But if I had known for sure that there were no police in a place, I had firm evidence of that, that there's no police in the place, I would not have gone to my Commander and said should we go ahead with the operation, I would have said this is the situation, there are no police there, it would not have been a target." To the best of his abilities, he uses the occasion of his public hearing to present his use of violence in the struggle as a moral choice. He calls for an interpretive approach to his self-reflective statements that acknowledges moral ambiguity and the contingent conditions in which decisions are made.

McBride also reminds his audience (lawyers, commissioners, and the viewing public) that the material effects of apartheid's racism made it impossible for him to make the reasoned and moral decisions advocated by Richard. At two different moments in his hearing, he calls attention to his inability to do full-scale reconnaissance missions while apartheid was still in effect. When the chairperson of the AC asks him to describe what he knew about the Why Not Bar, McBride says, "I attempted to enter the bar at one stage and I was told it was full when clearly it was not full.

So I was not allowed to get in there" (McBride). Later in his hearing, in response to Richard's pushing him to explain why he chose the Why Not Bar as his target, McBride states, "The information we had on those two were where Security personnel went to, because we were not—because of the peculiarities of South Africa we were not really in the white community so we couldn't pick up more information on other pubs." The ANC's nonracialism pervades McBride's response. Rather than state explicitly that the norms of apartheid prevented him from entering a white bar in downtown Durban, McBride refers euphemistically to the "peculiarities of South Africa." The elephant of racism sits in the hearing, influencing everything but not directly referenced, even by McBride.

McBride further calls attention to the performative dimension of Richard's questions, which aim not to deepen understanding of McBride's decisions—one of the putative goals of the hearings—but rather to underscore his supposed moral depravity for choosing a target in which civilians socialized. For example, Richard concludes one line of interrogation in which he gets McBride to state that the ANC was "overly concerned" about the possibility of civilian casualties: "We've been through this evidence and I don't want to labour the point, so I'm just simply establishing that it speaks for itself" (McBride). What Richard hopes "speaks for itself" is McBride's callousness about the possibility of civilian casualties. McBride does not have the opportunity to respond to that insinuation, but in response to Richard's questions about the number of security personnel who might have been in the Why Not Bar on a Saturday night, he asserts, "That is a *rhetorical question*. . . . Even if you were outside you wouldn't know the answer." Richard pushes further: "What percentage of people in your perception, inside there would be security personnel?" McBride then responds with sarcasm: "In my *perception*. I wasn't able to *perceive* in the bar, I was only able to *perceive* those which went to the bar very frequently" (McBride, my italics). McBride again calls attention to the fact that the realities of apartheid limited his ability to *perceive* as fully and accurately as the situation demanded. To make the same point, he references the differences in resources available to the apartheid government and those involved in the anti-apartheid struggle. He asserts, "We didn't have the billion rand intelligence budget that the government had and still made mistakes." Here McBride sarcastically refers to the South African security forces' raid in Botswana that occurred one year before and mistakenly led to the deaths of twelve civilians. He states, "The Security Forces had raided Gaborone in Botswana, killing 12 people, two Botswanan citizens, one Somalian, one six year old child from Lesotho and eight South Africans. Of all the South Africans, eight were ANC members, none of them were MK combatants." McBride's point: despite their abundant resources, the security forces still made a severe mistake. Given the constraints within which he was compelled to operate, McBride suggests that he in fact made quite reasoned, indeed moral, decisions. While he regrets the suffering that he caused, he maintains that he was and is in the moral right.

In his closing statement at the hearing, McBride emphasizes that he and the other amnesty applicants were not only perpetrators, but also, and just as significantly, victims of apartheid. He explains, "Apartheid as a system attacked non-white South Africans as a whole. In fact it attacked them because they were non-white. All the applicants in this hearing are victims of the apartheid system." McBride calls attention to the collective underpinnings of apartheid, which did not conceive of nonwhite South Africans as distinct individuals. He also challenges the justice of placing nonwhite participants in the struggle—"the applicants in this hearing"—in the same category as those who defended an unjust system, for not only was their cause just, but they were victims of that system as well. In sum, McBride compels the TRC to entertain arguments about morality, responsibility, and justice that challenge its even-handed approach and its assumptions concerning the existence of the liberal, autonomous, and raceless subject in apartheid South Africa.

Winnie Madikizela-Mandela:
From "Mother" to "Mugger" of the Nation

Winnie Madikizela-Mandela's apartheid existence exemplifies the crisscrossed boundaries between the individual and the collective, the private and the political, during the apartheid era. Her life was shaped both by the system of apartheid and by the struggle to end it. She became a public figure through her marriage to Nelson Mandela in 1958 and then a political figure in her own right during his imprisonment. She continued to play an active role in the ANC after their separation in 1992 and their divorce in 1996. As recently as 2009, she was elected to parliament as an ANC member. Madikizela-Mandela was herself detained and tortured by apartheid security forces for her political work after the Soweto uprisings in 1976, but she refused to testify about this abuse in the Commission's victims' hearings because of what she considered its mistreatment of her (TRC, *Report* 2: 580). Human rights abuses also allegedly occurred at Madikizela-Mandela's home, and, according to some, on her watch. Madikizela-Mandela's resistance to inquiries about these abuses made her notorious both within South Africa and internationally.

From the Soweto uprisings of 1976 though the mid-1980s, Madikizela-Mandela established herself as a prominent pro-democracy activist. She was attuned to the rising militancy of black South African youth, who were responding to the increasingly frequent and brutal states of emergency imposed by the apartheid regime. It was during this post-Soweto period through the mid-'80s that Madikizela-Mandela came to embody her honorific: Mama Wetu (Mother of the Nation). During this era, Madikizela-Mandela also became a vocal proponent of the ANC's use of strategic violence, a position she defended in a 1985 speech: "I will tell you why we are violent. It is because those who oppress us are violent. The Afrikaner knows only one language: the language of violence. The white man will not hand over power in talks around a table. They will use every trick in the white man's book to keep us from power. Therefore, all that is left to us is this painful process of violence" (qtd. in Holmes 95). The Nationalist government did eventually "hand over power in talks around a table," but, as some historians of South Africa argue, the violence that Madikizela-Mandela advocated in the mid-'80s might have driven those negotiators to that metaphorical table. Moreover, in the midst of the state oppression of 1985, such a future was inconceivable. Notwithstanding these speculations, there was a growing disjuncture between Madikizela-Mandela's stance toward violence and that of the ANC. The Nationalist government's brutal repression of the movement to end apartheid had justified her calls for violent resistance. As it became increasingly apparent that the end of apartheid and the transition to a constitutional liberal democracy were imminent, however, her advocacy of violence threatened the ANC's status as a viable political entity for the nation-to-be. Rachel Holmes observes, "Winnie Madikizela-Mandela's position on the ethics of violence fell increasingly out of step with the shifting political context of a South Africa moving towards political transition, wherein the ANC guided its international image away from that of 'terrorist' resistance movement to democratic government-in-waiting" (94).

Madikizela-Mandela's "precipitous fall from 'Mother of the Nation' to deviant 'Mugger of that Nation'" began in 1986 with her infamous statement regarding necklacing[9] (Holmes 96). In a speech in Munsieville, outside Johannesburg, she stated, "Together, hand in hand, with our boxes of matches and our necklaces we shall liberate this country" (qtd. in Holmes 96). Madikizela-Mandela increasingly became associated with violent recriminations against putative informants to and collaborators with the apartheid regime. In 1988, Nelson Mandela issued a request from Poolsmoor Prison that prominent political activists and church leaders form a "Crisis Committee" to oversee the activities of the "Madikizela-Mandela United Football Club" (MUFC), Madikizela-Mandela's team of bodyguards or gang of thugs, depending on one's perspective. In 1989, the Soweto community called upon the Crisis Committee to investigate the abduction of four youths who were being held at Madikizela-Mandela's home in Orlando West. Madikizela-Mandela claimed that the boys had been sexually abused by the Reverend Paul Verryn and that she had taken them to be examined by Dr. Abu-Baker Asvat. (Asvat was murdered in his office just as the story of the abduction began to appear in the press; his records indicated that he found no signs of abuse on the boys.) After resisting pressure from the Crisis Committee and the Soweto community for two weeks, Madikizela-Mandela released three of the four boys on 16 January 1988. One, however, remained missing: Stompie Moeketsi Seipei, a fourteen-year-old youth activist whom some had accused of being a police informant (Edelstein, *Truth and Lies* 43). Stompie's mother, Joyce Mananki Seipei, testified at Madikizela-Mandela's hearing that she had identified Stompie's corpse at a Soweto morgue on 13 February 1989. Jerry Richardson, the head "coach" of the MUFC, was sentenced to death for Stompie Seipei's murder in 1991, but his sentence was later commuted to life in prison. In their testimony at Richardson's trial, the three surviving youths accused Madikizela-Mandela of being present for and participating in the assaults against them and Stompie.

After these allegations against Madikizela-Mandela resurfaced in victims' testimony at the human rights violations hearings, the Commission subpoenaed her for a closed hearing. She in turn called for a public hearing, popularly referred to as the "Winnie hearing," to address the charges. This hearing was held in November 1997. Antjie Krog, who covered the TRC for the South African Broadcasting Corporation, notes that "as a South African media event it is compared to the release of Nelson Mandela from prison in 1990. The international news desks say: provided that Saddam Hussein isn't bombed in the next few days, the 'Winnie hearing' will be the biggest news story on the globe this week" (Krog, *Country* 261). The Winnie hearing was public in the vernacular sense of being seen by all interested parties. But it was also public in that it provided a platform for the encounter between the Commission's constructed remembrance of South Africa's apartheid past, i.e., as a series of incidents between individual victims and perpetrators who fell neatly into their designated categories and acted rationally and autonomously—and an alternative remembrance that accounted for the intermingling of these categories and that also highlighted the affective and collective dimensions of the struggle against apartheid.

The Commission claimed that Madikizela-Mandela's special hearing "was not a court of law, but a commission of enquiry—attempting to understand events rather than establish guilt or innocence" (TRC, *Report* 2: 558). However, according to witnesses, the mood of the Winnie hearing was decidedly legal and accusatory.[10] Krog notes the spectacular and gendered nature of the Winnie hearing: "The world has come to watch us burn a witch" (*Country* 245). Most observers described Madikizela-Mandela's attitude throughout her hearing as defiant and dismissive. Krog ultimately wills herself into believing Madikizela-Mandela's apology (259–60). However, the dominant emotions in her description of Madikizela-Mandela's behavior are frustration and disgust. She states, "Winnie Madikizela-Mandela denies every single allegation of human rights abuses made against her. In her responses she alternates between the words 'ludicrous' and 'ridiculous'" (257). Krog also recounts the angry observations of her fellow journalists about Madikizela-Mandela's apology: "She simply aped it for the benefit of international media . . . [or] to further her populist political career" (259). These responses suggest that Madikizela-Mandela mocked the Commission's project and that her statements at the hearing communicated nothing more than arrogance—a belief that she stood above the moral reckoning with the past that drove the Commission's project. They reveal frustration with Madikizela-Mandela's refusal to assume the position of shamed and repentant subject in the Commission's official memory of South Africa's past, and, in so doing, to participate in its redemptive narrative of restorative justice.

In addition to, or perhaps in lieu of, arrogance, scholars argue that Madikizela-Mandela's resistance to the Commission at her special hearing signals a political position. They contend that she was "out of step" with the ANC's evolving position on the legitimacy of violence in the anti-apartheid movement (Holmes 94). Or, as Richard Wilson explains, "Winnie Mandela never quite made the transition from the 1980s to the 1990s. . . . [She] became the symbol of a historical disjuncture, the ANC's own break with the past, the excesses of the 1980s struggle, and the new national historicity" (165). Robert Meister focuses on the TRC's figuring of Madikizela-Mandela as the "bad victim" (97), she who refused to acknowledge that apartheid had damaged her own moral compass. Had she acknowledged this moral damage, Meister argues, she would have relieved fears that she would inflict the resulting anger and resentment on those who had benefited under apartheid. He suggests, "To many South Africans, black and white, she represented the unreconciled victim for whom the anti-apartheid struggle was not yet over . . . the overall effect [of the hearing] was to construct her as the very figure that the TRC meant to marginalize" (86). Wilson and Meister rightly call attention to the Commission's figuring of Madikizela-Mandela and to the ways in which she came to represent a politics of violence and revenge that was incompatible with the democratic legalism of the new South Africa. Their analyses echo that of Rachel Holmes, who locates the origins of this rift in Madikizela-Mandela's advocacy of violence in the final years of the struggle against apartheid and the early days of the transition. For these scholars, Madikizela-Mandela epitomizes the eclipse of the moral order of the old South Africa.

I want to suggest that the contestation during the Winnie hearing might also result from Madikizela-Mandela's resistance to the Commission's rhetoric of accountability, which she conveys through a rhetorical strategy John Schilb has coined a "rhetorical refusal." Rhetorical refusals do not adhere to the audience's expectations, and thus they "deliberately challenge the frame that their audiences bring to the occasion" (6). Schilb emphasizes that these acts "are not indifferent to the audience. Rather, they are efforts to shape its thinking" (10). It is important to remember that Madikizela-Mandela volunteered to appear before the Commission to address the allegations lodged against her, despite having rejected the Commission's earlier invitation to speak as a victim at the hearings on gross human rights violations. As some of the aforementioned critics suggest, she might have done so merely to give herself a highly public platform from which to show her disdain for the TRC. Alternatively, she might have supported the Commission's historical endeavor, but wanted to revise its terms. If she participated in the reconciliation process as the Commission framed it and anticipated she would, she would have had to acquiesce to its individualistic framing of her actions and accept its moral condemnation, rather than exploring what Nesiah and Keenan describe as "the material and ideological structures and contestations that are the constitutive background conditions [of acts of violence]" (274). I argue below that her various rhetorical refusals during the Winnie hearing bring these "material and ideological structures and contestations" to the fore. In this regard, Madikizela-Mandela's intentions matter less than the consequences of her rhetoric.

At several points in the hearing, Madikizela-Mandela attempts to convey the particular context of the struggle in the mid-1980s so as to situate her actions in place and time. The phrase "at that time" appears frequently in her responses, as if she seeks to remind the Commission and the hearing audience that she is speaking of another reality, one that cannot be represented with, nor fairly subjected to, the norms of behavior and subjectivity that the Commission seeks to promote in the new South Africa. The repetition of this phrase reminds listeners of the differences between the possibilities for knowledge in the present and those during the struggle against apartheid. Her response to questions about her infamous statement concerning necklacing emphasizes the distinctiveness of the conditions during the struggle: "Well, statements made *at that time* under those conditions, during our struggle.... They were descriptive of *that time*" ("Human Rights," my emphasis). She further reminds the Commission that a climate of suspicion permeated the anti-apartheid movement, especially during the 1980s, when the violations under consideration took place. In this example as well, she repeats the phrase "at that time" to explain her actions: "*At that time,* I did not have official information about STRATCOM. All I knew *at that time,* was that there was this machinery used by the State to discredit the African National Congress and that I had been targeted for that" (my emphasis). Those under suspicion knew that someone or something was watching them, but who or what, precisely, they could not determine. The Commission's final *Report* acknowledges the potentially pernicious influence of this uncertainty: "The Commission cannot ignore the paranoia that existed at the time regarding informers. There is no doubt that being under constant surveillance and living under siege may have made a considerable contribution to what eventually happened" (2: 582). Nevertheless, the lawyers during the hearing sought to discredit Madikizela-Mandela for pointing to the historical specificity and context of her statements or actions, and the commissioners did not stop them from doing so.

An infamous exchange between Madikizela-Mandela and one of the victims' lawyers, S. L. Joseph, highlights the incompatibility between the Commission's investment in individual responsibility and forensic truth and its putative goal of "understand[ing] events" (TRC, *Report* 2: 558). In it,

CONTESTING ACCOUNTABILITY   89

Madikizela-Mandela engages in rhetorical refusals to thwart Joseph's use of legal logic to parse her statement about "necklacing." First, Joseph asks whether "horrific things were taking place all over the country," to which Madikizela-Mandela responds, "That is correct." He proceeds: "Necklacing was taking place. Is that correct?" Her noncommittal response: "That may also be correct." Next he inquires as to the primary victims of necklacing, to which she also responds evasively: "Well, I don't really know, I am not an expert in that part of your history.... I do not know who was necklaced at that stage and why." Though Madikizela-Mandela finally acknowledges that the victims were supposed to be collaborators or informants of the apartheid police, she parries Joseph's effort to link her "description of that time" to her personal involvement with the necklacings: "I did make mention of those words in describing the situation of the time. It was not in relation to any particular necklacing I had personally done.... I did not necklace anybody.... And a description of the events of the time, is not part of the perpetration of acts of atrocities." Joseph continues, pushing Madikizela-Mandela to acknowledge the effects of her "description": "Let me rather then ask you this, will you convey what you intended the ordinary reader should have understood by these words." She responds, "I did not intend anything, I was describing the situation at the time." He asks again, "You did not intend any person who heard these words, to understand anything from these words?" She again refuses to engage on his terms: "I was describing the situation at the time. And it is my final answer" ("Human Rights").

Madikizela-Mandela's rhetoric in this exchange might merely constitute her attempt to avoid culpability through a literal interpretation of the Commission's insistence on personal responsibility: since I personally did not place the tire around the victim's neck, I cannot be held responsible. At the same time, her literal interpretation of the Commission's prosecutorial logic imbues her response with a touch of irony. It is as if Madikizela-Mandela is pointing to the inadequacy of this discursive framework for the Commission's task of understanding South Africa's apartheid past. For the broader aim of the Commission is not solely to determine whether she literally placed a tire around a victim's neck, nor even whether she made a statement that encouraged such behavior. Rather, the intention is to understand the conditions that made the utterance of such a statement, and the action that it called into being, possible—a historical undertaking that requires far more than the Commission's "who did what to whom?" approach. By taking the Commission's emphasis on individual responsibility to its logical extreme, Madikizela-Mandela's rhetorical refusal reveals its limitations as a heuristic. Put simply, her responses imply that pressuring her to acknowledge her individual responsibility, with no attention to the context within which she was acting, would not enable the richer historical understanding that the Commission ostensibly sought.[11] To draw again from Nesiah and Keenan, this infamous exchange suggests how the Commission's framework for accountability, based on the dominant human rights framework, precluded an examination of "the social forces that enabled or sustained the broader political dynamics within which violence played its part" (275).

Events at the hearing testify to Madikizela-Mandela's representative status and the collective dimensions of the anti-apartheid struggle. According to Krog, "representatives of the Women's League of the African National Congress chanted outside the hearing hall: 'Winnie didn't kill alone! Winnie had a mandate from us to kill!'" (*Country* 246). At the time of her special hearing, Madikizela-Mandela literally represented these women, as she was elected president of the ANC Women's League in December 1993 and then again in April 1997. Her supporters demanded that the Commission see Madikizela-Mandela as one of them, as simultaneously a member and leader of their collective. They rejected the implication that she acted as an individual subject whom the Commission could or should hold solely accountable for her actions. Their actions at the hearing bolster claims about the disjuncture between the Commission's emphasis on individuals and the collective subject positions of those involved in the struggle against apartheid.

A Freer Rhetorical Scene: Njabulo Ndebele's
The Cry of Winnie Mandela

Njabulo Ndebele's novel *The Cry of Winnie Mandela* (2003), written in the wake of the Winnie hearing, helps illuminate the critiques of the TRC's approach implied by Madikizela-Mandela's rhetorical refusals. The novel creates a rhetorical situation wherein an *ibandla* (gathering), in this case of black South African women, poses questions of Winnie Madikizela-Mandela, to whom the women refer respectfully as Mother-of-the-Nation, *yena* (her), and *leleidi* (the lady), and affectionately as *notombi* (girl!) and *sana* (baby!). The novel presents and celebrates the individual history of each woman in the *ibandla,* whose members ask probing, difficult questions about each other's choices and decisions, culminating in their discussion with the fictional Winnie. This self-examination occurs in a collective and supportive setting in which the women seek to understand one another's emotional, logical, and circumstantial reasoning in addition to, or at times in lieu of, morally evaluating the decisions and actions that resulted. Before the *ibandla,* the fictional Winnie speaks about the erosion of her selfhood as she became a figurehead in the struggle against apartheid and about her vexed emotional response to the questions that were posed of her at the TRC hearing. The novel's mapping of the complex relationships among systemic oppression, historical experience, and consciousness, and its depiction of the everyday experience of nonwhite South Africans during apartheid, negatively highlights the TRC's tendency to conceive of individuals as decontextualized and nonracial free agents.

Ndebele's dissatisfaction with the Winnie hearing led him to write *Cry.* In our interview, he explained that he sought "a deepening of insight into a historic moment." He emphasized, however, that his primary goal was to understand the effect of that historic moment on Winnie Madikizela-Mandela: "I wanted also, and perhaps more significantly, to understand the impact of major events on her as an individual." The character Mamello Malete expresses the curiosity, concern, and admiration that motivate Ndebele's inquiry. She tells the fictional Winnie, "I'm unable to definitively resolve my doubts into contempt. Who are you, Mummy? . . . You leave me in confusion, torn between my love for you, and my loathing for the banalities and horrors associated with you in the name of freedom. Who are you? . . . It's me . . . who admires how you seem to have succeeded in suspending consciousness and feeling in favour of postures that have been as heroic as they were malignant" (Ndebele, *Cry* 77). Mamello's confusion haunts her. She seeks to reconcile the different versions of Winnie, the public and the private, the heroic and the villainous. Ndebele suggested in our interview, and then through the content of *Cry,* that the Winnie hearing did not generate this deeper understanding—otherwise, he would have had no need to write the novel—and that the Commission's inability to elicit her reflections about the imbrication of the personal and the political during apartheid prevented it from doing so.

In *Cry,* Ndebele does not pretend to speak directly for Madikizela-Mandela. However, in our interview, he relayed an anecdote that attests to her awareness of the novel's existence, and, perhaps, her acceptance of its representation of her. Ndebele recounted, "[Madikizela-Mandela] did come to the launch of the novel in Johannesburg. She told me she had not read the novel at the time . . . if she had not read it, she had probably been told about it and felt that it was okay to attend the launch. It could be that her attendance signals an approval or a high degree of comfort. All this is speculation on my part." Given her celebrity or notoriety, depending on one's perspective, the mere fact that Madikizela-Mandela chose to attend, and thereby implicitly support, the launch of the novel is significant. At a minimum, it suggests her belief that *Cry* is relevant and perhaps also conveys some degree of truth about her personal history and her experience before the TRC. The favorable response that Madikizela-Mandela received at the launch also reveals the interest, if not outright support, that she continues to receive from some South Africans. Ndebele recalled in our interview that "her queue of readers who had bought a copy of the book and wanted her autograph was longer than mine!!!" The interest in the novel demonstrates that many South Africans were dissatisfied with the memory work of the Winnie hearing, and that, in search of a more nuanced remembrance of that period, they turned to the novel. These readers endorsed Ndebele's imagined account of Madikizela-Mandela's memories and explanation of her actions. However, they also valued the autograph of the historical figure herself. Their enthusiastic reception of the novel and the real Madikizela-Mandela further blurs the boundaries between the real and the imagined.

Cry reproduces the Winnie hearing for these curious readers, but with a difference: a spirit of inquiry, focused on understanding why Madikizela-Mandela did what she did, animates the *ibandla,* not a prosecutorial animus. In proposing the "game" with Winnie (*Cry* 46), Mamello outlines the mood the *ibandla* hopes to create. She describes the *ibandla*'s interaction with Winnie as a "conversation" and proposes, "Let's ask her something we deeply want to know about her thoughts and desires" (46). The *ibandla* does not seek an account or justification, but a deep and intimate understanding of Winnie. Mamello reminds the women, "You can also tell her a story. About yourself, for example" (46). All share in the *ibandla,* creating an equal balance of power among the participants. Mamello concludes, "Let's invite Winnie into our membership and make her the fifth woman-in-waiting in this room" (46). The invitation to join the *ibandla* precedes and thus is not dependent on the content of Winnie's statements or explanations. For the *ibandla,* Winnie belongs by virtue of her experience as a fellow woman-in-waiting and her willingness to reflect on her experience with them, not because she adopts a particular moral stance toward her past.

Ndebele's Winnie comments indirectly on the ways in which the rhetorical scene created by the *ibandla* differs from that of the Winnie hearing. She says to the women of the *ibandla*, "You've done me the honor of asking me questions, not demanding that I confess" (*Cry* 110). Only a criminal "confesses." She begins her response to the women's questions by noting her lack of language and her resulting inability to express her identity and reflect on it. She attributes this lack of "the capacity for reflection and the vital sense of identity" both to the years she spent waiting for Nelson Mandela's release from prison and to the intrusion of the apartheid state on their home life that began before his arrest (104). She refers to this process as an "emptying out": "[It] began even before Nelson was arrested. It started with the systematic invasion of whatever dreams we had of a family life" (106). She describes the cumulative effects of apartheid's erosion on her selfhood and identity: "My law of resistance emerged from this gradual emptying out of my life. Here was my law: embrace disruption, and then rage against order instead of longing for it" (107). As she lost control over her daily life, and the stable self that consistency and order enable, the fictional Winnie suggests that she eventually succumbed to the all-encompassing force of her own "law of resistance." She asks rhetorically, "If one's very life becomes a weapon of resistance, something designed to negate repressive intent, raging against an imposed order, is there a point at which self-negation becomes a permanent feature of identity?" (114). Here she suggests that apartheid did not allow her the space or time to have an identity outside of the one required by the struggle.

Ndebele's Winnie's reflections do not directly challenge the Commission's emphasis on individual responsibility. Yet the consistency with which she refers to her lack of a coherent self during apartheid implies the need for a different rhetorical frame to understand her actions, and by extension those of other actors, during that time. Her reflections ask the reader-listener to conceive of her actions in context, rather than as the actions of a decontextualized free agent. She recalls that she was only one of many "trapped in the roles politics prepared them to take.... There are many out there who are not what they are but what politics has made them ... we have an acquired will to perform roles that do not accord with our being. The struggle re-routed many of us from our destinies" (*Cry* 137). Her reflections point to the ways in which the anti-apartheid movement superseded the desires and needs of the individual actors within it.

Ironically, it is precisely this kind of individual autonomy that the Commission required. That is, the Commission asked Madikizela-Mandela to speak from an individualized and autonomous subject position that was unavailable "at that time," and, at the same time, made it nearly impossible for her to explain why doing so posed such a challenge.

The zenith of *Cry* occurs with Winnie's proclamation of her "distrust" of the Commission's reconciliation-driven memory project. She states, "For me, reconciliation demands my annihilation. No. *You*, all of you, have to reconcile not with me, but with the meaning of me. For my meaning is the endless human search for the right thing to do" (137). Here she claims that there is no transhistorical morality, or "right thing to do," as the Commission implies through its positing of reconciliation via moralistic remembrance and retrospective judgment. Rather, Ndebele's Winnie suggests, the Commission must engage differently in its memory work, accounting for the collective dimensions of both apartheid and the political resistance it engendered, and the perhaps irreconcilable moral demands that South Africa's complex past placed on historical actors. Only in so doing might it approximate its goal of reconciliation.

Conclusion

Robert McBride's and Winnie Madikizela-Mandela's testimonies and Ndebele's *Cry of Winnie Mandela* highlight the particular challenges of accounting for oneself during a time of transition. The Commission's rhetoric of accountability assumed the presence of a coherent, unified, and ahistorical moral self with the ability to narrate his or her past. This assumption poses problems. It limits the range and depth of remembrances that participants share before a truth commission. A commission working under this assumption may thus be unable to hear those parts of perpetrator testimonies that attest to the collective identifications that often characterize the social and political movements that precede a transition. This inability to hear perpetrators' testimony might compromise a commission's aim of generating a fuller truth about the past. A truth commission needs to strike a delicate balance between its desire to cultivate a new subject position and morality in the present and its willingness to hear how participants understood themselves and their actions in the past.

Narrating the self is not easy under any conditions. As theorist Judith Butler explains, social norms provide the vocabulary with which one constructs and accounts for oneself (26). These norms both precede and enable the creation of the "I" (27). Butler observes that "this particular kind of transitivity is difficult, if not impossible, to narrate," thus making it hard to account for and justify oneself (37). The material examined in this chapter suggests that, on a more fundamental level, the notion of individual subjectivity is itself worthy of reconsideration, for the "I" is always an unstable construction, if not a fiction. Kopano Ratele, professor of psychology at the University of South Africa, explains the incongruity between the Western "I" and black South Africans' sense of self: "You are always formed by others, not by yourself, but because in, say, the black community, everybody is so close, you cannot make out what 'you' is. . . . To ask how the self is formed, to ask about borders, are the wrong questions. You should ask, what is the self in the family? Within the networks, the map of networks, where is the dot that is you? There is no dot without a connecting line" (Krog, Mpolweni, and Ratele 204). Ratele makes a dangerously essentialist statement about "the black community" in South Africa. However, his observation that all humans are social beings, made in and by our relationships with others, has the ring of truth. The body of scholarship clustered around the term "relational autonomy" similarly complicates the notion of individual and decontextualized autonomy by considering "the implications of the intersubjective and social dimensions of selfhood and identity for conceptions of individual autonomy and moral and political agency" (Mackenzie and Stoljar 4). The question becomes whether and how truth commissions, as liberal democratic institutions that assume the value and existence of individual subjects, can acknowledge the existence of selves—those blurred boundaries of the "I"—within that "map of networks."

These findings about subjectivity have methodological implications for scholars interested in understanding the complexity and layers of perpetrators' reasoning about the past and their evolving subjectivities. It has become a commonplace to state that "context matters," referring both to the historical context of the actions for which the speaker accounts and to the contemporary context wherein she provides that account. This chapter demonstrates that imaginative texts have the potential to illuminate both senses of context, providing insights that other textual sources cannot. Writing about post-TRC narratives, Njabulo Ndebele observes that they "may have less and less to do with the facts themselves and with their recall than with the revelation of meaning through the imaginative combination of those facts" ("Memory, Metaphor" 20–21). Here Ndebele suggests that "imaginative combination[s]" might in fact contribute more to meaning making than the facts alone do. The following chapter examines the contribution that Jillian Edelstein's *Truth and Lies*, a photographic essay that imaginatively combines images and texts from the TRC process, makes to the reconciliation process that the Commission instigated.

4
IMAGINING RECONCILIATION

Collective imagining does not proceed through fixed, teleological processes of discursive engagement; its images are not constant and eternal. Imaginings change. Controversy engenders moments especially amenable to changes in imagining by unsettling background understandings and engaging imagining as an active force.

—ROBERT ASEN

Joyce Mtimkulu, the woman in figure 1, has sought for more than twenty years to gain legal redress against Gideon Nieuwoudt, the man who murdered her son. In spite of her objections, the TRC granted Nieuwoudt's application for amnesty because he fully disclosed his violations and proved that they were politically motivated and met the "proportionality" requirement.[1] For Mtimkulu, Nieuwoudt's truth telling did not foster reconciliation. Even for viewers who do not know that she holds a chunk of her son's scalp and hair in her hand—the effects of his being given rat poison by the South African police while in custody—Mtimkulu's searing gaze exhorts viewers to question, if not critique, the reconciliatory process that the TRC sought to promote.

This chapter engages the *topos* of reconciliation, taking literally the "imagining" of its title through an analysis of Jillian Edelstein's *Truth and Lies: Stories from the Truth and Reconciliation Commission in South Africa*, a project comprising a series of imagetexts.[2] Inspired by Robert Asen's insight in the epigraph that opens this chapter, I argue that *Truth and Lies* "unsettles" easy assumptions about reconciliation by making available the complex, ambivalent, and at times contradictory responses of victims and perpetrators to the TRC process (Asen 352). These imagetexts capture what Erik Doxtader identifies as the "substance" of reconciliation: "the contingent communicative interaction that [reconciliation] constitutes and supports" (*With Faith* 15). The images in *Truth and Lies*, which depict ways of being and being-with-others, compel "imagining as an active force"

Figure 1 Joyce Mtimkulu Zwide, Port Elizabeth, February 1997.
Photo: Jillian Edelstein

(Asen 352). These striking photographs "offer a performance of social relationships that provides a basis for moral comprehension and response" (Hariman and Lucaites 44). Writing about the "subjunctive voice" of the visual, Barbie Zelizer observes that images have the power to "activat[e] impulses about how the 'world might be' rather than 'how it is'" (164). In other words, they energize the conditional—the "what if" as well as the "what is." The imagetexts of *Truth and Lies* do just that: they invite imaginings about the possibilities for coexistence and about the emergence of democratic norms in the new South Africa. Like the novelists whose work I analyze in the previous chapters, Edelstein capitalizes on the rhetorical power of her chosen genre—the imagetext—both to witness and to participate in the truth and reconciliation process that the TRC set in motion.

This chapter's methodology mirrors that of the previous chapters. I first analyze the TRC's development of an elastic and ambiguous notion of reconciliation that enabled a range of responses to its process. Reconciliation became a generative *topos* with which TRC participants could engage in a variety of ways, not a goal that was (or was not) achieved. The remainder of the chapter examines how *Truth and Lies* makes available participants' diverse—sometimes overlapping and sometimes opposing—perspectives on the TRC's reconciliatory logic and process. After explaining the genesis of *Truth and Lies* and discussing the rhetorical effects of Edelstein's highlighting of her vexed relationship to South Africa's apartheid past, I turn to five imagetexts in *Truth and Lies* that showcase TRC participants' perspectives on and engagement with reconciliation. These imagetexts reflect five distinct stances: (1) rejecting truth-as-path-to-reconciliation; (2) striving for reconciliation through truth; (3) contesting the terms of reconciliation; (4) manifesting indifference toward reconciliation; and (5) recognizing the ambiguity of reconciliation.

The TRC on Reconciliation

Reconciliation has a long history in South Africa, notably in the antiapartheid struggle and in the negotiations that culminated in the country's first democratic elections.[3] The word "reconciliation" appears in the Act that founded the TRC, Promotion of National Unity and Reconciliation, and in the name of the Commission itself. According to the Act, the TRC's central objective was "to promote national unity and reconciliation in a spirit of understanding which transcends the conflicts and divisions of the past" (Republic of South Africa). However, as Erik Doxtader observes, "the government's initial call for a truth commission did not proceed from a clear definition of reconciliation. Was it a process or goal? Was it both?" (*With Faith* 251). Once the Commission got under way, the commissioners, as well as many TRC participants, invoked reconciliation in their public statements. What reconciliation precisely meant to these speakers, and in the TRC process more generally, however, remains unclear. According to historian David Philips, "the evidence suggests that during the nearly three years of the Commission's existence, the Commission as a whole never had a clear idea of what was involved in the idea of 'reconciliation'" (part 2). Philips cites several sources from within the TRC as "evidence," including a researcher from the TRC Investigation Unit—"I don't think they grappled with it [reconciliation] adequately"—and a commissioner— "they [the commissioners] all had very different understandings" (part 2). That TRC insiders did not reach consensus about reconciliation is not surprising, given the many definitions made possible by the Commission's legal mandate and "reconciliation's characteristic ambiguity" (Doxtader, *With Faith* 296).

Though written at the conclusion of the TRC process, the *Report* reflects the existence of the Commission's multiple understandings of reconciliation rather than resolving them. The "Concepts and Principles" chapter in volume 1 offers a typology of reconciliation: first, intrapersonal reconciliation "of victims with their own pain" (1: 107); second, interpersonal reconciliation "between specific victims and perpetrators" (1: 107); third, communal reconciliation "within and between communities" (1: 107); and, finally, "national unity and reconciliation." It explains that this fourth notion, "national unity and reconciliation," could be understood in Christian terms, entailing "contrition, confession, forgiveness, and restitution . . . apologies" (1: 108), and also in political terms, entailing "peaceful coexistence, culture of human rights, shared citizenship" (1: 108). Charles Villa-Vicencio, former director of research for the TRC, argues that the TRC helped lay the foundation for the latter—reconciliation as a political goal—rather than the former because "[forgiveness] cannot be imposed" ("Getting on with Life" 209). The *Report* itself simply acknowledges the tension between the Christian and political notions of reconciliation. Indeed, theologian Piet Meiring argues that proponents of both notions of reconciliation continued the debate "right to the end of the life of the TRC" (124). At different moments, it seems, both notions of national reconciliation, as well as the three other forms of reconciliation, informed commissioners' and participants' engagement in the TRC process.[4]

The chapter entitled "Reconciliation" in the fifth volume of the *Report* likewise fails to clarify which of, or at what stages, these various notions of reconciliation took precedence during the TRC process. It instead reiterates that reconciliation is "a complex, long-term process with many dimensions" and then, for the remainder of the chapter, offers abundant examples of these dimensions of reconciliation as evidence that South Africa is on the "long road" toward "reconciliation" (TRC, *Report* 5: 350). The reasoning of the "Reconciliation" chapter is thus both tautological and guardedly laudatory of the TRC; the examples support the definition of reconciliation as multidimensional as well as the claim that the Commission, while not achieving reconciliation, promoted "significant steps in the reconciliation process" (5: 350).[5] The chapter concludes with a list of what it calls "stages or signposts on the reconciliation road" that reiterates central, and at times conflicting, claims (especially regarding forgiveness) of both the Christian and political notions of reconciliation (5: 435). The *Report* thus thwarts definitive interpretations of the TRC's particular definition of reconciliation as well as more general definitional claims about the term.

Not surprisingly, the TRC's multidimensional and sometimes contradictory notions of reconciliation have generated a good deal of criticism. Some fault the Commission for its failure to offer a coherent notion of reconciliation (Chapman), while others claim that its shaky theoretical and epistemological foundations served a higher moral purpose (Herwitz), or, more cynically, masked its political agenda and nation-building project (Wilson, Moon). More sympathetic critics, typically South Africans who were directly involved with the Commission, defend the TRC. Against Wilson's claim about the TRC's use of "Africanist wrappings to sell its reconciliatory version of human rights talk" (13), Antjie Krog argues that an African worldview, what she describes as an "interconnectedness toward wholeness," formed the interpretive foundation of the Commission's notion of reconciliation ("This Thing" 140). While noting that reconciliation and forgiveness are used interchangeably in many African languages, Pumla Gobodo-Madikizela suggests that *ubuntu* is in fact a "human concept," and that the TRC's ideas about reconciliation and forgiveness are "drawn from the universal values of care, compassion and empathy" (159, 165). Though she and Krog differ in their analysis of the source of the TRC's notion of reconciliation, both celebrate the "unprecedented moment of hope and moral imagination" that it inspired (Gobodo-Madikizela 152). As this condensed literature review demonstrates, criticism of the TRC ranges from cynical dismissals to adulation. Generally speaking, however, those who participated in the TRC process, either by working for the Commission directly or by covering it as a journalist, tend to shy away from harsh critiques even while they acknowledge its shortcomings.

There is evidence from the transcripts of the public hearings and the *Report* that could be used to support all of the above critics' interpretations of the TRC's notion of reconciliation. For that reason, I resist making definitive claims about the meaning of reconciliation in the TRC process. Instead, I focus on the ways in which reconciliation's "characteristic ambiguity" (Doxtader, *With Faith* 296) and the Commission's attempts to define the term made reconciliation a generative *topos*. For commissioners, participants, and observers of the TRC alike, the Commission's rhetorics of reconciliation became a resource for making arguments about how best to deal with South Africa's past and its bearing on the future. Some victims rejected outright the Commission's appeal that they accept truth as a form of justice or that they forgive those who had wronged them. Others seemed to be striving mightily to enact the Christian form of reconciliation articulated most powerfully by Archbishop Desmond Tutu, the TRC chairperson. Some perpetrators presented themselves as unrepentant for their actions but still committed to the creation of the new South Africa, while others seemed indifferent, dismissive, or disdainful of the entire process. Before turning to the imagetexts that capture these varied engagements with the TRC and collectively "imagine" the new South Africa, I discuss Jillian Edelstein's position vis-à-vis the Truth and Reconciliation Commission process. *Truth and Lies* foregrounds her need to come to terms with her role in South Africa's recent past as much as it documents, with no pretense of objectivity or disinterest, the efforts of her photographic subjects to do the same.

Jillian Edelstein—Motivations and Investment in *Truth and Lies*

From an early age, Jillian Edelstein experienced conflict about the privilege she enjoyed as a white South African during the apartheid era. As the following diary entry reveals, the conflict stemmed from a simultaneous awareness of her privilege and of the precarious lives of the black South Africans on whom that privilege depended. In this diary entry—one of many that Edelstein includes in *Truth and Lies*—form mirrors content, as Edelstein embeds her memory of the threats faced by Gertie, her black maid, within her recollection of Friday night dinners with her grandparents.[6] Edelstein recalls,

> When I made this my first trip to the Island[7] it was with mixed emotions—one of which was guilt, a common White South African theme. For years as a little girl growing up in White suburban Cape

> Town, I would look forward to Friday nights when we used to have dinner in Sea Point with my grandparents. From their balcony I would stare across the expanse of ocean all the way to Robben Island. . . . My earliest political memory is of my parents hiding Gertie, my black nanny, and her boyfriend, Ben, while the police were raiding homes searching for "illegal" migrant workers—those who were not carrying their passes, the document which the Blacks referred to as the "the dompas." These were the result of an inhuman piece of legislation designed to keep tabs on the movements of the black populace all the time. An early photograph shows me snug and secure, smiling as I straddle Gertie's chunky shoulders. I adored her and the fear of that raid and the thought that Gertie might disappear from my life began to make me understand a little of what politics was about. I certainly knew that Mandela was imprisoned on the Island but at that time—I must have been about five or six years old—my concerns were centred on the Cadbury's chocolate slab my grandfather used to give us children every Friday night. (*Truth and Lies* 62)

As a child, Edelstein's political analysis did not extend beyond a latent fear of losing Gertie. The adult Edelstein, the creator of *Truth and Lies,* is able to trace her nascent political consciousness to her awareness as a child that Gertie was subject to forces beyond her control.[8] The inclusion of this vexed remembrance reminds reader-viewers of her personal and highly emotional investment in the subject matter of *Truth and Lies.*

Edelstein's guilt and anger drove her to become a press photographer in Johannesburg in the early 1980s and provided the fuel for *Truth and Lies* a decade and a half later. She explains that "photography was a way, for me, of channeling these emotions" (*Truth and Lies* 12). The camera provided Edelstein with a tool with which she could put her indignation about the apartheid regime to work. She sought to bear witness to the violence that was necessary to maintain apartheid in order to forward the claim that it was brutal and unjust. Though she left South Africa in 1985 to take a photography course in London and ended up staying there, Edelstein returned frequently (12). In 1996, while in South Africa attending her sister's wedding, she was "gripped by the TV footage of the early scenes from the Truth Commission" and "promised [herself she] would return to document the process" (12). Edelstein recalls being "fueled by her drive and absolutely driven by her guilt about not being able to do anything more or better or braver" (interview). Chronicling the TRC's process constituted a contribution to that ongoing struggle, though, in her estimation, a meager one (interview). Over a period of four years, Edelstein traveled between her London home and South Africa to take photographs of deponents, the public hearings, and contemporary South Africa and South Africans. She sought demographic and geographic diversity and chose which public hearings to attend with these considerations in mind. She took photographs in the rooms adjacent to the hearing halls and in participants' homes and hometowns, spaces in which TRC participants had more freedom than they did in the actual hearings to express a range of sentiments and arguments about the TRC process.

Truth and Lies as Imagetext

The "stories" of the subtitle of *Truth and Lies*—*Stories from the Truth and Reconciliation Commission in South Africa*—consist of both the photographs and various written texts. For that reason, I describe *Truth and Lies* as a photographic essay comprised of "imagetexts": a "composite, synthetic work (or concept) that combines image and text" (Mitchell 89). Imagetexts call attention to the impurity of their form, and, in so doing, "permit a critical openness to the actual workings of representation and discourse" (91). The various fonts in *Truth and Lies* call attention to the differences among the written texts. The more purely objective or factual writings, such as historical background about South Africa, the TRC, and biographical information about the photographed subject, appear in Times Roman. Edelstein's entries from the diary she maintained during her trips to South Africa appear in Courier. Edelstein thus visually marks the difference in these writings, all of which she produced. In placing them on the same page with the photographs, she encourages reader-viewers to consider them simultaneously in juxtaposition and together, as constitutive of the broader rhetoric of the text. Edelstein includes the edges of the negative in the prints of the photographs, further denaturalizing these "stories" of truth and reconciliation by showing the artifice and staging of the photographic scene.

Truth and Lies is not organized into formal sections, nor does the text proceed chronologically or topically. Introductory materials include Edelstein's foreword; an introduction by the historian, writer, foreign policy expert, and Canadian politician Michael Ignatieff; and an essay, "Memory and Trauma," by psychologist and former TRC member Pumla Gobodo-Madikizela. The first set of imagetexts focuses primarily on famous and infamous people and places, such as the TRC chairperson, Archbishop Desmond Tutu; Winnie Madikizela-Mandela; Nelson Mandela; Steven Biko; and Robben Island. The second set of imagetexts, which Edelstein referred to informally during our interview as her "gallery of rogues," contains photographs of alleged perpetrators and their victims and families. The final set depicts the TRC's process of exhumations, which Edelstein describes as "one of the immediate results of the Truth Commission hearings" (*Truth and Lies* 211). The photographs capture the process of exhumation and the experiences of those who discovered the often mutilated and unidentified corpses. Edelstein's explanatory paragraph notes that many victims waited years to confirm the death and to determine the whereabouts of their disappeared loved ones.

In addition to her diary entries and writings about South Africa and the TRC, which provide sociohistorical context for the portraits that constitute the bulk of the text, *Truth and Lies* includes pre- and post-apartheid land- and urbanscapes. These varied images depict the complex reality of life during apartheid and the different, yet still vexed, conditions of existence in the new South Africa. On and between the title page and table of contents, four photographs suggest the continuities and discontinuities in everyday South African life before and after apartheid. The first three were taken after the transition in 2000, while the fourth was shot in 1984, during the apartheid era. The title page photograph shows the bleak landscape of Upington in the Northern Cape. Four black South Africans carrying heavy loads appear in the photograph, but they are not foregrounded. Nothing in the photograph suggests that it was taken in the post-apartheid era; in this photograph, at least, the lives of these laboring black men and women seem unaffected by the end of apartheid. The next photograph of Meadowlands, Soweto, in contrast, could only have been taken in the post-apartheid era. Its focal point is a multiracial advertisement for an unidentified product with the caption, "Share today. Be rich tomorrow." This image would not have been produced or used during apartheid. While it celebrates the overcoming of racial barriers, it does so in the service of the market economy. During apartheid, South Africa experienced numerous trade sanctions and boycotts. It was hoped that its entry into the global market would strengthen the previously constrained economy and buttress the new government's social goals and economic redistribution programs.

Progress has been uneven. Edelstein's photograph reminds viewers of the rainbow nation's embrace of the market and the resulting imbrication of democracy and capitalism in the new South Africa.[9]

The third photograph captures the vast township of Crossroads, Cape Town, its corrugated tin-roofed shacks and empty lots strewn with debris offering a reminder that the end of apartheid did not spell the end of poverty. Like the first photograph, this image calls attention to the continued socioeconomic disparities in the new South Africa. The final photograph of early morning workers, bundled in shawls and hats in a resettlement camp in what is now Orange Free State, is congruous with the prior images of the working poor, but Edelstein took it in 1984. Though much has changed in the new South Africa, this group of photographs reminds reader-viewers of all that has not. They contextualize the subsequent photographs of TRC deponents, demonstrating that they speak from neither a utopian rainbow nation nor an impoverished wasteland, but rather from a nation in the midst of an economic, political, and social transition, the future of which is still uncertain.

Blurred Boundaries

While Edelstein makes evident her opposition to apartheid, her desire "to educate people about a history that they would rather not know" (interview), and her commitment to a democratic South Africa, *Truth and Lies* does not offer a univocal perspective on the TRC process or judgments of the participants that it profiles. Rather, as South African writer and activist Gillian Slovo observes in her endorsement on the back cover of *Truth and Lies,* Edelstein conveys "the complex, contradictory, confusing process that was the Truth and Reconciliation commission." Paradoxically, it is Edelstein's explicitly subjective presence that makes the varied perspectives of the TRC participants whom she photographs available to viewers. Before turning to those participants' perspectives on reconciliation, here I analyze how Edelstein's artistic and editorial decisions bring her subjectivity as well as the participation of her photographic subjects to the fore.

Edelstein makes no pretense of objectivity or neutrality. She consistently calls attention to her personal need to reconcile with South Africa's past. In so doing, she distances herself from the traditional *ethos* of the objective photojournalist who seeks to obscure her presence and (to appear) to merely record what happens before her. As imagetexts, the photographs and diary entries work together to remind viewers of Edelstein's identifications and "dis-identifications." On the one hand, Edelstein establishes little distance from the perpetrators, those enthusiastic and unapologetic defenders of apartheid who "offered themselves up so willingly for a portrait, often proudly, as if they had played some heroic part in South Africa's history" (*Truth and Lies* 13). Though Edelstein refers to them as "rogues" (interview), she acknowledges their *shared* status as white South Africans, and, as such, equal "beneficiaries" of the systemic benefits of apartheid (Mamdani 181). As she writes in *Truth and Lies*, "growing up white in apartheid South Africa entitled one to massive and instant privilege" (12). She tells reader-viewers that these "rogues" could plausibly consider her a potential ally, or, at the very least, a drinking buddy. For example, in the diary entry that accompanies the photograph of Gideon Nieuwoudt, Edelstein recalls that Nieuwoudt (whom I will discuss later in more detail) invited her to join him for a drink in Belville, a conservative area of Cape Town in which black South Africans would still feel unwelcome, but that she, as a white woman, could go unmolested (56). Edelstein declines Nieuwoudt's offer, but her response matters less than the offer itself, as it calls attention to their shared identity as white South Africans. By placing diary excerpts such as this one next to the photographs of these "rogues," Edelstein avoids presenting them as completely alien or herself as somehow untainted by apartheid.

Edelstein's reflections on the self-interested attitude of the photographer reveal, perhaps unintentionally, the rhetorical agency of the photographer's subjects. Her account of the photographer's single-minded quest to turn the subject into the ideal photographic object attests to the potential for photographers to dehumanize their subjects. Edelstein recounted to me the questions that run through her mind, and, she alleges, through the minds of most photographers, during a shoot: "What else have you got? What else can you give me?" In other words, what additional facial expressions, gestures, or evidence of violence can you present that I can capture with my camera? And, only occasionally, their opposite: "What am I taking?" Edelstein concluded ruefully, "I was astounded at the level to which I would go to get the shot" (interview). While this interior monologue conveys Edelstein's attitude toward her subjects, it also conveys the subject's role in the production of a photograph. Portrait photographers evidently need the subject to participate in the production of "the best shot." The subjects of a portrait can choose what to offer to the photographer and the extent to which they will collaborate with her. At the moment of production, at least, the relation between photographer and subject thus seems more collaborative than predatory, as it involves a dynamic negotiation between two people.[10]

Edelstein's subjects had some degree of control over the images they created of themselves for *Truth and Lies*. In their portrait sessions, many of which took place in the rooms adjacent to the hearing halls and in participants' homes and hometowns, they were not subject to the TRC's rhetorics of truth and reconciliation, the pressures of the highly mediatized environment of its hearings, or its labels—victim or perpetrator. Moreover, they had the opportunity to prepare for the photograph. Even when telling their stories made them cry, participants could choose whether to appear in portrait with tears in their eyes. As we will see in the next section, none of the victims whom Edelstein photographed—and decided to include in *Truth and Lies*—chose to pose while crying. In this regard, *Truth and Lies* provides alternative images to those of weeping black women, images that appeared frequently in the media coverage of the TRC and threatened to confirm long-held stereotypes of black women as highly emotional and irrational.[11]

Why Edelstein's subjects agreed to participate in her photographic project remains unclear even to her. In the foreword to *Truth and Lies*, she ruminates on their reasons, echoing the Commission's assumptions about the healing effects of "speaking truth": "I guessed it might have been because they wanted to reclaim their dignity, their past, or to feel acknowledged for the part they had played. Largely it seemed to me they were grateful to have had the opportunity to share their experiences and to make public their painful stories. Perhaps this process of being in front of the camera was part of that ritual" (12). However, in our interview, which occurred several years after the publication of *Truth and Lies*, Edelstein offered a different interpretation. She spoke of victims' frustration with journalists (like her) who took their stories without offering anything substantive in return. It is possible that some of her subjects appreciated the opportunity to testify photographically, and yet also wanted something more from both Edelstein and the Commission. During the time period in which she took these photographs, victims remained cautiously optimistic that they would receive material reparations from the Commission. In the end, however, few did, and none to the extent that they had hoped. At the time Edelstein took the photographs, they may have simultaneously felt gratitude for the opportunity to share their story in another venue (in addition to the TRC) and frustration that this opportunity to testify was all that she offered them. As with Thandi Shezi (see chapter 2), their attitudes toward the

TRC process and the opportunity "to speak their truths" likely evolved over time in response to changing circumstances.[12] Whatever their long-term response, what matters is that Edelstein sought their consent and needed their participation to create *Truth and Lies*. Moreover, in the photographic event, they had the opportunity to present themselves in ways that corresponded to their self-understanding rather than in ways that fit the Commission's categories of "victim" and "perpetrator."

I return now to the jarring photograph of Joyce Mtimkulu, mother of Siphiwo, who died at the hands of Gideon Nieuwoudt. Few images suggest the potential incompatibility of truth and reconciliation as well as this one. Edelstein recalled that "[the shoot] took a long time that day" (interview), as she and Mtimkulu spoke for several hours before she took out her camera. During their pre-shoot conversation, Edelstein broached the topic of Siphiwo's poisoning and subsequent hair loss, in response to which she recalls Mtimkulu saying, "I kept the hair. It is what I have left of my son. This is what happened to him. It came off in my hand" (interview). Edelstein asked if she could photograph her with the chunk of hair. Mtimkulu acquiesced, and, without prompting, held it in her raised fist for the camera.[13] Mtimkulu displays her son's hair to call attention to what she considers the TRC's abuse of justice. She speaks through her visual presentation: "This is what they did." The chunk of hair in the portrait functions metonymically, representing the depravity and immorality of the police. Mtimkulu's decision to display it indicates her unwillingness to forget and perhaps her inability to forgive as well. The gesture compels the viewer to reflect on the ultimate inequity of the TRC's exchange of amnesty for full disclosure, as it provides visual proof of the terms of that exchange: for Mtimkulu, nothing but a chunk of her son's hair, and, for Nieuwoudt, freedom.

Two written texts collaborate with the portrait; together, they produce the necessary conditions—what in rhetorical terms we might call *kairos*—for Joyce Mtimkulu to convey her opposition to the TRC's too-facile linking of truth, amnesty, and reconciliation. Edelstein's diary entry from the day of the shoot reproduces the context of the photographic scene. Without these details about the history of the physical place in which Mtimkulu stands and Edelstein's personal experience of seeing this material evidence of apartheid's brutality, Mtimkulu's brandishing of Siphiwo's hair would not be so suggestive or powerful. Edelstein explains that she shot the photograph in the same room in the house in which Nieuwoudt had sought Mtimkulu's forgiveness. While Nieuwoudt stood in the living room, Siphiwo's son, Sikhumbuzo (which means "remembrance" in Xhosa), threw a stone through the window, hitting Nieuwoudt in the head, terminating his visit and suggesting the family's attitude toward his efforts at reconciliation. Mtimkulu did not offer Nieuwoudt forgiveness the day he came to her home, and she opposed his application for amnesty. Despite her objections, the TRC granted Nieuwoudt amnesty because he fully disclosed his politically motivated violation of Siphiwo's human rights.

In addition to providing the historical context of the photograph, Edelstein's diary entry clarifies and concretizes, making us "see" the photograph differently. The first sentence of the diary entry explains that when Mtimkulu held up the fistful of Siphiwo's hair, Edelstein thought that it "looked as if it was still attached to part of his scalp" (*Truth and Lies* 128). Without this detail, the viewer might not know what precisely Mtimkulu displays in her raised fist. The rhetorical power of the photograph increases when we understand that Mtimkulu is a mother who holds onto the sole remains of her son. Edelstein's words also remind the reader-viewer of the materiality of this sign. It is first and foremost Siphiwo's hair and scalp, and only later, in the hands of his mother, a symbol of the abuses of the apartheid era and of a mother's ceaseless vigil for her son. Edelstein's words thus facilitate the transformation of Mtimkulu's gesture into a political and personal statement.

The more formal "objective" writing provides background information about Joyce Mtimkulu's contested relationship to Gideon Nieuwoudt and to the TRC process. It informs reader-viewers that her son, Siphiwo, was a member of the Council of South African Students, and that the security police had arrested, detained, and tortured him in the year preceding his death. Before releasing Siphiwo, the police gave him rat poison in the hopes that he would die of seemingly natural causes. This poison caused Siphiwo to lose his hair, the "chunk" of which Mtimkulu saved and displays in the photograph (Edelstein, *Truth and Lies* 128). Edelstein recounts how three policemen revealed during their amnesty hearing that Siphiwo and his friend, Topsy Madaka, were ultimately shot execution-style and their bodies burned on a pyre. Finally, she explains that Mtimkulu did not believe that Siphiwo's murderers drugged him before killing him, for "they would never have spared him the terror of knowing that he was about to die" (128). Michael Ignatieff, who sat next to Mtimkulu during Nieuwoudt's amnesty hearing, confirms Edelstein's account of Mtimkulu's response. In his introduction to *Truth and Lies*, he describes Mtimkulu as "corrosively skeptical of everything she was told" and claims that she was "disgusted" with Nieuwoudt's testimony at his amnesty hearing, as "he had not said anything" (19). Edelstein, however, claims that at the conclusion of the hearings, Mtimkulu told her, "At least now we know what happened" (13). These anecdotes convey Mtimkulu's commitment to grapple with as much of the truth of her son's murder as she can access, a resolve that manifests itself visually in the photograph via her severe expression and straightforward gaze. We see the pain and determination etched in the lines of her face.

The amnesty hearing did not provide Mtimkulu with an opportunity to represent the treatment of her son at the hands of the police, nor did it enable her to elaborate fully her case against Nieuwoudt's amnesty application. In contrast, the photographic scene, in her home, on her turf, enabled Mtimkulu to decry visually the Commission's logic and telos of truth and reconciliation. She could express her anger outside of the scripted space of the public hearings hall. For her portrait session with Edelstein, Mtimkulu aired her grievances freely and unequivocally, both verbally in her comments and visually via the camera. In her living room, Mtimkulu was a grieving and angry mother with a particular history and the desire to speak it on her own terms, not a citizen-participant in the new South Africa's project of national reconciliation.

What does the photograph of Joyce Mananki Seipei (fig. 2), the mother of the murdered, and Jerry Richardson, the murderer, do? Does it haunt? Educate? Goad? In the photograph, Seipei and Richardson stand side by side. Richardson was the leader of the Mandela United Football Club when Stompie, Joyce Seipei's son, was murdered at the hands of its members. In the photograph, their faces look directly outward, but Seipei's body is square to the camera and upright, whereas Richardson stands at a slight angle, his shoulders hunched, and his body tilted slightly toward Seipei. Richardson wears thick gold rings on three of the four fingers that are visible in the picture, a watch, and a colorful shirt with a button displaying the image of a girl's face, and he holds a small football that he considers "his good luck charm" (Edelstein, *Truth and Lies* 49). Seipei, in contrast, wears a simple dark dress with small polka dots, with the Commission's interpretation equipment attached to the collar, and a head scarf. Richardson's pensive expression and slight inclination toward Seipei and the camera suggest humility and perhaps constitute his attempt to win the viewer's sympathy. Seipei's locked jaw, erect posture, and frontal stance hint at the effort she must exert to stand next to him.

As with the portrait of Joyce Mtimkulu, the writings that accompany this photograph provide context that enhances its rhetorical potential. Earlier

Figure 2 Mrs. Seipei and Jerry Richardson, Johannesburg, 1997.
Photo: Jillian Edelstein

on the day that the photograph was taken, Richardson testified to torturing Stompie, Mrs. Seipei's son, and other youth, putatively upon the orders of Winnie Madikizela-Mandela. In the excerpt of his testimony included in *Truth and Lies*, Richardson recalls the events leading to Stompie's death. It is difficult to determine which horrifies most, the brutality of his actions or his honesty in recounting them: "The first thing that I did to Stompie was to hold him with both sides, throw him up in the air and let him fall freely on to the ground. . . . He was tortured so severely that at some stage I could see that he would ultimately die. . . . There was a lot of things that we did to Stompie. We kicked him, we just kicked him like a ball" (qtd. in Edelstein, *Truth and Lies* 43). The small football that Richardson carries as a good luck charm in this photograph scarily evokes a mental image of this group of men kicking Stompie "like a ball."

Edelstein's diary entry, placed opposite the photograph, captures the banality of the context as well as the genesis of this particular image. She notes that the room in which she set up her studio lay right behind the one that housed the witnesses, Richardson among them. It was lunchtime, and they were eating "bunny chow": "large loaves of white bread with the interior gouged out and replaced with beef or lamb stew with lots of garlic and potatoes" (*Truth and Lies* 49). Richardson appeared in the room where she was waiting to do the portrait of Seipei. Edelstein writes, "He wants to be photographed with Mrs. Seipei. She agrees. A strange silence accompanies the picture-taking" (49). In our interview, Edelstein emphasized again, almost incredulously, that Seipei and Richardson did not exchange a single word during the photographic event.

Unlike Mtimkulu, Seipei does not give us an account of her wishes, thoughts, or feelings when this photograph was taken. Edelstein felt that Seipei, in agreeing to stand next to Richardson in the photograph, was "trying mightily to take to heart the Commission's goal of reconciliation" (Edelstein exchange). Terry February, the director of communications for the TRC who arranged for Edelstein to take this photograph, echoed Edelstein's interpretation of Seipei's motivations. In our interview, I asked February why Seipei "wanted" to have her photograph taken with Richardson, and he corrected me: "No, she didn't want to have it taken. I asked her if she would. There is a big difference in that. There is a big difference in that [*sic*]. Stompie's mother didn't necessarily object to being photographed. But it wasn't necessarily her wish to be photographed" (Hallett and February interview). Thus corrected, I asked again: Why did she acquiesce to Richardson's request? His response: "Because she was well on the road to reconciliation. She wanted to reconcile. She wanted also to hear the truth. She also wanted to have a look and talk to the person that she felt killed her son" (Hallett and February interview).

Though Seipei's intentions remain unknown, I can suggest the potential effects of this photograph. First, it captures a moment in time. Two individuals, both intimately linked to Stompie, though in violently opposed relations, inhabit the same frame. Their co-presence in the photograph concretizes abstract discussions of reconciliation between victims and perpetrators. It demands that viewers reckon with the reality of reconciliation on the ground: Joyce Seipei has to coexist with Jerry Richardson, with the knowledge that he brutally murdered her son. She tacitly acknowledges their unavoidable coexistence by agreeing to appear in the photograph with him. Ironically, the photograph humanizes Richardson as much as it does Seipei. He looks like a normal man, not the monster that his testimony creates in the reader's imagination. He has a thoughtful expression, and his clothes are nothing out of the ordinary. He seems a man like any other. It is difficult to reconcile the banality of Richardson's image with the horrific actions he relates in his verbal testimony. While the normalcy of the image prevents us from seeing Richardson as a monster, the accompanying text prevents us from denying what he did. Bound together, image and words challenge the reader-viewer to acknowledge the existence of an average-looking man who did something beyond imaginable.

Historical understanding constantly changes. Rhetorical analysis of images must account for their circulation and the resulting changes in interpretation as they move across time and space (Finnegan and Kang 395). This photograph, however, forestalls the overshadowing of an earlier reality by the present historical moment, as it visually captures a unique moment in South Africa's transition. It testifies to the daily and intimate challenge faced by the individuals charged with enacting the goal of intra- and inter-personal reconciliation, a challenge mitigated, but not wholly eradicated, by the TRC. When South Africans look back at this transitional moment, this powerful image has the potential to evoke in them a memory of the struggle for reconciliation that followed the struggle against apartheid. In his foreword to the *Report*, Tutu writes, "Having looked the beast of the past in the eye, having asked and received forgiveness and having made amends, let us shut the door on the past—not in order to forget it but in order not to allow it to imprison us" (1: 22). This photograph arrests the forgetting or amnesia (with its etymological connection to amnesty) that Tutu's and, by extension, the Commission's notion of reconciliation runs the risk of enabling.

Were viewers unable to recognize the face of Robert McBride, they could easily mistake figure 3 for an album cover or celebrity photo shoot. This reception would not be entirely misguided. As McBride walked to his amnesty hearing in Durban, crowds of mostly black South Africans thronged around him and cheered. Sharon Welgemoed, the sister of one

Figure 3 Robert McBride, Pretoria, 29 May 1997. Photo: Jillian Edelstein

of McBride's victims, complained to the Commission about his celebrity status: "He is seen in some circles as being seen as some sort of liberation activist, people's hero, but in our opinion all he did was contribute to the violence, hatred, and segregation that we all wanted to disappear. . . . Mr. McBride is a cold blooded murderer who can never wipe away the pain, sorrow and anguish and destruction he caused" (Reid and Hoffmann). The case of Robert McBride, perpetrator of the 1986 bombing of the Why

Not Bar in Durban, which killed three and left sixty-nine injured, inflamed passions from all sectors of South Africa's divided population.

Since I discuss Robert McBride at length in chapter 3, "Contesting Accountability," I will only review briefly here the nature of his anti-apartheid activism and his explanation of the ANC's turn away from nonviolent resistance. My aim here is to demonstrate how the imagetext in *Truth and Lies*—the photograph of McBride and his supporters in conjunction with the two written texts—makes available his perspective on reconciliation and provokes speculation about how South Africans might remember and account for apartheid's violence.

Edelstein explains that McBride worked in the special operations unit of Umkhonto we Sizwe, the military wing of the ANC. In the portion of McBride's testimony excerpted in *Truth and Lies*, he acknowledges the tragic loss of life caused by the Why Not Bar bombing, but he does not disavow what was then his ongoing commitment to strategic acts of violence. To the contrary, he reports that upon viewing an image of the child orphaned by the bombing, his resolve to end apartheid through violent means was only strengthened: "My immediate reaction was to be obsessed with doing sabotage operations so that I could get rid of apartheid as quickly as possible, because the way I saw it, apartheid was responsible for the tragedy" (Edelstein, *Truth and Lies* 133). McBride's logic exculpates him, without negating his empathy for his victims. His popularity, evident in his reception at the TRC hearing, suggests that a large portion of the black South African community endorsed his analysis of the political (im)possibilities under apartheid and the need to turn to violent resistance.

Though he was released from prison in 1992 during negotiations between the liberation movement and the apartheid government, and no suits had been brought against him (yet), he nevertheless applied for amnesty to show his commitment to the process. Though McBride voluntarily participated in the amnesty process, he insisted on doing so on his own terms. In interviews and during his testimony before the Commission, he articulately and forcefully critiqued the TRC's "even-handed" approach to the violence committed by apartheid's defenders and liberation forces. McBride considered his violent actions justifiable, given that they were directed against an unjust system, and he resented having to apologize for them in the same manner as those who committed violent acts to defend apartheid.

Edelstein's portrait does not unveil McBride's resistance, as he clearly made no attempt to disguise it during the amnesty hearing, but it does convey that resistance visually. McBride sits among his supporters. He wears sunglasses, and his head is turned away from the camera. His posture in this photograph suggests that he is at a slight remove from the photographic scene, just as his verbal testimony established his distance from the national narrative being woven by the Commission. In the photograph, as in the hearing hall and interviews, he appears unruffled and unperturbed by the furor around his case—some might say aloof. His visual testimony and his verbal testimony complement each other; in both, he is firm and unapologetic. Despite his stated commitment to participating in the process of reconciliation and his decision to appear before the Commission, he withholds his full endorsement of its logic and process.

Edelstein's photograph does more than provide a visual complement to McBride's verbal testimony; it also conveys the existence of popular support for his "just war" argument, popular support for which McBride could not provide evidence during his amnesty hearing. McBride stood alone before the commissioners, but the photograph demonstrates that on the streets of South Africa, he has the backing of at least some South Africans. In the photograph, he is flanked by four unnamed black men and one black woman. Though he sits slightly in front of the group and the sun hits his face, two factors that set him apart, he is nevertheless fully surrounded, a seating arrangement that establishes his belonging and symbolic centrality. His supporters look directly at the camera with confident, perhaps even slightly smug, expressions. Their bodily rhetoric—arms resting on McBride's shoulders and their physical proximity to him—convey respect for McBride. It is as if, with their bodies, they seek to shield him from criticism or condemnation. This visual evidence of at least some black South Africans' endorsement of McBride's actions strikes the viewer forcefully and perhaps differently from the statistics that record black South Africans' lack of regret for violence wreaked against white South Africans during the anti-apartheid struggle.

In *Picturing Poverty*, Cara Finnegan observes that "the photograph's ability to freeze time and construct a bounded, static space enables the image to serve as a kind of witness to that moment" (xvi). In this instance, as with the photograph of Joyce Seipei and Jerry Richardson, what is valuable is precisely the photograph's ability to capture this moment in South Africa's transition. In this moment, the TRC's project of establishing a culture for the new South Africa in which conflicts are dealt with politically, rather than violently, confronts the ideology of righteous violence of those who struggled against apartheid. To be clear, McBride does not advocate the use of violence in the post-apartheid era, but he does object to a truth and reconciliation process that considers all acts of apartheid-era violence equally immoral. This photograph testifies to his resistance to an ideological transition that entails the uniform application of its morality in its judgment of the past.

Wouter Basson (fig. 4) is the man frequently referred to in the media as "Dr. Death" or "Evil Einstein." Basson founded and directed Project Coast, the South African army's secret biological and chemical warfare program from 1981 to 1993. The background writing that accompanies Basson's portrait details the heinous scope of Project Coast: the manufacture of "'murder weapons' such as food and cigarettes contaminated with anthrax, milk contaminated with botulinum, poisoned chocolate . . . [and] muscle-relaxants [to drug POWs who were then dumped from planes at sea]" (Edelstein, *Truth and Lies* 196). Project Coast also conducted research on vaccines that would sterilize and bacteria that would ostensibly infect only black South Africans, as well as on the use of drugs such as Mandrax, anthrax, LSD, Ecstasy, and marijuana as a form of crowd control (196). In 1992, a government-appointed commission found Basson guilty of "unauthorized activities," and he was forced to retire from the army (196).

Basson provided evidence at the TRC's inquiry into biological and chemical warfare in 1998, but he opted not to apply for amnesty, showed utter contempt for the truth and reconciliation process, and subsequently denied all allegations against him both to the media and in his later trial before the High Court in Pretoria. He appeared for the TRC inquiry in a "Madiba" shirt, the colorful batik print made popular by Nelson Mandela—a mocking appropriation of the style of the man who personifies South Africa's transition and reconciliation. Then, during a drunken bout on the evening of the inquiry, Basson wrote "Truth Above All, Dr. Death," on the walls of a Cape Town coffeehouse frequented by ANC leaders (W. Finnegan 6–7). Because Basson had not received amnesty from the TRC, he was subject to prosecution. In 1999, at a trial before the High Court, he pleaded not guilty in response to charges of "sixty-one counts of murder, conspiracy to murder, [and] possession of addictive drugs, and fraud" (Edelstein, *Truth and Lies* 196). This trial, described by *The New Yorker*'s William Finnegan as "pure old South Africa" because "anyone with any standing or authority [was] white" (2), was in process at the time that Edelstein took this photograph. In 2002, Basson was acquitted of all charges.[14] If Basson's acquittal does not represent the epitome of injustice, it certainly suggests that the South African judicial system has yet to be affected fully by the transition.

Figure 4 Dr. Wouter Basson, Pretoria, November 2000. Photo: Jillian Edelstein

Neither Basson's actions nor his self-presentation in Edelstein's portrait suggest any interest in reconciliation, let alone contrition. In the photograph, he sits on a park bench, looking directly at us with the barest whisper of a smile, hands folded demurely in his lap. His suit is crisp and his shoes well shined. Basson seems not to fear retaliation, legal or extralegal, as he sits unprotected in the park, nor does it seem as though his routines have changed in response to his legal travails. Edelstein's diary entry tells us that this park, Magnolia Dell, is near Basson's favorite restaurant, Huckleberry's, where he and his family dine on "hake, grilled, and rock shandy" every Thursday at 5:00 P.M. (*Truth and Lies* 196). The park setting—nature domesticated—and the "rock shandy" cocktail, described by *Food and*

Wine as "a holdover from colonial times . . . the sparkling cooler of choice at many African safari camps" (Pépin), suggest South Africa's colonial past and the Afrikaner's central role within it. Basson remains squarely within that tradition, which seems largely unaffected by South Africa's transition from apartheid to democracy. What does it mean for South Africans that Dr. Death remains free, and, at least from his appearance in this photograph, untroubled by his past? How might one imagine a new South Africa in which one of the perpetrators of the worst of apartheid's crimes remains so unconcerned?

The anecdote that Edelstein recounts in her diary entry undercuts any benignity suggested by the parklike setting. She recalls that Basson said to her in a low voice, "'I hate you. I really hate you.' Why? 'Because I agreed to do this. I am going to disappear you. . . . I will vanish you and your family.' A pause. 'No, only joking'" (*Truth and Lies* 196). Basson's chilling taunt recalls what he has done and suggests what he is still capable of doing. His power derives both from his ability to terrorize and from his knowledge that he has gotten away with doing so. Having avoided accountability thus far, he feels he can dismiss morality itself. Basson's amorality calls into question the entire truth and reconciliation process. If Basson can sit on this park bench, unmolested and unafraid, what does reconciliation mean? When the process is premised on the existence of conscience, empathy, and moral values, what can it do with a man like Basson, who seems to eschew all of that? Edelstein asks reader-viewers to ponder these questions, which her imagetext raises but not does answer.

While South Africans might not recognize the faces of the mothers of the Gugulethu Seven (fig. 5), most are familiar with this infamous case, which epitomizes the abuses of the apartheid state. For those who are not, Edelstein's accompanying text explains that in 1986, policemen shot and killed seven young men from the Gugulethu township whom they accused of being ANC guerrillas. The police claimed that they fired in self-defense, but eyewitnesses insisted that the boys tried to give themselves up peacefully, and that one had been shot dead as he lay wounded on the ground. The South African networks covered the story extensively and showed gory footage of the carnage that resulted. One of the mothers, Eunice Miya, recalls experiencing disbelief when she saw her son's mutilated body on the television screen: "No, it can't be him, . . . I prayed, I said, 'Oh Lord . . . I wish—I wish this news could rewind" (Edelstein, *Truth and Lies* 144). The TRC's investigation revealed that black askaris (former guerrillas recruited by the security forces) had in fact "recruited, trained, and armed" the young

Figure 5 Ntombomzi Piet, Mrs. Ngewu, and Cynthia Bablwa Ngewu, Guguletu Township, 22 February 1997. Photo: Jillian Edelstein

men who believed that they were becoming guerrillas and forming a real ANC cell (143), and that the police had planned the attack on them long in advance. Worse still, the secret police files contained a photograph of a senior superintendent "with his foot on the body of one of the dead guerrillas as if he had just returned from a hunting expedition" (143). Only two of the police officers involved in the murder of the Gugulethu Seven, Sergeant Riaan Bellingan and Constable Thapelo Mbelo, applied for amnesty, claiming that their participation in the killings of the seven young men was "politically motivated."

The background information that Edelstein provides about the setup and ambush of these young unarmed men, and the details conveying the callousness with which the police engaged in the operation, prime viewers to expect that Cynthia Ngewu would respond to the policemen's amnesty applications as Joyce Mtimkulu did. The testimony that Edelstein includes in *Truth and Lies* reinforces this expectation. In it, Ngewu recalls watching the news the night of the attack and thereby learning of the death of her son: "I saw my child. I actually saw them dragging him, there was a rope around his waist, they were dragging him with the van" (143). With this statement in mind, how could we not read disgust and dismay in Ngewu's expression in the photograph? It would seem that the brutality of the killing, and the pain that she must have experienced as she witnessed it on the evening news, could generate nothing but this response and the desire for retribution. That Ngewu would or could forgive her son's murderers is inconceivable, and, consequently, unseeable in the photograph.

Ngewu, however, made powerful and unequivocal statements endorsing the TRC's notion of Christian reconciliation. Indeed, she has become "one of the key formulators on conceptions of forgiveness and reconciliation" (Krog, Mpolweni, and Ratele 12). For example, the "Reconciliation" chapter in the Commission's *Report* cites Ngewu as a moral emblem: "We do not want to return the evil that perpetrators committed to the nation. We want to demonstrate humaneness towards them, so that they in turn may restore their own humanity" (5: 367). Another widely circulated statement by Ngewu defines reconciliation: "This thing called reconciliation . . . if I am understanding it correctly . . . if it means this perpetrator, this man who has killed Christopher Piet, if it means he becomes human again, this man, so that I, so that all of us, get our humanity back . . . then I agree, then I support it all" (Krog, *Country* 109). Had Edelstein included these other statements in *Truth and Lies*, viewers might arrive at a radically different interpretation of the photograph.[15] We might initially attribute them to Ntombomzi Piet, Ngewu's daughter-in-law, as her sideways glance and slightly downturned eyes suggest vulnerability, sadness, and compassion, while Ngewu's frontal stance, wrinkled brow, and direct gaze more readily suggest defiance and anger. The photograph's rhetorical availability to multiple interpretations is what makes it truthful, for Ngewu's various statements suggest that she feels all of these emotions. Rather than containing her to one unified, coherent, and reconciled stance, this imagetext testifies to anger and mercy—and to their irresolution.

This photograph leaves itself open to many understandings of the substance and texture of the reconciliatory process. This makes it more truthful than any one statement in isolation, for Ngewu has felt all of these emotions, though perhaps not simultaneously. The photograph's ambiguity reflects the ambiguity at the core of reconciliation, a process in which emotions of anger and pain, and various political commitments, coexist with the desire to see the humanity in those who have wronged and to participate in the construction of a truly new South Africa. When accompanied by statements—all Ngewu's—this photograph yields different, yet equally reasonable, meanings. These varying interpretations reflect the contradictions and ambivalences inherent in the reconciliation process. In heralding this photograph's polysemicity, I do not mean to suggest that the photograph can mean anything and everything. As Cara Finnegan observes, "photographs are not simply free-floating signifiers awash in a sea of relativistic meaning" (xvi). They circulate within particular material, sociocultural, and historical contexts that determine the boundaries of reasonable interpretations. The irony is that visual media's polysemicity, which some rhetoricians find problematic, is what makes this photograph more "truthful" than Ngewu's verbal testimony, the precision of which in fact misrepresents the complexity of her feelings toward the men responsible for the death of her son. Ngewu is frequently held up as an example of victims' support for the TRC's logic of reconciliation. This photograph does not explicitly convey her opposition to that logic, nor does it convey her willingness or ability to comply with it. It instead compels a moment of reflection, a pause in the whirlwind that is South Africa's transition. It captures the many layers and complexity of the process of reconciliation and thus seems a fitting endpiece for my exploration of the *topos* of reconciliation.

Conclusion

All truth commissions seek to inspire deeper historical understanding of the time period covered by their mandate and to create a new "collective imaginary" that includes the stories and experiences of those who were treated unjustly (and, in the case of South Africa's TRC, of those who committed those injustices) under the previous government or regime (Asen 352). By enabling participants to call into question the assumptions and practices of the TRC, *Truth and Lies* critiques, and, in so doing, furthers the Commission's aims of truth and reconciliation. Edelstein's photographic subjects took advantage of the rhetorical repertoire of photography and of the unofficial spheres in which they collaborated with Edelstein to make an array of arguments about the meaning of reconciliation. Through the inclusion of their verbal testimony, details about the photographic scene, and photographs that lend themselves to particular interpretations because of their juxtaposition to specific texts, *Truth and Lies* makes available TRC participants' arguments about the past and the conditions of reconciliation and enables those arguments to circulate literally and figuratively in the collective imaginary of the new South Africa.

Transitions to democracy are often accompanied by abstract, idealistic, and goal-driven rhetoric, such as reconciliation, democratization, truth, and justice. In his introduction to *Truth and Lies*, Michael Ignatieff argues that Edelstein's photographs challenge the TRC's rhetoric by giving it an embodied form. He contrasts the Commission's "abstractions" of truth and reconciliation with her photographs of "the reality of the process," claiming that "her pictures take us back to the way it really was" (15). That "reality," Ignatieff reminds readers, was experienced by flesh-and-blood individuals, who, while committed to the process of truth telling and aware of the Commission's important role in the transition, were "scarred by the past and corroded by mistrust" (17). The hard work of turning the TRC's abstractions of truth and reconciliation into a lived reality fell on these individuals' already burdened shoulders. Their faces remind us of the daily work of the transition. In some instances, these images, which capture a particular moment in time, also serve as intransigent reminders that the transition did not occur seamlessly or without resistance. They are grains of sand in the historical memory, irritating reminders of the rough texture of transition.

CONCLUSION

It is no accident that the periods in which power relations are changing will prove especially rich in new rhetorics.

—JAMES BERLIN

In the 1990s, power relations in South Africa changed dramatically. That period was indeed "rich in new rhetorics." The architects of the TRC, an institutionalized set of rhetorics, hoped it would facilitate South Africans' movement from the culture, politics, and violence of an apartheid past toward a democratic and rights-based future. The Commission was a rhetorical experiment—an attempt to marshal speech to address and heal from past wrongs, to fulfill a desire for justice, and to create a new set of political vocabularies and practices. Not surprisingly, its efforts to persuade South Africans of speech's *dunamis* generated impassioned responses. TRC participants challenged the Commission's varied efforts to promote "unity and reconciliation" and to put the apartheid past behind them (Republic of South Africa). They insisted on their distinctive modes of recovery, the righteousness of their historical actions, and their particular understandings and enactments of reconciliation. TRC participants' challenges to the Commission contributed to the "new rhetorics" of the period. By showcasing both the diversity of the TRC's rhetorics and the responses they provoked, *From Apartheid to Democracy* demonstrates that the South African TRC, rather than "closing the book," kept the past and South Africans' different relationships to it open. Indeed, the Commission's various failures—to produce a fair history of the period covered by its mandate, to maintain philosophical and methodological coherence, or to persuade all South Africans to acknowledge the inherent injustice of apartheid—were generative. These failures fomented deliberation both within the TRC hearings and in their imaginative receptions, and, in so doing, strengthened civic culture in the new South Africa. This deliberation, not closure, is the hope and promise of a truth commission.

Due in part to the outsized influence of the South African TRC, truth commissions have become a standard component in transitional "first aid" packages (Shaw 2). In the twenty years between the first truth commission in Uganda in 1974 and the South African TRC, there were only fifteen truth commissions. In the nearly twenty years since the South African TRC, there have been twenty-five. Some practitioners claim that truth commissions now serve as "the official symbol of a political transition" (Chapman and Van der Merwe 1). While truth commissions constitute a genre in the sense that they organize language in a particular way so as to accomplish a specific action or aim (Miller 151), they are not one-size institutions. How truth commissions organize language and what, specifically, they seek to accomplish reflect the particular conditions of their time and place. While we have yet to determine the precise boundaries of truth commissions, one defining characteristic is their adaptation and recirculation of principles of past commissions and contemporary human rights rhetoric. As James Beitler demonstrates in his study of the Truth and Reconciliation Commission in Greensboro, North Carolina, advocates of a truth commission deploy and reaccentuate aspects of what is now a transitional justice rhetorical tradition to address local needs and aims (19–20). Future studies might examine the deliberation that occurred in the creation of, during, and in response to truth commissions that took place before and after the South African TRC in an effort to deepen understanding of this new rhetorical genre and to chart the capacities and limitations of public rhetorics aimed at national transformation.

The permeable boundaries of truth commissions demand attention to the full circuit of responses they generate. Rhetorical studies of civic deliberation have traditionally focused on nonfiction texts such as speeches, political pamphlets, meeting minutes, legal documents, newspaper articles, and the like. We must expand the archive of civic deliberation. My readings of *Bitter Fruit*, *The Cry of Winnie Mandela*, and *Truth and Lies: Stories from the Truth and Reconciliation Commission in South Africa* show that deliberation occurs in imaginative texts, far beyond the sites where it has been traditionally thought to take place. These imaginative texts are part of the "new rhetorics" generated by a transition. Literary scholars have already issued a call for a method of "cross-reading" that "play[s] across different genres and modes of address rather than remaining trapped within those protocols of symbolic exchange that thrive on an endless series of tired oppositions: 'the novel' versus 'history'; 'aesthetics' versus 'raw experience'; 'committed' versus 'formalist'" (Twidle 24). Memories often find expression in genre-bending texts that lie at the intersection of these various oppositions. It is not surprising, then, that truth commissions generate texts that demand this kind of "cross-reading." Indeed, contemporary South African writing certainly reflects the influence of the TRC. The Commission's acknowledgment of multiple truths has contributed to an explosion of texts that defy generic conventions in form and content. In different ways, Jacob Dlamini's *Native Nostalgia* (2010), Hugh Lewin's *Stones Against the Mirror: Friendship in the Time of the South African Struggle* (2011), and Patrick Flanery's *Absolution* (2012) acknowledge the TRC's significance while simultaneously exposing its shortcomings and addressing gaps in its engagement with South Africa's recent past. Like the imaginative texts I examine in *From Apartheid to Democracy*, these works continue the deliberative processes that the Commission set into motion and are worthy of inclusion in future studies of South Africa's unfinished reckoning with its past.

My call for the inclusion of imaginative texts in studies of civic deliberation follows naturally from rhetoric's historic role "as a meta-discipline through which a whole spectrum of language uses and their outcomes as social action can be refracted for analysis and combination" (Jarratt 14). As Susan Jarratt explains, the Sophists "predated the establishment of sharp distinctions between the techniques and effects of poetry and language use in other fields" (xx). These first theorists of language and progenitors of our discipline understood that all genres of discourse could support and provoke reflection, judgment, and dissent. Contemporary institutional arrangements support an interdisciplinary approach to the study of deliberation. Rhetorical scholars find themselves in English and communications departments, or, in some instances, in departments that house both disciplines. We are thus uniquely positioned to draw on a broad range of media, materials, and methods in our efforts to track circuits of deliberation across diverse genres. Finally, an ecumenical approach to the study of deliberation is timely. Universities seek to build bridges across departments and disciplines. *From Apartheid to Democracy* demonstrates that civic deliberation—comprising arguments that travel across genres—constructs these bridges. Future studies of civic deliberation must account for the links between, as well as the intermingling of, a wide variety of genres if they aim to capture arguments that run against the grain, cannot be voiced in traditionally deliberative realms, or perhaps cannot be voiced at all.

NOTES

Introduction

1. The first truth commission took place in Uganda in 1974. Since the Ugandan experiment, there have been more than thirty truth commissions in Africa, Asia, Europe, Australia, South America, and North America (Greensboro, North Carolina). As I write, there are calls for additional commissions to be held in Kenya, Iraq, and the United States.

2. Don Foster credits the TRC for its "novel" acknowledgment that "ideological language is a major factor in gross human rights violations" (224).

3. The Promotion of National Unity and Reconciliation Act charged the TRC with producing a final report. The first five volumes of the *Truth and Reconciliation Commission of South Africa Report* were released in 1998. The final two volumes were released in 2003. While the *Report* does not speak with one voice about many aspects of the TRC process (and indeed includes a "Minority Position" submitted by Commissioner Wynand Malan), the significance and intentionality of the public dimensions of the TRC process were never in dispute. The *Report* states unequivocally that "unity and reconciliation could be achieved only . . . if the truth about past violations became *publicly* known" (1: 53, my emphasis).

4. See also Simpson.

5. There is a movement in political theory to shift away from notions of reconciliation as "communitarian social harmony" (Hirsch 1) toward a specifically political notion of reconciliation as "passionate and often agonistic discourse about the world we share in common" (Schapp 4). Proponents of "political reconciliation" defined thus would concur with Payne's, Miller's, and my advocacy for an agnostic deliberative public sphere. As I discuss in more detail in chapter 4, the TRC entertained the notion of "political reconciliation," but not to the exclusion of other, more irenic notions of reconciliation, such as Christian reconciliation, with which political reconciliation stood in tension. The Commission never resolved the tension between its competing notions of reconciliation.

6. Despite a decided lack of clarity about the TRC's definition of "reconciliation," a problem that I examine in chapter 4, "the commission's success was judged in part on whether and how much 'reconciliation' was perceived to have resulted from its work, and in its last months, especially, was criticized for its lack of success" (Hayner, "Same Species" 40).

7. Umkhonto we Sizwe (abbreviated as MK) was the armed wing of the African National Congress. It is translated in English as "Spear of the Nation."

Chapter 1

1. The conference proceedings were published as books, titled *Dealing with the Past: Truth and Reconciliation in South Africa* (ed. Boraine, Levy, and Scheffer) and *The Healing of a Nation?* (ed. Boraine and Levy). In this chapter, I make parenthetical references to various individuals' contributions as they appear in these two publications.

2. For an incisive analysis of the rhetorical opportunities created by the question of amnesty in the early 1990s, prior to the creation of the TRC, see Doxtader, "Easy."

3. Chile's Comisión Nacional de Verdad y Reconciliación (1990–1991) was the first truth commission to include "reconciliation" in its title. The South African TRC was the second.

4. The TRC was mandated to conclude its process in eighteen months, but the deadline was extended until October 1998, when the first five volumes of the *Report* were presented to then President Mandela. The work of the AC continued until 2001, and it was not until 2003 that the Commission issued the sixth and seventh volumes of its *Report*.

5. In the chapter "Truth Commission Journal and Notes" in his *Ambiguities of Witnessing*, Mark Sanders traces the etymology of *ubuntu* and its connection to related terms in various African languages.

Chapter 2

1. See *Facing the Truth with Bill Moyers*; Krog, *Country*; and Lynn Burke's "Consequences of Truth." Shezi was also an oft-cited complainant in a lawsuit for apartheid reparations that was filed against multinational corporations and banks by the Khulumani Support Group, an NGO that represents survivors of apartheid violence ("South Africa: Apartheid Debt"). Shezi was also one of three lead actors in *The Story I Am About to Tell*, a play that focuses on human rights violations committed during apartheid ("Play Focuses on Racism and Reconciliation").

2. While the Commission considered using the term "survivor" rather than "victim," it concluded that the "intentions and actions of the perpetrator [not the survivor's response] create the condition of being a victim" (TRC, *Report* 1: 59).

3. Four regional offices in Durban, Johannesburg, East London, and Cape Town directed the statement gathering in all nine provinces of South Africa. The rate of statement taking was not the same in each province. The *Report* attributes this inconsistency to the fact that each province experienced different levels of violence during the period covered by the Commission's mandate and to the Commission's differing ability to access deponents from province to province (1: 167–68). Another potential reason for the differing rates is the fact that the HRVC relied on self-selection; that is, it gathered the statements of those who responded on their own volition to the Commission's appeals rather than gathering statements from target populations so as to get a probabilistic sample. Statement takers asked deponents to use apartheid-era terminology drawn from the Population Registration Act No. 30 of 1950 to identify their "population groups." Those who identified as Africans made more statements (90 percent) than those who identified as Coloureds, Asians, or Whites (TRC, *Report* 1: 169). The *Report* suggests that the antipathy of some members of the white community to the Commission might account in part for the minimal participation of white South Africans, but that the primary reason for their low numbers is that "the conflicts of the past affected very few whites in comparison to the rest of the population" (1: 169).

4. Kulumane, which means "speak out" in Zulu, was "founded on the premise that encouraging people to 'speak out' about the atrocities of the past was psychologically beneficial" (Hamber et al., para. 3).

5. I collected biographical information about Dangor from the Kagiso Trust and Synergos websites.

6. Dangor's preoccupation with the challenge of representing women's experience of sexual violations echoes that of other post-apartheid South African writers whose work also critically, though more indirectly, engages the TRC and its attempt to narrate the past. *Bitter Fruit* includes excerpts of Lydia's diary entry about the rape and gives voice to her explicit rejection of the invitation to speak at the TRC's Women's Hearings. Two other contemporary South African novels, J. M. Coetzee's *Disgrace* and Zoë Wicomb's *David's Story*, in contrast, contain no such direct representations of the sexual violations, nor do they explicitly critique the TRC's attempt to solicit women's stories. They nevertheless address similar issues: women's ability and desire to speak of their experience of sexual violations and others' willingness to bear witness.

7. Silas describes 1998 as a transition within the transition: "This year was the last but one of the century; they were facing a twilight period, an interregnum between the old

century and the new, between the first period of political hope and the new period of 'managing the miracle'" (Dangor, *Bitter Fruit* 255). Silas's slightly cynical description contrasts with the Commission's idealistic statements. He calls attention to the inevitable bureaucratization of the struggle's goals.

8. Silas unknowingly, and thus ironically, calls attention to the direct parallels between the TRC's process and his own family's engagement with the legacy of apartheid. He tells himself, "Enough of this nightmarish obsession with Mikey's sex life. Life was going on, sins were being confessed, murder, rape. Assassins confessing to the Truth Commission" (Dangor, *Bitter Fruit* 148). Unbeknownst to Silas, Mikey's worrisome sex life relates directly to the TRC process, as he is sleeping with Kate, Silas's colleague, to gain access to the TRC's file on Du Boise, his biological father, who has submitted an amnesty application.

9. "The struggle" is a shorthand reference to the anti-apartheid movement. It is typically used by those who favored ending apartheid, not by apartheid's defenders.

10. The Combahee River Collective Statement, which discusses the ways in which feminists' concerns were sidelined in the black nationalist, liberation, and anti-racist movements—thus precluding the kind of "intersectional" analysis called for later by Kimberlé Crenshaw—is one of the best-known examples.

11. The narrator's frequent comments about Silas's ironic distance from Nelson Mandela, the "Old Man," and the un-named "Minister" for whom he works—and more generally about his cynicism about the new South Africa—suggest that Lydia's perception of Silas is not wholly accurate. Indeed, Silas feels that he is beginning to lose his "true north": "He has a grudging sympathy for his Minister, and for the Old Man, the President, both of whom embody, in their personal integrity, the 'value system' of the liberation movement. Being in government, having to make decisions that accord not with their own wishes but with the 'needs of the country' makes demands on their personal principles" (Dangor, *Bitter Fruit* 165). The inaccuracy of Lydia's perception of Silas only underscores the distance that has grown between them. In any case, the "truth" of his feelings matters less than Lydia's perceptions, as they are what influence her thoughts and subsequent actions.

12. Fiona Ross emphasizes the "paucity of currently existing grammars ... the need for a new language of social suffering that ... recognizes the fragmented and unfinished nature of social recovery, and does not presume closure" (165).

13. Silas interrupts a moment of intimacy in which Mikey has his head in Lydia's lap. Though nothing physical transpires between them at this moment, all three of them are aware that the moment is sexually charged. Later in the novel, Lydia does in fact kiss Mikey, but Silas does not discover this, and she and Mikey never discuss the kiss or the sexual tension between them.

Chapter 3

1. Philippe Salazar analyzes how this new national culture was forged through traditional political rhetoric as well as through popular culture, fashion, and sport.

2. For example, Deborah Posel faults the TRC's methodology, arguing that it offered "a primarily descriptive rendition of the past, uneven in its discernment of detail and indifferent to the complexities of social causation" (148). Mahmood Mamdani similarly claims that the Commission offered "an institutionally produced truth [that] was established through narrow lenses, crafted to reflect the experience of a tiny minority" (177–78). A different interpretation of the mandate, Mamdani suggests, might have "illuminated apartheid as a reality lived by the majority, a reality that produced racialized poverty alongside racialized truth, both equally undeserved" (180).

3. In total, the AC received 7,116 amnesty applications. However, this number is misleadingly large (Harris et al. 4). The AC denied roughly 5,000 of these applications for administrative reasons, as many ordinary criminals made submissions for acts that clearly did not meet the "political motivations" requirement (Fullard and Rousseau 198). Individuals

responsible for acts committed on behalf of the apartheid state submitted fewer than half of the approximately 2,000 legitimate applications. The majority of these came from members of the police and the security forces, not the South African Defence Force (199). Of the applications received for acts committed on behalf of the anti-apartheid struggle, the vast majority came from individuals associated with the ANC. Both the Inkatha Freedom Party (IFP) and Pan Africanist Congress (PAC) opposed the amnesty process and the TRC more generally, and, as a result, their members submitted relatively few applications. Members of the ANC submitted 998 applications, while members of the IFP and PAC submitted roughly 240 (200).

4. The TRC used an "even-handed" approach in its dealings with victims as well. The Commission considered "victims" all those harmed in defense of apartheid or in the attempts to dismantle it.

5. For the intricate legal reasoning supporting their judgment, see Asmal, Asmal, and Roberts.

6. The anti-apartheid movement used the adjective "black" to refer to all people, including whites, who were committed to dismantling apartheid. To be "black" became a political descriptor, not a racial one.

7. The transcripts of McBride's amnesty hearing only provide the last names of the lawyers, Mr. Richard and Mr. Prior.

8. See chapter 4 for a brief remark by Sharon Welgemoed about McBride's status.

9. This refers to the practice of lighting on fire a gas-filled car tire that has been placed around the neck of a (supposed) informant.

10. The content and visual representation (extensive use of bold headings and capital letters) of the summary of the Winnie hearing in the *Report* confirm this impression: "[Madikizela-Mandela] did not use the hearings as a forum to take the Commission and the nation into her confidence in order to shed light on the circumstances that resulted in the chaos and violence that emanated from her household. . . . [Her] testimony before the Commission was characterized by a blanket denial of all allegations against her . . . the picture that she sought to paint of herself was that she was right and that everybody else was wrong . . . she refused to take responsibility for any wrongdoing. It was only at the end of her testimony . . . that she reluctantly conceded that 'things had gone horribly wrong'" (2: 578–82).

11. Time constraints also influenced the rhetorical situation of the Winnie hearing. Before the exchange discussed above, Alex Boraine, deputy chair of the TRC, states that "to ask Mrs Madikizela-Mandela to give a lecture on how the situation was, would take her hours and we haven't got that sort of time," to which Mr. Joseph responds: "All right, let me help. It wouldn't take hours, it can be done in minutes." Mr. Joseph's confidence that the discussion would only take minutes highlights the limited nature of his goals. He does not hope to inspire the deep understanding of events that the Commission ostensibly sought to elicit through the Winnie hearing.

Chapter 4

1. The AC considered criteria such as the perpetrator's motive, the context wherein the act took place, and the proportionality of the act to the objective pursued. For more details on the logic and process of the AC, please see chapter 2.

2. In *Truth and Lies*, Edelstein juxtaposes texts (her diary entries, background information about the TRC, South African history, and excerpts of TRC participants' testimony) alongside the photographs themselves. W. J. T. Mitchell coined the term "imagetext" to "designate composite, synthetic works (or concepts) that combine image and text" (89 n. 9).

3. For a thorough examination of reconciliation's history in South Africa through the creation of the TRC, see Doxtader, *With Faith*.

4. Critics frequently point to Desmond Tutu's praise of victims who expressed a willingness to forgive and of perpetrators who expressed contrition in a manner consistent with

the Christian notion of reconciliation. However, Tutu just as strongly promoted political reconciliation. At one hearing, he said, "one of the things about a new dispensation on all of our democratic and constitutional rights is, is that we have, all of us, points of view which have to be respected" ("Human Rights Hearing").

5. Deborah Posel makes a similar argument about the *Report* as a historical text. She writes, "Underlying the report's claims for the authority of its findings [about gross human rights violations] then, is a self-effacing, circular process in terms of which the past is recorded only insofar as it is necessary to produce moral judgment; and the only basis for these judgments is the version of the past as it is written in the report" (161).

6. Edelstein never states that she is Jewish, although her last name and the ritual of Friday night dinners with her grandparents suggest that she is. For more on the particular experience of Jewish South Africans, who enjoyed "white status" under apartheid but were nevertheless socially marginalized, see Adler.

7. Robben Island sits in Table Bay within sight of Cape Town. It has been the site of a prison since the late 1700s. Nelson Mandela, as well as many other anti-apartheid activists, spent decades imprisoned there.

8. The adult Edelstein, the writer of the reflection, interestingly does not choose to address the problematic history of the black nanny.

9. Responding to his own rhetorical question about how anti-apartheid activists who consider themselves communists and socialists can explain their propagation of the free market, Neville Alexander says, "Suffice it to say that these men and women mostly genuinely believe that they have the acumen and the leverage in the international arena to change the manner in which the world economy actually operates, and, thus, to negotiate the best possible place for themselves, for South Africa, and for their allies in Africa and in the rest of the South in the global system" (3).

10. In our interview, Edelstein spoke of the "power of suggestion" through which she encouraged her subjects to present themselves in particular ways before the camera. She recalled that in some instances, Liz Jobey, her editor, feared that viewers would interpret the photographic results of this "power of suggestion" as manipulation. For example, Edelstein wanted to include a portrait of Chairperson Tutu with his hands cradling his head in a position suggestive of dismay, hopelessness, and exhaustion. Though Tutu frequently adopted this posture as he listened to testimony during the hearings, it was only in response to Edelstein's reminding him of it that he did so during the shoot—a nice example of photographer and subject engaging in a "dynamic exchange," as discussed earlier. Jobey, however, determined that the photograph's seemingly staged nature would interrupt the apparent spontaneity that characterizes the other portraits in *Truth and Lies*. She insisted that Edelstein use a different photograph, in which Tutu's body and head incline slightly toward the camera, but his eyes look directly out at the viewer.

11. Njabulo Ndebele feared that "the TRC hearings may confirm the image of blacks as helpless victims, suffering complainants before whites who claim to understand their plight and declare themselves to be willing to help" ("Memory, Metaphor" 27). Indeed, an anecdote in Antjie Krog's memoir, *Country of My Skull*, testifies to the enduring power of stereotypes and the ways in which well-intentioned efforts to challenge them can ironically end up reinforcing them. Krog recalls an Afrikaner farmer's response to the images of black women crying during the TRC's victims' hearings: "I cannot take the crying in front of the Commission any longer.... If I see a black woman crying, then I remember two expressions from my youth: 'to cry like a *meid*' and 'to be as scared as a *meid*.' What do I do with this? The most despicable behavior, cowardice and loss of control, we have equated with the actions of a black woman. Now the Commission just reinforces the stereotype" (190). Despite the Commission's focus on victims' words, this farmer responded most powerfully to the image of black women deponents, images that he presumably saw on television. Ironically, given the aims of the victims' hearings to promote empathy and understanding, he claims that this visual reinforces his long-held negative stereotype about overly emotional black African women. Rather than considering her an equal and worthy of his respect and understanding,

and attempting to understand the source of her tears, he succumbs to (or, more generously, becomes subject to) that negative stereotype. While Edelstein's portraits of defiant women still fall within the broader category of "suffering mothers," *Truth and Lies* offers a more varied collection of images than those generated during the public hearings in which victims responded to a predetermined set of questions about their victimhood.

12. Though Edelstein sent a copy of *Truth and Lies* to each of her subjects, she has not returned to gauge their reactions to it.

13. The gesture hearkens back to the African National Congress's rallying cry, "Amandla," to which the crowd would reply, "Ngawethu," loosely translated as "power of the people."

14. In November 2008, the Health Professions Council of South Africa held a hearing in which additional charges were leveled against Basson. In September 2011, due to lack of evidence, the Council dismissed the charges relating to the testing of incapacitating agents on members of the special forces troops and the South African Police Task Force. The charges concerning the production of cyanide capsules and tranquilizers are still pending at the time of writing (http://news.yahoo.com/charges-dropped-against-africas-dr-death-193821725.html).

15. Edelstein claims that she does not know why she did not include Cynthia Ngewu's endorsements of reconciliation in *Truth and Lies*; in retrospect, she claims that she wishes she had.

WORKS CITED

Adler, Franklin Hugh. "South African Jews and Apartheid." *Macalester International* 9.2 (2000): 185–97. Print.
Alexander, Neville. *An Ordinary Country: Issues in the Transition from Apartheid to Democracy in South Africa.* Pietermaritzburg: U of Natal P, 2002. Print.
Andrews, Robert. *The Columbia Dictionary of Quotations.* New York: Columbia UP, 1993. Print.
Arendt, Hannah. *The Human Condition: A Study of the Central Dilemmas Facing Modern Man.* Chicago: U of Chicago P, 1958. Print.
Asen, Robert. "Imagining in the Public Sphere." *Philosophy and Rhetoric* 35.4 (2002): 345–65. Print.
Asmal, Kader. In Boraine and Levy 26–30.
———. In Boraine, Levy, and Scheffer 138–40.
———. "Victims, Survivors, and Citizens—Human Rights, Reparations, and Reconciliation." *South African Journal on Human Rights* 8.4 (1992): 491–511. Print.
Asmal, Kader, Louise Asmal, and Ronald Suresh Roberts. "When the Assassin Cries Foul: The Modern Just War Doctrine." Villa-Vicencio and Verwoerd, *Looking Back* 86–98.
Atwill, Janet. *Rhetoric Reclaimed: Aristotle and the Liberal Arts Tradition.* Ithaca: Cornell UP, 1998. Print.
Beitler, James Edward, III. *Remaking Transitional Justice in the United States: The Rhetorical Authorization of the Greensboro Truth and Reconciliation Commission.* New York: Springer, 2013. Print.
Berlin, James. "Postmodernism, Politics, and Histories of Rhetoric." *PRE/TEXT: A Journal of Rhetorical Theory* 11.3–4 (1990): 170–87. Print.
Bickford, Louis. "Transitional Justice." *Encyclopedia of Genocide and Crimes Against Humanity.* Ed. Dinah Shelton. Vol. 3. Farmington Hills: Macmillan Reference USA, 2004. 1045–47. Print.
———. "Unofficial Truth Projects." *Human Rights Quarterly* 29.4 (2007): 994–1035. Print.
Boraine, Alex. Introduction. Boraine and Levy xiv–xxiii.
———. "Truth and Reconciliation in South Africa: The Third Way." *Truth v. Justice.* Ed. Robert I. Rotberg and Dennis Thompson. Princeton: Princeton UP, 2000. 141–57. Print.
Boraine, Alex, and Janet Levy, eds. *The Healing of a Nation?* Cape Town: Justice in Transition, 1995. Print.
Boraine, Alex, Janet Levy, and Ronel Scheffer, eds. *Dealing with the Past: Truth and Reconciliation in South Africa.* Cape Town: IDASA, 1994. Print.
Bruffee, Kenneth A. "Collaborative Learning and the 'Conversation of Mankind.'" *College English* 46.7 (1984): 635–52. Print.
Bundy, Colin. "The Beast of the Past: History and the TRC." *After the TRC: Reflections on Truth and Reconciliation in South Africa.* Ed. James Wilmot and Linda Van De Vijver. Claremont: David Philip Publishers, 2000. 9–26. Print.
Burke, Lynn. "The Consequences of Truth: Post-traumatic Stress in New South Africa." *South Africa in Transition.* N.d. University of California, Berkeley Graduate School of Journalism. 10 June 2011 <http://journalism.berkeley.edu/projects/southafrica/news/news.html>.

Burton, Mary. In Boraine, Levy, and Scheffer 120–24.
Butler, Judith. "Giving an Account of Oneself." *Diacritics* 31.4 (2001): 22–40. Print.
Buur, Lars. "Monumental Historical Memory: Managing Truth in the Everyday Work of the South African Truth and Reconciliation Commission." In Posel and Simpson, *Commissioning* 66–93.
Canas, Roberto. In Boraine, Levy, and Scheffer 54–56.
Casey, Edward S. "Public Memory in Place and Time." *Framing Public Memory*. Ed. Kendall Phillips. Tuscaloosa: U of Alabama P, 2004. 17–43. Print.
Chapman, Audrey R., and Hugo van der Merwe. "Introduction: Assessing the South African Transitional Justice Model." *Truth and Reconciliation in South Africa: Did the TRC Deliver?* Ed. Audrey R. Chapman and Hugo van der Merwe. Philadelphia: U of Pennsylvania P, 2008. 1–20. Print.
Coetzee, Martin. "An Overview of the TRC Amnesty Process." *The Provocations of Amnesty: Memory, Justice, and Impunity*. Ed. Charles Villa-Vicencio and Erik Doxtader. Claremont: David Philip Publishers, 2003. 181–94. Print.
Cole, Catherine. *Performing South Africa's Truth Commission: Stages of Transition*. Bloomington: Indiana UP, 2010. Print.
Comaroff, Jean. "The End of History, Again? Pursuing the Past in the Postcolony." *Postcolonial Studies and Beyond*. Ed. Ania Loomba, Suvir Kaul, Matti Bunzl, Antoinette Burton, and Jed Esty. Durham: Duke UP, 2005. 125–44. Print.
Cruikshank, Barbara. *The Will to Empower: Democratic Citizens and Other Subjects*. Ithaca: Cornell UP, 1999. Print.
Dangor, Achmat. *Bitter Fruit*. New York: Grove/Atlantic, 2001. Print.
———. Interview. *Bold Type*. N.d. Random House LLC. 14 Mar. 2008 <https://www.randomhouse.com/boldtype/0399/dangor/interview.html>.
———. Interview. *The Ledge*. N.d. 26 Mar. 2008 <http://www.the-ledge.com/HTML/conversation.php?ID=57&lan=n>.
De Lange, Johnny. "The Historical Context, Legal Origins, and Philosophical Foundation of the South African Truth and Reconciliation Commission." Villa-Vicencio and Verwoerd, *Looking Back* 14–31.
Dorfman, Ariel. *Death and the Maiden*. New York: Penguin Books, 1991. Print.
Doxtader, Erik. "Easy to Forget or Never (Again) Hard to Remember? History, Memory, and the 'Publicity' of Amnesty." *The Provocations of Amnesty: Memory, Justice, and Impunity*. Ed. Charles Villa-Vicencio and Erik Doxtader. Claremont: David Philip Publishers, 2003. 121–54. Print.
———. *With Faith in the Work of Words: The Beginnings of Reconciliation in South Africa, 1985–1995*. East Lansing: Michigan State UP, 2009. Print.
Dube, Pamela Sethunya. "The Story of Thandi Shezi." Posel and Simpson, *Commissioning* 117–30.
Du Toit, Andre. In Boraine, Levy, and Scheffer 130–33.
———. "The Moral Foundations of the South African TRC: Truth as Acknowledgment and Justice as Recognition." *Truth v. Justice: The Morality of Truth Commissions*. Ed. Robert I. Rotberg and Dennis Thompson. Princeton: Princeton UP, 2000. 122–40. Print.
Du Toit, Louise. "A Phenomenology of Rape: Forging a New Vocabulary for Action." *(Un)thinking Citizenship: Feminist Debates in Contemporary South Africa*. Ed. Amanda Gouws. Burlington: Ashgate, 2005. 253–74. Print.
Eberly, Rosa A. *Citizen Critics: Literary Public Spheres*. Urbana: U of Illinois P, 2000. Print.
Edbauer, Jenny. "Unframing Models of Public Distribution: From Rhetorical Situation to Rhetorical Ecologies." *RSQ* 35.4 (2005): 5–24. Print.
Edelstein, Jillian. Exchange with the author. 12 Sept. 2006. E-mail.
———. Personal interview. London, 16 July 2006.
———. *Truth and Lies: Stories from the Truth and Reconciliation Commission in South Africa*. New York: New Press, 2001. Print.

Esterhuyse, Willie. In Boraine and Levy 30–32.
Facing the Truth with Bill Moyers. Public Affairs Television, Inc., 1999.
Finnegan, Cara A. *Picturing Poverty: Print Culture and FSA Photographs.* Washington: Smithsonian Books, 2003. Print.
Finnegan, Cara A., and Jiyeon Kang. "'Sighting' the Public: Iconoclasm and Public Sphere Theory." *Quarterly Journal of Speech* 90.4 (2004): 377–402. Print.
Finnegan, William. "The Poison Keeper." *The New Yorker* 15 Jan. 2001: 58–74. Print.
Foster, Don. "What Makes a Perpetrator? An Attempt to Understand." Villa-Vicencio and Verwoerd, *Looking Back* 219–29. Print.
Fullard, Madeline. "Dis-placing Race: The South African Truth and Reconciliation Commission (TRC) and Interpretations of Violence." Race and Citizenship in Transition Series. Johannesburg: Center for the Study of Violence and Reconciliation, 2004. 8–63. Web. 19 Aug. 2004 <http://www.csvr.org.za/docs/racism/displacingrace.pdf>.
Fullard, Madeline, and Nicky Rousseau. "Truth, Evidence, and History: A Critical Review of Aspects of the Amnesty Process." *The Provocations of Amnesty: Memory, Justice, and Impunity.* Ed. Charles Villa-Vicencio and Erik Doxtader. Claremont: David Philip Publishers, 2003. 195–216. Print.
Gibson, James L. *Overcoming Apartheid: Can Truth Reconcile a Divided Nation?* New York: Russell Sage Foundation, 2004. Print.
Glenn, Cheryl. *Unspoken: A Rhetoric of Silence.* Carbondale: Southern Illinois UP, 2004. Print.
Gobodo-Madikizela, Pumla. "Working Through the Past: Some Thoughts on Forgiveness in Cultural Context." *Memory, Narrative, and Forgiveness: Perspectives on the Unfinished Journeys of the Past.* Ed. Pumla Gobodo-Madikizela and Chris van der Merwe. Newcastle upon Tyne: Cambridge Scholars, 2009. 148–69. Print.
Goldblatt, Beth, and Sheila Meintjes. "Gender and the Truth and Reconciliation Commission: A Submission to the Truth and Reconciliation Commission." *Truth and Reconciliation Commission.* Official website. May 1996. Republic of South Africa, Department of Justice and Constitutional Development. 13 Jan. 2014 <http://www.justice.gov.za/trc/hrvtrans/submit/gender.htm>.
Goldstone, Richard. In Boraine and Levy 120–27.
Goodman, Tanya. *Staging Solidarity: Truth and Reconciliation in a New South Africa.* Boulder: Paradigm Publishers, 2009. Print.
Gready, Paul. *The Era of Transitional Justice: The Aftermath of the Truth and Reconciliation Commission in South Africa and Beyond.* New York: Routledge, 2011. Print.
Habermas, Jürgen. *The Structural Transformation of the Public Sphere: An Inquiry into a Category of Bourgeois Society.* Trans. Thomas Burger with Frederick Lawrence. Cambridge: MIT P, 1991. Print.
Hallett, George, and Terry February. Personal interview. Cape Town, 29 Sept. 2007.
Hamber, Brandon. "Does the Truth Heal? A Psychological Perspective on Political Strategies for Dealing with the Legacy of Political Violence." *Burying the Past: Making Peace and Doing Justice After Civil Conflict.* Ed. Nigel Biggar. Washington, D.C.: Georgetown UP, 2007. 131–48. Print.
Hamber, Brandon, Ntombi Mosikare, Maggie Friedman, and Traggy Maepa. "Speaking Out: The Role of the Khulumani Victim Support Group in Dealing with the Past in South Africa." Psychosocial Programmes After War and Dictatorship Conference. Frankfurt, Germany. June 2000. Web. 7 May 2012 <http://www.brandonhamber.com/publications/pap_khulumani.doc>.
Hariman, Robert, and John Lucaites. "Public Identity and Collective Memory in U.S. Iconic Photography: The Image of 'Accidental Napalm.'" *Critical Studies in Media Communication* 20 (2003): 35–66. Print.
Harris, Bronwyn, Nahla Valji, Brandon Hamber, and Carnita Ernest. "Introduction to the Race and Citizenship in Transition Series." Johannesburg: Center for the Study of

Violence and Reconciliation, 2004. 1–7. Web. 19 Aug. 2004 <http://www.csvr.org/za/wits/papers/paprctp6.htm#series>.

Hartley, L. P. *The Go-Between*. New York: NYRB Classics, 2002. Print.

Hayner, Priscilla. "Same Species, Different Animal: How South Africa Compares to Truth Commissions Worldwide." Villa-Vicencio and Verwoerd, *Looking Back* 32–41.

———. *Unspeakable Truths: Facing the Challenge of Truth Commissions*. New York: Routledge, 2002. Print.

Henry, Yazir. "Where Healing Begins." Villa-Vicencio and Verwoerd, *Looking Back* 166–73.

Hermann, Judith. *Trauma and Recovery: The Aftermath of Violence—from Domestic Abuse to Political Terror*. New York: Basic Books, 1992. Print.

Herwitz, Daniel. *Race and Reconciliation: Essays from the New South Africa*. Minneapolis: U of Minnesota P, 2003. Print.

Hesford, Wendy. "Global Turns and Cautions in Rhetoric and Composition Studies." *PMLA* 121.3 (May 2006): 787–801. Print.

Hirsch, Alexander Keller. "Introduction: The Agon of Reconciliation." *Theorizing Post-Conflict Reconciliation: Agonism, Restitution, and Repair*. Ed. Alexander Keller Hirsch. New York: Routledge, 2012. 1–10. Print.

Holiday, Anthony. "Forgiving and Forgetting: The Truth and Reconciliation Commission." *Negotiating the Past: The Making of Memory in South Africa*. Ed. Sarah Nuttall and Carli Coetzee. Cape Town: Oxford UP, 1998. 43–56. Print.

Holmes, Rachel. "All Too Familiar: Gender, Violence, and National Politics in the Fall of Winnie Mandela." *No Angels: Women Who Commit Violence*. Ed. Alice Myers and Sarah Wight. London: Pandora, 1996. 85–100. Print.

"Human Rights Hearing into the Activities of the Mandela United Football Club." *Truth and Reconciliation Commission*. Official website. Apr. 1997. Republic of South Africa, Department of Justice and Constitutional Development. 27 Jan. 2006.

Ignatieff, Michael. "Articles of Faith." *Index on Censorship* 25 (1996): 100–22. Web. 10 Sept. 2005.

———. "Human Rights as Idolatry." *Human Rights as Politics and Idolatry*. Ed. Amy Gutmann. Princeton: Princeton UP, 2001. 53–98. Print.

———. Introduction. *Truth and Lies: Stories from the Truth and Reconciliation Commission in South Africa*. New York: The New Press, 2001. 15–21. Print.

Isocrates. *Isocrates 1*. Trans. David Mirhady and Yun Lee Too. Austin: U of Texas P, 2000. Print.

James, Wilmot. In Boraine, Levy, and Scheffer 133–36.

Jarratt, Susan. *Rereading the Sophists: Classical Rhetoric Refigured*. Carbondale: Southern Illinois UP, 1991. Print.

Kagiso Trust. "CEOs." *Kagiso Trust*. Official website. N.d. 2 Oct. 2010 <http://www.kagiso.co.za/features/ceos/>.

Krog, Antjie. *Country of My Skull*. Johannesburg: Random House, 2002. Print.

———. In Boraine and Levy 112–19.

———. "This Thing Called Reconciliation: Forgiveness as Part of an Interconnectedness-Toward-Wholeness." *In the Balance: South Africans Debate Reconciliation*. Ed. Fanie du Toit and Erik Doxtader. Auckland Park: Jacana Media, 2010. 140–47. Print.

Krog, Antjie, Nosisi Mpolweni, and Kopano Ratele. *There Was This Goat: Investigating the Truth Commission Testimony of Notrose Nobomvu Konile*. Scottsville: U of Kwa-Zulu Natal P, 2009. Print.

Liatsos, Yianna. "Keeping Faith with the Dead: Restorative Justice, *Ubuntu*, and the Morality of National Reconciliation." *"Coming to Terms" with Reconciliation: Critical Perspectives on the Practice, Politics, and Ethics of Transitional Justice*. Madison, WI. 10 Nov. 2006.

———. "Truth, Confession, and the Black Post-Apartheid Consciousness in Njabulo Ndebele's *The Cry of Winnie Mandela*." *Modern Confessional Writing: New Critical Essays*. Ed. Jo Gill. New York: Routledge, 2006. 115–36. Print.

Macdonald, Michael. *Why Race Matters in South Africa.* Cambridge: Harvard UP, 2006. Print.

Mackenzie, Catriona, and Natalie Stoljar. "Introduction: Autonomy Refigured." *Relational Autonomy: Feminist Perspectives on Autonomy, Agency, and the Social Self.* Ed. Catriona Mackenzie and Natalie Stoljar. New York: Oxford UP, 2000. 3–32. Print.

Maier, Charles S. "Doing History, Doing Justice: The Narrative of the Historian and the Truth Commission." *Truth v. Justice: The Morality of Truth Commissions.* Ed. Robert I. Rotberg and Dennis Thompson. Princeton: Princeton UP, 2000. 261–78. Print.

Mailloux, Steven. *Reception Histories: Rhetoric, Pragmatism, and American Cultural Politics.* Ithaca: Cornell UP, 1998. Print.

Mamdani, Mahmood. "The Truth According to the TRC." *The Politics of Memory: Truth, Healing, and Social Justice.* Ed. Ifi Amadiume and Abdullahi An-Na'im. London: Zed Books, 2000. 176–83. Print.

Mandela, Nelson. "I Am Prepared to Die." *In His Own Words.* Ed. Kader Asmal, David Chidester, and Wilmot James. New York: Little, Brown, 2003. 27–42. Print.

Marback, Richard C. *Managing Vulnerability: South Africa's Struggle for a Democratic Rhetoric.* Columbia: U of South Carolina P, 2012. Print.

McBride, Robert. Transcripts of Robert McBride Amnesty Hearing. *Truth and Reconciliation Commission.* Official website. 27 Sept.–13 Oct. 1999. Republic of South Africa, Department of Justice and Constitutional Development. 27 Jan. 2006 <http://www.justice.gov.za/trc/amntrans/am1999.htm>.

Meiring, Jean. "Tasting the Sweet Fruit of Literary Success." *Lit Net: No Secret Too Big.* 22 Oct. 2004. Web. 17 Oct. 2008 <http://www.oulitnet.co.za/nosecret/achmat_dangor.asp>.

Meiring, Piet. "The Baruti Versus the Lawyers: The Role of Religion in the TRC Process." Villa-Vicencio and Verwoerd, *Looking Back* 123–31.

Meister, Robert. "Ways of Winning: The Costs of Moral Victory in Transitional Regimes." *Modernity and the Problem of Evil.* Ed. Alan D. Schrift. Bloomington: Indiana UP, 2005. 81–111. Print.

Mendez, Juan. In Boraine, Levy, and Scheffer 35–40.

Michnik, Adam. In Boraine, Levy, and Scheffer 15–18.

Miller, Carolyn R. "Genre as Social Action." *Quarterly Journal of Speech* 70 (1984): 151–67. Print.

Minow, Martha. *Between Vengeance and Forgiveness: Facing History After Genocide and Mass Violence.* Boston: Beacon, 1998. Print.

———. "The Hope for Healing: What Can Truth Commissions Do?" *Truth v. Justice: The Morality of Truth Commissions.* Ed. Robert I. Rotberg and Dennis Thompson. Princeton: Princeton UP, 2000. 235–60. Print.

Mitchell, W. J. T. *Picture Theory: Essays on Verbal and Visual Representation.* Chicago: U of Chicago P, 1994. Print.

Moon, Claire. *Narrating Political Reconciliation: South Africa's Truth and Reconciliation Commission.* Lanham: Lexington Books, 2008. Print.

Moriarty, Thomas A. *Finding the Words: A Rhetorical History of South Africa's Transition from Apartheid to Democracy.* Westport: Praeger, 2003. Print.

Ndebele, Njabulo. *The Cry of Winnie Mandela.* Banbury: Ayebia Clarke, 2003. Print.

———. Exchange with the author. 2006. E-mail.

———. "Memory, Metaphor, and the Triumph of Narrative." *Negotiating the Past: The Making of Memory in South Africa.* Ed. Sarah Nuttall and Carli Coetzee. Cape Town: Oxford UP, 1998. 19–28. Print.

Neier, Aryeh. "What Should Be Done About the Guilty?" *New York Review of Books* 1 Feb. 1990: 32–35. Print.

Nesiah, Vasuki, and Alan Keenan. "Human Rights and Sacred Cows: Framing Violence, Disappearing Struggles." *From the Margins of Globalization: Critical Perspectives on Human Rights.* Ed. Neve Gordon. Lanham: Lexington Books, 2004. 261–95. Print.

Nora, Pierre. "Between Memory and History: Les Lieux de Memoire." *Memory and Counter-Memory*. Spec. issue of *Representations* 26 (1989): 7–24. Print.
Ntoubandi, Faustin Z. *Amnesty for Crimes Against Humanity Under International Law*. Boston: Martinus Nijhoff, 2007. Print.
Nuttall, Sarah. "Telling 'Free' Stories? Memory and Democracy in South African Autobiography Since 1994." *Negotiating the Past: The Making of Memory in South Africa*. Ed. Sarah Nuttall and Carli Coetzee. Cape Town: Oxford UP, 1998. 75–88. Print.
Omar, Dullah. In Boraine and Levy 2–8, 130–36.
Payne, Leigh A. *Unsettling Accounts: Neither Truth Nor Reconciliation in Confessions of State Violence*. Durham: Duke UP, 2008. Print.
Pépin, Jacques. "Rock Shandy." *Food and Wine* March 2000. Web. 2 Nov. 2011 <http://www.foodandwine.com/recipes/rock-shandy>.
Phelps, Teresa Godwin. *Shattered Voices: Language, Violence, and the Work of Truth Commissions*. Philadelphia: U of Pennsylvania P, 2004. Print.
Philips, David. "A Reassessment by David Philips of the Truth and Reconciliation Commission: Parts 1–3." *Londongrip.co.uk: The International Online Cultural Magazine*. 2007/2008. Web. 12 Nov. 2012 <http://londongrip.co.uk/?s=david+philips>.
Phillips, Kendall R. Introduction. *Framing Public Memory*. Ed. Kendall R. Phillips. Tuscaloosa: U of Alabama P, 2004. 1–14. Print.
"Play Focuses on Racism and Reconciliation." 4 Sept. 2001. PANAPRESS: Pan-African News Agency. Web. 10 June 2011 <http://www.panapress.com/Play-focuses-on-racism-and-reconciliation--12-560888-34-lang2-index.html>.
Posel, Deborah. "The TRC Report: What Kind of History? What Kind of Truth?" Posel and Simpson, *Commissioning* 147–72.
Posel, Deborah, and Graeme Simpson, eds. *Commissioning the Past: Understanding South Africa's Truth and Reconciliation Commission*. Johannesburg: Witwatersrand UP, 2002. Print.
———. "The Power of Truth: South Africa's Truth and Reconciliation Commission in Context." Posel and Simpson, *Commissioning* 1–13.
Potgieter, Febe. In Boraine and Levy 21–23.
Povinelli, Elizabeth. *The Cunning of Recognition: Indigenous Alterities and the Making of Australian Multiculturalism*. Durham: Duke UP, 2002. Print.
Ramphele, Mamphela. In Boraine and Levy 32–36.
Reid, Frances, and Deborah Hoffmann, dirs. *Long Night's Journey into Day*. Iris Films, 2000.
Republic of South Africa. Promotion of National Unity and Reconciliation Act 34 of 1995. South African Department of Justice. N.d. Web. 10 Oct. 2012 <http://www.justice.gov.za/legislation/acts/1995-034.pdf>.
Rostron, Bryan. *Till Babylon Falls*. Sevenoaks: Coronet, 1991.
Romano, Susan. "The Historical Catalina Hernandez." *Rhetoric Society Quarterly* 37.4 (2007): 453–80. Print.
Ross, Fiona C. *Bearing Witness: Women and the Truth and Reconciliation Commission*. London: Pluto, 2003. Print.
Sachs, Albie. In Boraine and Levy 103–9.
———. In Boraine, Levy, and Scheffer 126–30.
Salazar, Philippe-Joseph. *An African Athens: Rhetoric and the Shaping of Democracy in South Africa*. Mahwah, N.J.: Lawrence Erlbaum Associates, 2002. Print.
Sanders, Mark. *Ambiguities of Witnessing: Law and Literature in the Time of a Truth Commission*. Stanford: Stanford UP, 2007. Print.
Sarkin-Hughes, Jeremy. *Carrots and Sticks: The TRC and the South African Amnesty Process*. Antwerp: Intersentia, 2004. Print.
Schaap, Andrew. *Political Reconciliation*. New York: Routledge, 2005. Print.
Schaffer, Kay, and Sidonie Smith. *Human Rights and Narrated Lives: The Ethics of Recognition*. New York: Palgrave Macmillan, 2004. Print.

Schilb, John. *Rhetorical Refusals: Defying Audiences' Expectations*. Carbondale: Southern Illinois UP, 2007. Print.

Shaw, Rosalind. "Rethinking Truth and Reconciliation Commissions: Lessons from Sierra Leone." *United States Institute of Peace*. Special Report 130. 13 Feb. 2005. 1–12. Web. 12 Dec. 2012 <http://www.usip.org/publications/rethinking-truth-and-reconciliation-commissions-lessons-sierra-leone>.

Shezi, Thandi. Transcripts of Thandi Shezi Hearing. *Truth and Reconciliation Commission*. Official website. 28 July 1997. Web. 4 May 2011 <http://www.justice.gov.za/trc/special/women/shezi.htm>.

Simpson, Graeme. "'Tell No Lies, Claim No Easy Victories': A Brief Evaluation of South Africa's Truth and Reconciliation Commission." Posel and Simpson, *Commissioning* 220–51.

Slaughter, Joseph R. "A Question of Narration: The Voice in International Human Rights Law." *Human Rights Quarterly* 19.2 (1997): 406–30. Print.

"South Africa: Apartheid Debt and Reparations, 1/2." 12 Nov. 2002. University of Pennsylvania: African Studies Center. 10 June 2011 <http://www.africa.upenn.edu/Urgent_Action/apic-111202.html>.

Stanley, Elizabeth. "Evaluating the Truth and Reconciliation Commission." *Journal of Modern African Studies* 39.3 (2001): 526–46.

Steiner, Henry J., ed. *Truth Commissions: A Comparative Assessment*. Transcript of an international meeting organized by the World Peace Foundation and the Harvard Law School Human Rights Program. Cambridge, Massachusetts, 1997. Print.

Strauss, Helene. "Intrusive Pasts, Intrusive Bodies: Achmat Dangor's *Bitter Fruit*." *Postcolonial Text* 1.2 (2005). Web. 14 Mar. 2008 <http://postcolonial.org/index.php/pct/article/view/436>.

Synergos. "Achmat Dangor." N.d. Web. 20 May 2012 <http://www.synergos.org/bios/adangor.htm>.

Thompson, Leonard. *A History of South Africa*. 3rd ed. New Haven: Yale UP, 2000. Print.

Truth and Reconciliation Commission (TRC). *Truth and Reconciliation Commission of South Africa Report*. Ed. Department of Justice. Vols. 1–5. Cape Town: Juta, 1998. Print.

Tutu, Desmond Mpilo. *No Future Without Forgiveness*. New York: Image, 1999. Print.

Twidle, Hedley. "In a Country Where You Couldn't Make This Shit Up? Literary Non-Fiction in South Africa." *Safundi: The Journal of South African and American Studies* 13.1–2 (2012): 5–28. Print.

Van der Merwe, Hugo. "The Role of the Church in Promoting Reconciliation in Post-TRC South Africa." *Religion and Reconciliation in South Africa: Voices of Religious Leaders*. Ed. Audrey R. Chapman and Bernard Spong. Philadelphia: Templeton Foundation P, 2003. 269–81. Print.

Villa-Vicencio, Charles. "Getting on with Life: A Move Toward Reconciliation." Villa-Vicencio and Verwoerd, *Looking Back* 199–209.

———. "On the Limitations of Academic History: The Quest for Truth Demands Both More and Less." *After the TRC: Reflections on Truth and Reconciliation in South Africa*. Ed. Wilmot James and Linda van de Vijver. Claremont: David Philip Publishers, 2000. 21–33. Print.

Villa-Vicencio, Charles, and Wilhelm Verwoerd. Introduction. Villa-Vicencio and Verwoerd, *Looking Back* xiv–xxi.

———, eds. *Looking Back, Reaching Forward: Reflections on the Truth and Reconciliation Commission of South Africa*. Cape Town: U of Cape Town P, 2000. Print.

Vivian, Bradford. *Public Forgetting: The Rhetoric and Politics of Beginning Again*. University Park: Penn State UP, 2008. Print.

Walker, Jeffrey. *Rhetoric and Poetics in Antiquity*. Oxford: Oxford UP, 2000. Print.

Warner, Michael. *Publics and Counterpublics*. New York: Zone Books, 2002. Print.

Wilson, Richard. *The Politics of Truth and Reconciliation in South Africa: Legitimizing the Post-Apartheid State*. Cambridge: Cambridge UP, 2001. Print.

Zalaquett, José. In Boraine, Levy, and Scheffer 8–15.

Zarefsky, David. "Four Senses of Rhetorical History." *Doing Rhetorical History: Concepts and Cases*. Ed. Kathleen J. Turner. Tuscaloosa: U of Alabama P, 1998. 19–32. Print.

Zelizer, Barbie. "The Voice of the Visual in Memory." *Framing Public Memory*. Ed. Kendall Phillips. Tuscaloosa: U of Alabama P, 2004. 157–85. Print.

INDEX

Absolution (Flanery), 127
AC. *See* Amnesty Committee
accountability. *See also* rhetoric of accountability in TRC hearings
  as issue in Interim Constitution, 18
  in restorative justice, 61, 70–71
An African Athens (Salazar), 11
African National Congress (ANC). *See also* violence against apartheid
  on amnesty, conditions for granting, 18, 72–73
  ideology of, and individualized human rights rhetoric, 69
  and just cause *vs.* just means, 72–73
  liberalism of, influence on TRC's rhetoric of accountability, 61, 65
  and negotiations leading to TRC, 17–18
  nonracialism of: as fundamental ANC principle, 61, 65; influence on TRC's rhetoric of accountability, 61, 62–63, 65–66; and race as taboo subject in democratic South Africa, 66
  prisoners, releases of, 18
  turn to violence by, 72–73
  Women's League, support for Madikizela-Mandela, 90
  Youth League, 26
African worldview, and TRC's definition of reconciliation, 101. *See also* identity, South African; *ubuntu*
agonistic deliberation. *See also* contestation
  advantages over irenic deliberation, 9
  and deepening of TRC process, 10
  and political reconciliation, 129nI:5
  TRC process as, 9–10
Alexander, Neville, 133n4:9
Ali, Lydia. *See Bitter Fruit* (Dangor)
Ali, Mikey. *See Bitter Fruit* (Dangor)
Ali, Silas. *See Bitter Fruit* (Dangor)
amnesty
  ANC conditions for, 18, 72–73
  criteria considered in, 18, 21, 69, 132n4:1

  as focus of third stage of TRC process, 21
  full disclosure as condition for, 4, 18, 21, 23, 68, 70–71, 97, 109, 110
  Further Indemnity Act of 1992 and, 18
  for Gideon Nieuwoudt, 97, 110
  for Guguletha Seven massacre policemen, 120–21
  as incentive for full disclosure, 68
  Indemnity Act of 1990 and, 17, 18
  individualized pardon process, 21
  individuals not applying for, 118
  as issue in negotiations leading to TRC, 17–19
  and just end *vs.* just means, 72–73, 78, 117
  as necessary for reconciliation, 23
  and political motivation, proof of, 21, 68, 69–70, 73–74, 77, 80, 97, 110, 122, 131–32n3:3
  proportionality requirement for, 69, 78, 97, 132n4:1
  provisions for in interim constitution, 1, 18–19
  vs. punishment: balancing of, 2; as inadequate result for some victims, ix, 109, 120; as issue in negotiations leading to TRC, x, 17–19, 23; and meaning of reconciliation, 119–20; restorative justice principles and, 61, 70–71; TRC as "third way" between, 1
  real and symbolic benefits of, 74
  secret hearings under Further Indemnity Act of 1992, 18
amnesty applications
  number of, 131
  persons filing, 131–32n3:3
  separate filings for each act, 68–69
Amnesty Committee (AC), 20
  as focus of third stage of TRC process, 21
  and forensic (factual) truth, 27, 30
  identification of politically motivated violations and, 68–69
ANC. *See* African National Congress

anti-apartheid movement. *See also* African National Congress (ANC); violence against apartheid
  and Communist influence, white fear of, 65, 72
  constraints on strategy under apartheid, 74, 82–83
  and just cause *vs.* just means, 72–73, 78, 117
  most violent phase of (1980s-early 90s), 60–61
apartheid. *See also* violence against apartheid
  as crime against humanity, 67, 72–73, 79
  defense of, as just cause, 72
  homelands (Bantustans) under, 64
  ideology of, 63–64
  Jewish South Africans and, 133n4:6
  life under, and TRC rhetoric of accountability, incompatibility of, 60–62, 66–71, 72, 74, 82, 88–90, 93–94, 95, 131n3:2
  most violent phase of (1980s-early 90s), 60–61
  and race, adoption of biological constructions of, 63
  racial groups recognized under, 63
  racial legislation, broad, deep, reach of, 64–65
  as system per se, as outside HRVC focus, 38, 39, 66–68, 125
Apelgren, Greta, 76
Arendt, Hannah, 34, 37
art. *See* imaginative texts
Asen, Robert, 97
Asmal, Kader, 22, 24, 65, 73
Asmal, Louise, 73
Asvat, Abu-Baker, 85
audience for confession
  in Dangor's *Bitter Fruit* (Dangor), 52–53, 56
  in Ndebele's *Cry of Winnie Mandela*, 62, 93
  Thandi Shezi and, 43, 52
Azanian People's Liberation Army, 73

Bantu Authorities Act of 1951, 64
Bantu Education Act of 1953, 64
Bantustans (homelands), apartheid ideology and, 64
Basson, Wouter, 118–20, 119, 134n4:14
Bechet College, protests as, 75–76
Beitler, James, 126
Bellingan, Riaan, 120–21

Berlin, James, 125
Bickford, Louis, 2
Biehl, Amy, 60
Biko, Steven, 105
Bisho massacre (1992), 17
Bitter Fruit (Dangor), 49–59. *See also specific characters*
  critical reception of, 47
  dissolution of Ali family in, 57–58
  Du Boise; murder of, 57; rape of Lydia, 49; Silas's later encounter with, 48, 49
  inspiration for writing of, 47–48
  on limitations of empathy, 56
  Lydia: incestuous episode with Mikey, 54–55, 131n2:13; perception of Silas's motives, 51–52, 131n2:11; rape of, 49, 52; readers' response to, 48; Silas's encounter with Du Boise and, 48, 49; Silas's prioritization of his needs over hers, 50–51; transformation of, 57–58
  Lydia's diary: dates of as parallel to those of TRC hearings, 49; as type of voicing, 49
  Lydia's silence: as challenge to link between speech and healing, 46, 48, 51–55; as challenge to link between speech and identity, 33, 59; as choice of audiences, 52–53, 56; as critique of TRC nationbuilding, 33, 52–55, 57–59; as effort to reclaim female agency, 51; as imposed "zone of silence," 49–50; as protective sphere, 53, 55, 57–58; as refusal to prioritize Silas's needs over her own, 50–51; as response to earlier imposed silence, 50–51
  Mikey: affair with Kate, 53, 131n2:8; as bitter fruit of rape, 49; desire to leave history behind, 59; incestuous episode with Lydia, 54–55, 131n2:13; murder of Du Boise, 57, 131n2:8; research into family background by, 55–57; silence of, 46, 55; transformation to adulthood, 55–56
  proposed alternative responses to abuses, 46
  readers' response to, 48
  sexual encounters in; explicitness of, 48, 130n2:6; overlay of power and race in, 48
  Silas: ANC involvement of, 49; efforts to save marriage, 58; encounter with Du Boise, 48, 49; extramarital affair of, 50, 131n2:8; later encounter with Du Boise, 48, 49; motivations, Lydia's perception

of, 51–52, 131n2:11; political views, as critique of TRC, 130–31nn2:7–8; prioritization of his needs over Lydia's, 50–51; rape of Lydia and, 49; silence of, 49, 50, 54, 55
silence as isolating, protective sphere in, 53–58
silence of Ali family in, as critique of TRC nationbuilding, 54–55, 57
Black Sash, 24
black women, stereotypes of, TRC hearings and, 108, 133–34n4:11
Boipatong massacre (1992), 17
Boraine, Alex, 19, 22–23, 132n3:11
Bundy, Colin, 5, 10
Burton, Mary, 24, 25, 76
Butler, Judith, 94–95
Buur, Lars, 37

Canas, Roberto, 23
Center for the Study of Violence and Reconciliation, 66, 68
Chapman, Audrey R., 9
Chilean National Commission on Truth and Reconciliation, ix, 4, 129n1:3
Christian *vs.* political forms of reconciliation, 100, 101, 132–33n4:4
citizen participation in TRC, as goal of Commission, 19–20
citizen trust, regaining of, through truth telling, 3, 36
civic deliberations, cross-reading of, 126–27
civilization, speech as basis of, 33–34
CODESA. *See* Convention for a Democratic South Africa
Coetzee, J. M., 130n2:6
Cole, Catherine, 10
collective imagining, as fluid process, 97
colonial past
 ongoing relevance of, 119–20
 and special features of South African context, 24
coloureds
 as racial designation, 63, 75
 and tricameral parliament, 75
Combahee River Collective Statement, 131n2:10
communal reconciliation, as goal of TRC, 100
community as South African value
 incompatibility with individualized human rights rhetoric, 60–62, 66–71, 72, 74, 82, 88–90, 93–94, 95, 131n3:2
 TRC definition of reconciliation and, 101

ubuntu concept and, 27–29, 69, 101
compensation for victims
 efforts to obtain, 130n2:1
 as motive for testifying, 108
 recommended *vs.* paid amount of, 21
concentration camps of Second Anglo-Boer War, psychological effect of, 24, 25–26
confrontation of past
 in Dangor's *Bitter Fruit*, 55–58
 as necessity for political transition, 2, 21–22
conspiracy of silence, truth commissions and, 3
Constitution, Interim (1993)
 amnesty provisions in, 1, 18–19
 and issue of accountability, 18
 on reconciliation, need for, 28–29
 writing of, 18
contestation. *See also* agonistic deliberation
 in artistic responses to TRC, 10, 126–27
 TRC generation of, and national discourse of reconciliation, 2, 7, 9, 10, 30, 36, 97, 99, 102, 125
 TRC typology of truths and, 30
context, and meaning of actions
 imaginative texts' potential to illuminate, 95–96, 126–27
 nonracialism of TRC rhetoric, and impossibility of explaining actions under apartheid, 60–62, 66–71, 72, 74, 82, 88–90, 93–94, 95, 131n3:2
Convention for a Democratic South Africa (CODESA), 17–18
Council of South African Students, 110
Crenshaw, Kimberlé, 131n2:10
Crisis Committee, Winnie Madikizela-Mandela's excesses and, 85
cross-reading in rhetorical studies, 126–27
The Cry of Winnie Mandela (Ndebele), 90–94
 and choice of audience for confession, 62, 93
 as critique of Madikizela-Mandela hearing, 91, 93–94
 emphasis on understanding *vs.* individual responsibility, 91
 and incompatibility of individual accountability with group identity under apartheid, 62, 93–94
 Ndebele's goal in writing, 91
 plot of, 90–91
 popularity of, and South Africans' search for understanding, 92–93

The Cry of Winnie Mandela (continued)
  on radicalization of Madikizela-Mandela, 93
  on reconciliation, 94
  on selfhood of Madikizela-Mandela, erosion of, 91, 93
  on trans-historical morality, absence of, 94
cultural rhetoric approach, 30

Dangor, Achmat. *See also Bitter Fruit* (Dangor)
  background and career of, 46–47
  on *Bitter Fruit*, issues addressed in, 47–48
  on consequences of abuses, importance of understanding, 47
  critique of TRC, 47
  political activism of, 46
  and writing of *Bitter Fruit*, 48
Danieli, Yael, 3
Das, Veena, 42
David's Story (Wicomb), 130n2:6
Death and the Maiden (Dorfman), ix–x
De Klerk, F. W., 17
de Klerk, Marike, 75
deliberation
  agonistic (*see also* contestation):
    advantages over irenic deliberation, 9;
    and deepening of TRC process, 10; and political reconciliation, 129nI:5; TRC process as, 9–10
  as central South African value, 11
  irenic, 9, 12
democracy, transition to
  and burdens and risks of belonging, 12
  and deliberation as central South African value, 11
  and market economy, 106–7, 133n4:9
  and new rhetorics, 11–12, 125
democratic commons, creation of
  as goal of TRC, 20
  and rhetorical studies, 11
  TRC generation of debate and, 7, 9, 10, 30, 36, 125
dialogic *vs.* microscopic truth, 26
Disgrace (Coetzee), 130n2:6
Dlamini, Jacob, 127
Dorfman, Ariel, ix–x
Doxtader, Erik
  on democratic commons, creation of, 7, 11
  on reconciliation, 97
  on South Africa and rhetorical studies, 10–11
  on TRC, 16, 19
  on TRC definitions of reconciliation, 99
  on TRC rhetoric of accountability, 69
Dube, Pamela Sethunya
  characterization of Shezi as naturally-gendered victim, 44
  interpretations of Shezi's story, 43–45
  interviews of Shezi, 32, 40, 43–45
  and Shezi's self-characterization as survivor, 44–45
Du Toit, Andre, 20–21, 24
Du Toit, Louise, 34–35

Edelstein, Jillian. *See also Truth and Lies* (Edelstein)
  on Joyce Mtimkulu's response to perpetrator's testimony, 111
  personal past in South Africa, efforts to come to terms with, 102–4, 106–7
  on Wouter Basson, threats from, 120
elections of 1948, and National Party rise to power, 63
elections of 1984, and tricameral parliament, 75
elections of 1994
  as first democratic election, 1
  and nonracialism of ANC, triumph of, 66
epideictic discourse, political facets of, x
Esterhuyse, Willie, 25
even-handed approach of TRC
  in perpetrator hearings: McBride's critique of, 77, 83, 116, 118; as morally questionable, 74
  in victims' hearings, 132n3:4
exhumations, imagetexts of, in Edelstein *Truth and Lies*, 105

fact finding by truth commissions. *See also* forensic (factual) truth
  vs. interpretation or evaluation, 4–7
  as minimum function, 2–3
February, Terry, 113
Finding the Words (Moriarty), 11
Finnegan, Cara, 116, 123
Finnegan, William, 118
Flanery, Patrick, 127
forced relocations
  Achmat Dangor's experiences with, 46
  Dangor's *Bitter Fruit* on, 56–57
  legislation enabling, 64
  McBride family and, 75
forensic (factual) truth. *See also* fact finding by truth commissions; rhetoric of accountability in TRC hearings

conflict with other forms of truth, 29–30
as focus of third stage of TRC process, 21
TRC focus on, *vs.* efforts to understand historical events, 60–62, 66–71, 72, 74, 82, 88–90, 93–94, 95, 131n3:2
in TRC truth typology, 26–27
Fullard, Madeline, 67
Further Indemnity Act of 1992, 18

Gaborone, Botswana, Security Forces raid on, 82–83
"Gender and the Truth and Reconciliation Commission" (Goldblatt and Meintjes), 39–40
Gibson, James L., 9
Gobodo-Madikizela, Pumla, 27–28, 101, 105
Goldblatt, Beth, 39–40
Goldstone, Richard, 22–23
Goodman, Tanya, 10
Gready, Paul, 30, 35
Group Areas Act of 1950, 64, 75
Gugulethu Seven, 29, 120–23

Hartley, L. P., 60
Hayner, Priscilla, 3, 31
healing. *See also* reconciliation
effects of truth commissions on, 5
speech as source of: critique of in Dangor's *Bitter Fruit*, 46, 48, 51–55; human rights discourse on, 35; women's narratives of abuse and, 31, 34, 42–43, 44
healing and restorative truth, in TRC truth typology, 26, 27
Health Professions Council of South Africa, 108, 134n4:14
hearings. *See* perpetrator hearings; victims' hearings; Women's Hearings
Henry, Yazir, 35
Hermann, Judith, 34
Herwitz, Daniel, 5, 10
historians views on truth commissions, 5
histories, as working out of resistance and survival in present, 59
history of apartheid era
TRC effort to understand: Dangor's *Bitter Fruit* as critique of, 46, 53–54, 56–59; as embodied experience, Dangor on, 47–48; and incompatibility of cultural context with TRC terms of inquiry, 60–62, 66–71, 72, 74, 82, 88–90, 93–94, 95, 131n3:2; and nature of truth, as issue, 24–30; *vs.* reconciliation, as issue, 25–26; shaping of testimony and, 10, 32–33, 36, 38, 40, 41, 42–43
TRC's failure to develop, as generative, 125
Hoffmann, Deborah, 60
Holiday, Anthony, 29
Holmes, Rachel, 87
Holocaust
lessons learned in, as influence on TRC, 71
and value of truth telling, 21–22
homelands (Bantustans), apartheid ideology and, 64
HRVC. *See* Human Rights Violations Committee
human rights discourse
assumed link between speech and empowerment in, 35
emphasis on truth telling, 21–22, 23
focus on individual action and responsibility, 68–69
influence on TRC process, 1, 16–17, 21–23
influence on TRC's rhetoric of accountability, 61, 65–66, 68–69
influence on truth commissions, 126
life narratives as tools of, 35
South African context and, 16–17, 24–30
human rights violations
history of efforts to address, 2
TRC definition of, as purely physical, 38
Human Rights Violations Committee (HRVC), 20. *See also* victims' hearings; Women's Hearings
distinction between primary and secondary witnesses, 32, 38–39
as focus of second TRC stage, 21
hearings by, as substitute for more substantial action, 36–37
and narrative truth, 27, 30
ubuntu concept and, 28

identity, individual
complexity of narrating, 94–95
speech as basis of, 33–35, 59
TRC focus on: and definition of reconciliation, 101; *vs.* efforts to understand historical events, 88–90, 94, 131n3:2; incompatibility with South African concepts of identity, 60–62, 66–71, 72, 74, 82, 88–90, 93–94, 95, 131n3:2; and relational autonomy, 95
truth commission testimony and, 6
unavailability of under apartheid, 74

identity, South African
  as group-directed, 60–62, 66–71, 72, 74, 82, 88–90, 93–94, 95, 131n3:2
  TRC definition of reconciliation and, 101
  ubuntu concept and, 27–29, 69, 101
IFP. *See* Inkatha Freedom Party
Ignatieff, Michael
  on human rights discourse, 68
  introduction to Edelstein's *Truth and Lies*, 104, 110, 124
  on truth commissions, 4, 5, 26
images, power of to energize the conditional, 98. *See also* photography
imaginative texts
  potential to illuminate real-life events, 95–96, 126–27
  and purging of collective, ix–x
  in South Africa, TRC and, 127
Immorality Act of 1950, 64
Indemnity Act of 1990, 17, 18
individual identity. *See* identity, individual
Inkatha Freedom Party (IFP), amnesty process and, 132n3:3
Institute for Contextual Theology, 28
Institute for Democracy in South Africa, 23, 24
International Declaration of Human Rights, speech and empowerment in, 35
interpersonal reconciliation, as goal of TRC, 100
irenic deliberation, 9, 12
Isocrates, 2, 33

James, Wilmot, 24
Jarratt, Susan, 127
Jewish South Africans, 133n4:6
Joseph, S. L., 88–89, 132n3:11
jus ad bellum vs. jus in bello, perpetrator hearings and, 72–73, 78, 117
Justice in Transition Institute, 22
  and global influence on TRC process, 17, 22–24
  Justice in Transition conference (February, 1994), 22–24, 63
  South African Conference on Truth and Reconciliation (July, 1994), 24–27, 63
just war thesis, 73, 78–79, 117. *See also jus ad bellum vs. jus in bello*

Keenan, Alan, 87, 90
Khulumani Support Group. *See* Kulumane Support Group
Krog, Antjie, 6–7, 25–26, 27, 35, 85, 86, 90
  on stereotypes, 133n4:11

  on TRC's definition of reconciliation, 101
Kulumane Support Group, 43, 130n2:1

Lecordier, Matthew, 76
legitimacy of new government, TRC hearings and, 36
Lewin, Hugh, 127
Liatsos, Yianna, 28, 70
liberation struggles, sidelining of women's issues during, 50
life narratives
  appropriation by others, 35
  as tool of human rights advocacy, 35
logos, faith in power of, as basis of truth commissions, 1–2, 7–8
Long Night's Journey into Day (film), 60

Mabuza, Wesley, 28
Macdonald, Michael, 66
Madaka, Topsy, 110
Madikizela-Mandela, Winnie, 83–90. *See also The Cry of Winnie Mandela* (Ndebele)
  on acts of violence, importance of context of, 60–61
  as advocate of violence, 84; accusations of excessiveness, 84–85, 86–87, 88; lack of repentance for, 86–87; Women's League of ANC support for, 90
  alleged human rights abuses by, 84, 85, 112; ANC concerns about, 85; Madikizela-Mandela's denial of knowledge about, 89, 132n3:10; resistance to inquiries about, 84
  as "bad victim," 87
  career as activist, 83–84
  in Edelstein's *Truth and Lies*, 105
  and individual *vs.* collective identity, 83–90
  limited legal exposure of, 62
  South Africans' ongoing support for, 92
  testimony at perpetrators' hearings, 85–90, 87; accusatory atmosphere of, 86, 132n3:10; challenging of TRC's rhetoric of individual accountability, 62, 73, 85–90, 94; as defiant and dismissive, 86; gendered nature of, 86; Madikizela-Mandela's insistence on open hearing, 85; Madikizela-Mandela's location of events in specific place and time, 88; as rhetorical refusal, 87, 88–89; time constraints on, 132n3:11; as voluntary, 87
  and victims' hearings, refusal to testify at, 83–84

Madikizela-Mandela United Football Club
    (MUFC), 85, 111
Maier, Charles S., 5
Makana, Sizwe, 60
Malan, Wynand, 129n1:3
Malete, Mamello (Ndebele character), 91,
    92
Mamdani, Mahmood, 5, 131n3:2
Managing Vulnerability (Marback), 11–12
Mandela, Nelson
    Dangor's *Bitter Fruit* on, 131n2:11
    in Edelstein's *Truth and Lies*, 105
    election as president, 1
    on justice of anti-apartheid cause, 72
    and nonracialism of ANC, triumph of,
        66
    release from prison, 17
    and TRC, 17, 19
    white South Africans' awareness of, 103
    and Winnie Madikizela-Mandela, 83, 85,
        93
Marback, Richard, 11–12
Mbelo, Thapelo, 120–21
McBride, Robert, 75–83
    arguments against amnesty for, 77–78,
        80
    background of, 75
    bombings conducted by, 76
    in Edelstein's *Truth and Lies*, 114–18, 115
    indemnity of, 62, 76, 116
    meeting with victims' families, 77
    radicalization of, 75–76
    strong public views on, 115–16
    support of black South Africans for,
        114–15, 116
    testimony at perpetrator hearings,
        76–83; on all non-white South
        Africans as victims, 83; aloofness of,
        116; challenging of TRC's rhetoric
        of accountability, 62, 73, 77–78,
        81–82, 94; critique of TRC's even-
        handed approach, 77, 83, 116, 118; as
        demonstration of support for TRC,
        76–77, 116; emphasis on context of
        actions, 81–82; and pragmatism *vs.*
        idealism, 79–80
    Why Not Bar/Magoo Bar bombing, 76;
        justification of as act of war, 77–79,
        81–83, 116; McBride's feelings about,
        79, 80–81, 83, 116; sentencing and
        indemnity, 62, 76, 116
media coverage of TRC, 20
Meintjes, Sheila, 39–40
Meiring, Piet, 100
Meister, Robert, 87

Mendez, Juan, 23
Michnik, Adam, 23
microscopic *vs.* dialogic truth, 26
Minow, Martha, 3
Miya, Eunice, 120
Moon, Claire, 9, 17
moral authority of truth commissions,
    objectivity and, 4–5
Moriarty, Thomas A., 10–11
Mphahlele, Letlapa, 73
MPNF. *See* Multi-Party Negotiating Forum
Mpolweni, Nosisi, 27
Mtimkulu, Joyce, 97, 98, 109–11
Mtimkulu, Sikhumbuzo, 109–10
Mtimkulu, Siphiwo, 109, 110
Mtintso, Thenjiwe, 34–35
Multi-Party Negotiating Forum (MPNF),
    18

narrative truth, in TRC truth typology, 26,
    27
National Party (NP)
    and negotiations leading to TRC, 17–18,
        19
    rise to power, 63–64
National Unity and Reconciliation Bill, 19
nationbuilding goal of TRC, 100. *See also*
    reconciliation
    Dangor on, 31
    Dangor's *Bitter Fruit* as critique of, 33,
        52–55, 57–59, 130–31nn2:7–8
    use of victim narratives in, 31, 32, 36, 37,
        40
Native Nostalgia (Dlamini), 127
Nazis, comparisons of apartheid
    government to, 71, 74, 77
Ndebele, Njabulo, 91–92, 93–94, 133n4:11.
    See also The Cry of Winnie Mandela
    (Ndebele)
Neier, Aryeh, 3
Nesiah, Vasuki, 87, 90
Neville, Alexander, 5
New Yorker magazine, 118
Ngewu, Cynthia, 29, 121, 122–23, 134n4:15
Ngewu, Cynthia Bablwa, 121
Nieuwoudt, Gideon, 97, 107, 109–10
novels about apartheid-era violence,
    130n2:6. *See also Bitter Fruit* (Dangor)
NP. *See* National Party
Nuremberg trials, 2
Nuttall, Sarah, 31, 59, 61

Omar, Dullah, 7, 19, 22, 26
Open Society Institute, 3
Overcoming Apartheid (Gibson), 9

Pan Africanist Congress (PAC), 132n3:3
parliament
  and amnesty issue, debate on, 19, 24
  and TRC, debate on, 24
Pass Laws of 1952, 64, 67
Payne, Leigh A., 9
perpetrator hearings. *See also* amnesty; Madikizela-Mandela, Winnie, testimony at perpetrators' hearings; McBride, Robert, testimony at perpetrator hearings; rhetoric of accountability in TRC hearings
  adversarial atmosphere of, 73–74
  distinction between just end and just means in, 72–73, 78, 117
  even-handed approach of; McBride's critique of, 77, 83, 116, 118; as morally questionable, 74
  nonracialism of, and impossibility of explaining context of actions, 60–62, 66–71, 72, 74, 82, 88–90, 93–94, 95, 131n3:2
  opposing lawyers' strategy in, 74
  and political motivation, necessity of proving, 21, 68, 69–70, 73–74, 77, 80, 97, 110, 122, 131–32n3:3
perpetrators. *See also* amnesty
  in Edelstein *Truth and Lies*, 105, 107, 111–14, *112*, 114–18, *115*, 118–20, *119*
  molding of commission processes by, 6
  motive and perspectives of, TRC charge to discover, 7
  required public disclosure by, 4, 18, 21, 23, 68, 70–71, 97, 109, 110
  TRC generalization of perpetratorship and, 28
  unwillingness to disclose actions; in prosecutions, 3, 4; to truth commissions, ix, 4
Phelps, Teresa Godwin, 3–4, 34, 37
Philips, David, 100
philosophers, views on truth commissions, 5
Phosa, Matthews, 73
photography
  collaboration of subject and photographer in, 107–8
  complex, bounded meanings in, 123
  power of to energize the conditional, 98
Picturing Poverty (Finnegan), 116
Piet, Christopher, 122
Piet, Ntombomzi, *121*, 122
poison and drug research in apartheid South Africa, 118, 134n4:14

political leaders of South Africa, and deliberation as social value, 11
political *vs.* Christian forms of reconciliation, 100, 101, 132–33n4:4
Population Registration Act of 1950, 64
Posel, Deborah, 10, 29, 131n3:2, 133n4:5
Potgeiter, Febe, 26
Povinelli, Elizabeth, 36–37
Prohibition of Mixed Marriages Act of 1949, 64
Project Coast, 118
Promotion of National Unity and Reconciliation Act (1995)
  drafting and enactment of, 19, 20
  final report requirements, 129nI:3
  irenic impulse of, 9
  provisions for victim testimony, 35–36
  on reconciliation, need for, 28–29, 99
  tasks charged to TRC by, 7, 19
prosecutions. *See* punishment
psychoanalytic theory, on therapeutic value of narrative, 34
psychologists, views on truth commissions, 5
public memory, x–xi
public nature of TRC proceedings. *See also* democratic commons, creation of; speech
  ANC insistence on, 18
  goals of, 8, 19–20
  required public disclosure by perpetrators, 4, 18, 21, 23, 68, 70–71, 97, 109, 110
  transformative effects expected from, 8, 70, 129nI:3
publics, multiple, truth commissions and, 5–6
punishment
  vs. amnesty: balancing of, 2; as issue in negotiations leading to TRC, x, 17–19, 23; and meaning of reconciliation, 119–20; restorative justice principles and, 61, 70–71; TRC as "third way" between, 1
  political difficulties surrounding, 2
  as poor means toward truth, 3
  reconciliation as substitute for, ix, 109, 120
  truth commissions as alternative to, x, 3–4; TRC efforts to persuade public on, 8

race. *See also* apartheid
  biological constructions of under apartheid, 63

cultural understanding of, pre-apartheid, 63
ongoing importance of in South Africa, 66
as taboo subject in democratic South Africa, 66
racism, as motive, incompatibility of with nonracialist emphasis of TRC hearings, 60–62, 66–71, 72, 74, 82, 88–90, 93–94, 95, 131n3:2
Ramphele, Mamphela, 25
rape. *See also Bitter Fruit* (Dangor); Shezi, Thandi
speech and subjectivity in literature on, 34
taboo against discussing, Dangor on, 31–32
Ratele, Kopano, 95
reconciliation. *See also* nationbuilding goal of TRC
as ambiguous concept, 100, 102
amnesty as necessary for, 23
calls for, complexity of answers to, 102
Christian *vs.* political forms of, 100, 101, 132–33n4:4
as complex, long-term process: Dangor's *Bitter Fruit* on, 59; Edelstein's *Truth and Lies* on, 97, 99, 107, 113–14, 123, 124; and ongoing civic debate, 2, 7, 9, 10, 30, 36, 97, 99, 102, 125; TRC recognition of, 100–101
in Edelstein's *Truth and Lies*: as complex, long-term process, 97, 99, 107, 113–14, 123, 124; individuals accepting, 122–23; individuals contesting terms of, 116–18; individuals indifferent to, 118–20; individuals reluctantly accepting, 113–14; individuals unwilling to accept, 97, 109–11
as focus of first phase of TRC investigation, 20
as generative *topos*, 97, 99, 102, 125
as goal of TRC, 7–8, 10, 23, 129nnI:5–6
political *vs.* communitarian versions of, 129nI:5
vs. punishment: balancing of, 2; as inadequate result for some victims, ix, 109, 120; meaning of reconciliation and, 119–20; restorative justice principles and, 61, 70–71
rhetorical culture of South Africa and, 11
TRC definitions of: critiques of, 101–2; and danger of forgetting, 114; as generative, 125; as resource for debate on South African future, 102; types

of reconciliation, 100; vagueness of, 99–101
and truth telling, relationship between, as issue, 25–26
ubuntu concept and, 27–29, 69, 101
Record of Understanding (1992), 17–18
Reid, Frances, 60
relational autonomy, and identity, 95
Reparations and Rehabilitation Committee (RRC), 20, 21
repressed memories, and therapeutic value of narration, 34
Reservation of Separate Amenities Act of 1953, 64
restorative justice concept
influence on TRC's rhetoric of accountability, 61, 70–71
principles of, 70, 71
retributive justice measures. *See* punishment
revolutionary times, and moral norms, crumbling of, 60–61
rhetoric
inclusion of poetry and poetics in, x
as meta-discipline, 127
rhetorical culture of new South Africa. *See also* democratic commons, creation of
contested terms in search for common denominator, 11–12
and ongoing civic debate, 2, 7, 9, 10, 30, 36, 97, 99, 102, 125
transition to democracy and, 11–12, 125
rhetorical hermeneutics, as method, xi
rhetorical scholarship on South Africa, 10–11
rhetorical studies
cross-reading in, 126–27
global turn of, 15
21st-century, South Africa and, 10–11
rhetoricity, of truth commissions, 5–12
rhetoric of accountability in TRC hearings
challenging of by perpetrators, 62, 73, 77–78, 81–82, 85–90, 94
as deracialized, 67, 74
focus on isolated individual acts *vs.* racial or group identities, 60–62, 66–71, 72, 74, 82, 88–90, 93–94, 95, 131n3:2
origins of underlying ideology, 61, 65–66, 68, 70–71
rhetorics, new, in South African transition to democracy, 11–12, 125
Richardson, Jerry, 85, 111–14, 112
Rivonia Trial, 72
Roberts, Ronald Suresh, 73
Roberts-Miller, Patricia, 9

Ross, Fiona, 31, 39, 42, 131n2:12
Roston, Bryan, 80
RRC. *See* Reparations and Rehabilitation Committee

Sachs, Albie, 23, 24, 26
Salazar, Philippe, 10–11, 131n3:1
sanctions against South Africa, lifting of, 105–6
Sanders, Mark, 10, 28, 130n1:5
Schilb, John, 87
Second Anglo-Boer War concentration camps, psychological effect of, 24, 25–26
Security Forces, errors made by, 82–83
Seipei, Joyce Mananki, 85, 111–14, *112*
Seipei, Stompie Moeketsi, 85, 111, 112–13
selfhood. *See* identity, individual
separate development policy under apartheid, 64
Separate Representation of Voters Act of 1951, 65
Seroke, Joyce, 41, 44
Sharpeville Massacre (1960), 67
Shaw, Rosalind, 34
Shezi, Thandi
 ANC involvement of, 32
 Dube's interviews of, 32, 40, 43–45; interpretations of Shezi's story in, 43–45; Shezi as naturally-gendered victim in, 44; Shezi's self-characterization as survivor in, 33, 44–45
 as public figure after Hearings, 32
 and reparations, 130n2:1
 and silence; as choice of audiences, 43, 52; initial silence about rape, 42; strategic wielding of, 42, 59
 testimony at Women's Hearings, 32, 40–43; challenging of TRC's interpretation of, 33; efforts to control selfhood in, 45; motives for, 108–9; self-characterization as strong survivor, 33, 41–42; Shezi on experience of, 31, 45; TRC characterization of as naturally-gendered victim, 41, 43
 torture and rape of, 40; conflicting accounts of, 44; initial silence about, 42
silence. *See also* Bitter Fruit (Dangor); women's refusal to speak
 human need for breaking, 31
 potential eloquence of, 59
 of Thandi Shezi: as choice of audiences, 43, 52; initial silence about rape, 42; strategic wielding of, 42, 59
Slovo, Gillian, 107
Slovo, Joe, 18
social suffering, grammar of, 131n2:12
social (dialogic) truth
 conflict with other forms of truth, 29–30
 as one of four types recognized by TRC, 26, 27
Sophists, 127
South African Conference on Truth and Reconciliation (July, 1994), 24–27
South African identity
 as group-directed, 60–62, 66–71, 72, 74, 82, 88–90, 93–94, 95, 131n3:2
 TRC definition of reconciliation and, 101
 ubuntu concept and, 27–29, 69, 101
South African nationals, influence on TRC structure, 1
Soweto Youth Congress (SOYCO), 32
SOYCO. *See* Soweto Youth Congress
speech. *See also* silence; women's narratives of abuse; women's refusal to speak
 as basis of civilization, history of concept, 33–34
 and empowerment, assumed link between, 35, 48
 and identity, assumed link between, 33–35, 59
 as source of healing: critique of in Dangor's *Bitter Fruit*, 46, 48, 51–55; human rights discourse on, 35; women's narratives of abuse and, 31, 34, 42–43, 44
stases, addressing of by truth commission
 inevitability of, 6–7
 as issue, 4–5
 promotion of identification and, 8
Steiner, Henry, 4–5, 26
stereotypes of black women, TRC hearings and, 108, 133–34n4:11
Stones Against the Mirror (Lewin), 127
stories of past, as working out of resistance and survival in present, 59
The Story I Am About to Tell (play), 130n1
"The Story of Thandi Shezi" (Dube)
 characterization of Shezi as naturally-gendered victim in, 44
 Dube's interviews for, 32, 40, 43–45
 interpretations of Shezi's story in, 43–45
 Shezi's self-characterization as survivor in, 44–45
 writing of, 32

Strauss, Helene, 51
subject-formation. *See entries under* identity
sunset clause, 18
Suppression of Communism Act of 1951, 65

texts
　diverse, value of in interpreting political projects, x, 126–27
　imaginative: potential to illuminate real-life events, 95–96, 126–27; and purging of collective, ix–x; in South Africa, TRC and, 127
'Till Babylon Falls (McBride), 80
Tokyo trials, 2
transformative storytelling, potential for in truth commissions, 4
transitional justice theories
　emergence of, 2
　influence on truth commissions, 126
　and range of mechanisms for transition, 2
transition from apartheid, complexity of
　Dangor's Bitter Fruit on, 59
　Edelstein's *Truth and Lies* on, 97, 99, 107, 113–14, 123, 124
　and ongoing civic debate, benefits of, 2, 7, 9, 10, 30, 36, 97, 99, 102, 125
　TRC recognition of, 100–101
transition to new order, as function of peace commissions, 3
TRC. *See* Truth and Reconciliation Commission
truth. *See also* forensic (factual) truth; history of apartheid era
　four types recognized by TRC, 16, 26–27; and conflicts between types, 29–30; and generation of contestation in public hearings, 30; as necessity of political realities, 16
　post-modern conceptions of, 30
　vs. retribution, Tutu on, x
　role of human perception in, TRC recognition of, 26
truth, revelation of. *See also* contestation; public nature of TRC proceedings
　and citizen trust, regaining of, 3, 36
　conceptual conflict between types of truth and, 29–30
　emphasis of global human rights movement on, 21–22, 23
　imperfect, and agonistic deliberation, 10
　individual's fear of, 3
　as insufficient for some victims, ix, 109, 120

　possibility of, as issue, 6–7, 25
　and reconciliation, relationship between, as issue, 25–26
　truth commissions as best means towards, 3–4
Truth and Lies (Edelstein)
　collaboration of subjects and photographer in, 107–8, 133n4:10
　continuity and change in South Africa as theme of, 105–6
　as critique of TRC, 124
　Edelstein's decision to document TRC process, 103–4
　Edelstein's diary entries in, 102–3, 104, 109–10, 113, 119–20
　and Edelstein's own past, effort to come to terms with, 102–4, 106–7
　Edelstein's subjectivity as unifying element in, 107–8
　imagetexts in, 132n4:2; as captured moments of reconciliation struggle, 113–14, 116–17, 122–23, 124; and complex ambiguity of reconciliation, 122–23, 124; and danger of forgetting, 114; interplay of text and image in, 110, 111–13, 116–18; as invitation to imagine reconciliation, 97–99; rhetorical availability to multiple interpretations, 104, 122–23
　individuals portrayed in: ambivalence and complex responses of, 97; control of over circumstances of photograph, 108, 109, 124, 133n4:10; Gideon Nieuwoudt, 107, 109–10; Jerry Richardson, 111–14, *112*; Joyce Mananki Seipei, 111–14, *112*; Joyce Mtimkulu, 97, 98, 109–11; overview of, 105; perpetrators, 105, 107, 111–14, *112*, 114–18, *115*, 118–20, *119*; reasons for cooperating, 108–9; rhetorical agency of, 107–8; Robert McBride, 114–18, *115*; Wouter Basson, 118–20, *119*
　introductory material in, 104–5, 105–6, 108, 124
　reconciliation in: as complex, long-term process, 97, 99, 107, 113–14, 123, 124; individuals accepting, 122–23; individuals contesting terms of, 116–18; individuals indifferent to reconciliation, 118–20, *119*; individuals reluctantly accepting, 113–14; individuals unwilling to accept, 97, 109–11

Truth and Lies (continued)
   stereotypes of black women and, 108, 133–34n4:11
   structure of, 104–5
Truth and Reconciliation Commission (TRC). *See also specific topics*
   commissioners of, 20
   committees of, 20
   convergence of global and local in, 15–16, 16–17, 24–30
   creation of national discourse of reconciliation by, 2, 7, 9, 10, 30, 36, 97, 99, 102, 125
   Dangor's critique of, 47
   dates of operation, 20, 130n1:4
   diversity of responses to, as generative, 125
   establishment of, 1, 19
   four types of truths recognized by, 16, 26–27; and conflicts between types, 29–30; and generation of contestation in public hearings, 30; as necessity of political realities, 16
   influence on South African imaginative writing, 127
   influence on subsequent truth commissions, 126
   irenic impulses of, 9, 12
   maximum publicity policy of, 19–20
   negotiations leading to, 16, 17–19, 22–23
   nonracialism of, as product of ANC influence, 62–63, 65–66
   period covered by mandate of, 67
   phases of investigation, 20–21
   powers of, 19
   and public memory, x
   reconciliation as central goal of, 7–8; as constraint on testimony, 10; definition of reconciliation and, 129nnI:5–6; and emphasis of practical action, 23
   responsibilities given to, 19
   as rhetorical experiment, 125
   scholarship on, 8–10
   shaping of testimony by, 10, 32–33, 36, 38, 40, 41, 42–43
   as technology of citizenship, 20
   as "third way" between amnesty and prosecutions, 1
Truth and Reconciliation Commission of South Africa Report
   on apartheid as systemic and pervasive, 74
   on apartheid per se as human rights violation, 67
   on definitions of reconciliation, 100–101
   on four types of truth, 27
   as historical text, 133n4:5
   on Holocaust, lessons learned in, 71
   Minority Position report in, 129nI:3
   on paranoia within anti-apartheid movement, 88
   on perpetrator hearings, public nature of, 70
   on reconciliation, x
   shaping of victim narratives to conform to, 38
   summary of Madikizela-Mandela testimony in, 132n3:10
   on *ubuntu* concept, 27, 29
   on value of truth telling, 21–22
   on victims' stories, as legacy of nation, 37
   volumes, release dates of, 20, 129nI:3, 130n1:4
Truth and Reconciliation in South Africa (Chapman and Van der Merwe), 9
truth commissions
   as alternative to prosecutions, 3–4; TRC efforts to persuade public on, 8
   and assumed coupling of speech and identity, 59
   and collective imaginary, creation of, 123–24
   convergence of global and local in, 15–16
   critiques of, 4–5, 6
   cross-reading of texts generated by, 126–27
   deliberation, not closure, as goal of, 125
   and demands of political *vs.* scholarly inquiry, 5
   and faith in power of *logos*, 1–2, 7–8
   functions of, 2–4
   ideological influences on, 126
   increasing numbers of, 1, 3, 126, 129nI:1
   influence of TRC on, 126
   as inherently rhetorical, 1
   interpretation or evaluation by; inevitability of, 6–7; as issue, 4–5
   and multiple publics, demands of, 5–6
   rhetoricity of, 5–12
   tailoring of to specific conditions, 126
Truth Commission Special Report (TV show), 20
Tutu, Desmond
   and ANC amnesty, as issue, 73
   critique of in Dangor's *Bitter Fruit*, 56
   in Edelstein's *Truth and Lies*, 105, 133n4:10

on public shaming, effectiveness of, 70
on reconciliation, 102, 114, 132–33n4:4
on respect among democratic citizens, 20
on truth telling, value of, x, 21–22
and *ubuntu* concept, 28, 29

ubuntu
definition of, 27
as guiding principle of TRC, 27–29
and individualized human rights rhetoric, 69
legitimacy of concept as issue, 28
as nonracialized term, 29
and TRC's conception of reconciliation, 101
Umkhonto we Sizwe
bombings conducted by, 76
Mandela on, 72
McBride in, 76, 116
persons killed by, 29
Universal Declaration of Human Rights, focus on individuals in, 68–69

van der Merwe, Hugo, 9
van der Merwe, Susan, 29
van Heerden, Andries, 43–44
Verryn, Paul, 85
Verwoerd, Hendrik, 63, 64
victims. *See also* women victims of abuses
compensation for: efforts to obtain, 130n2:1; as motive for testifying, 108; recommended *vs.* paid amount of, 21
molding of commission processes by, 6
motive and perspectives of, TRC charge to discover, 7
trauma of prosecutions and, 3
victims' hearings. *See also* Women's Hearings
conceptual conflict with forensic form of truth, 29–30
even-handed approach of TRC in, 132n3:4
Madikizela-Mandela's refusal to testify at, 83–84
as narrative truth, 27
number testifying, 21, 37
TRC screening of, 37–38
Villa-Vicencio, Charles, 100
violence against apartheid. *See also* Why Not Bar/Magoo Bar bombing
alleged human rights abuses by Madikizela-Mandela, 84, 85, 112; ANC concerns about, 85;
Madikizela-Mandela's denial of knowledge about, 89, 132n3:10; resistance to inquiries about, 84
black South Africans' support of, 116
cultural context of, as incompatible with TRC ideology, 60–62, 66–71, 72, 74, 82, 88–90, 93–94, 131n3:2
justifications of, 72–73, 74, 77–79, 81–83, 117
Madikizela-Mandela as advocate of, 84; accusations of excessiveness, 84–85, 86–87, 88; and importance of context for understanding, 60–61; lack of repentance for, 86–87; Women's League of ANC support for, 90
Umkhonto we Sizwe bombings, 76
voting rights, restriction of to white South Africans, 64–65

Walker, Jeffrey, x
Webster, Gordon, 76
Welgemoed, Sharon, 114–15
white community in South Africa
apathy toward apartheid, culpability of, 74
coalescing of around racial identity, 63–64
concerns about TRC, 25
white right, and negotiations leading to TRC, 19
white supremacy, history of in South Africa, 63–65
Why Not Bar/Magoo Bar bombing, 76
McBride's feelings about, 79, 80–81, 83, 116
McBride's justification of as act of war, 77–79, 81–83, 116
McBride's sentencing and indemnity, 76
Wicomb, Zoë, 130n2:6
Wilson, Richard, 28, 65–66, 69, 86–87, 101
With Faith in the Works of Words (Doxtader), 11, 16
Women's Hearings, 37–40. *See also* women's narratives of abuse; women's refusal to speak; women victims of abuses
assumed link between speech and empowerment in, 34–35
Dangor on, 47–48
Dangor's *Bitter Fruit* on, 52
reasons for establishment of, 32, 39–40
regional rates of reporting and, 130n2:3

Women's Hearings (*continued*)
  Thandi Shezi's testimony at, 32, 40–43; challenging of TRC's interpretation of, 33; efforts to control selfhood in, 45; motives for, 108–9; self-characterization as strong survivor, 33, 41–42; Shezi on experience of, 31, 45; TRC characterization of as naturally-gendered victim, 41, 43
  TRC's shaping of testimony in, 32–33, 36, 38, 40, 41, 42–43
women's issues
  sidelining of during liberation struggles, 50
  typical subordination of to broader agenda, 51
Women's League of ANC, support for Madikizela-Mandela, 90
women's narratives of abuse. *See also* Women's Hearings; women's refusal to speak
  human need for breaking silence and, 31
  inclusion in national community through, 31, 32, 36
  and restoration of dignity, 31, 36
  as source of healing, 31, 34, 42–43, 44
  suffering of family members as focus of, 32, 38–39
  TRC's assumptions about meaning of, 35–37; shaping of remembrance by, 32–33, 36, 38, 41, 42–43; women's resistance to, 32, 33, 41
  TRC screening of, 37–38
  TRC's misinterpretations of, 39
  TRC's special effort to collect, 32, 39–40
  and TRC's truth recovery project, influence on interaction with victims, 32, 36
  validation received from, 31
women's refusal to speak, 32. *See also* silence
  assumed link between speech and identity and, 33, 59
  Dangor's *Bitter Fruit* as effort to give voice to, 48
  as form of prudery, 47–48
  rhetorical power of, 32, 33, 42
  as threat to TRC's nation-building project, 32, 39
  TRC's interpretation of, 38–39
women victims of abuses
  TRC characterization of as voiceless, 35
  TRC characterization of naturally-gendered victims, 41, 43, 130n2:2
  TRC objectification of, 35
  TRC's focus on sexual violations, 39, 41

Zalaquett, José, 4, 5, 23
Zelizer, Barbie, 98

RHETORIC AND DEMOCRATIC DELIBERATION

EDITED BY CHERYL GLENN AND J. MICHAEL HOGAN
THE PENNSYLVANIA STATE UNIVERSITY

Books in the series:

Karen Tracy *Challenges of Ordinary Democracy: A Case Study in Deliberation and Dissent* / VOLUME 1

Samuel McCormick, *Letters to Power: Public Advocacy Without Public Intellectuals* / VOLUME 2

Christian Kock and Lisa S. Villadsen, eds., *Rhetorical Citizenship and Public Deliberation* / VOLUME 3

Jay P. Childers, *The Evolving Citizen: American Youth and the Changing Norms of Democratic Engagement* / VOLUME 4

Dave Tell, *Confessional Crises: Confession and Cultural Politics in Twentieth-Century America* / VOLUME 5

David Boromisza-Habashi, *Speaking Hatefully: Culture, Public Communication, and Political Action in Hungary* / VOLUME 6

Arabella Lyon, *Deliberative Acts: Democracy, Rhetoric, and Rights* / VOLUME 7

Lyn Carson, John Gastil, Janette Hartz-Karp, and Ron Lubensky, eds., *The Australian Citizens' Parliament and the Future of Deliberative Democracy* / VOLUME 8

Christa Olson, *Constitutive Visions: Indigeneity and Commonplaces of National Identity in Republican Ecuador* / VOLUME 9

Damien Pfister, *Networked Media, Networked Rhetorics: Attention and Deliberation in the Early Blogosphere* / VOLUME 10

www.ingramcontent.com/pod-product-compliance
Lightning Source LLC
Chambersburg PA
CBHW021408290426
44108CB00010B/433